THE TREE WITH LIGHTS

"One day I was walking along Tinker Creek thinking of nothing at all and I saw the tree with the lights in it. I saw the backyard cedar where the mourning doves roost charged and transfigured, each cell buzzing with flame. I stood on the grass with the lights in it, grass that was wholly fire, utterly focused and utterly dreamed. It was less like seeing than like being for the first time seen, knocked breathless by a powerful glance . . . I had been my whole life a bell, and never knew it until at that moment I was lifted and struck."

—ANNIE DILLARD

Pilgrim at Tinker Creek

Annie Dillard

BANTAM BOOKS, INC.
Toronto / New York / London

RLI: VLM 8 (VLR 8-9)
       ———————————————
       IL 9-adult

PILGRIM AT TINKER CREEK

*A Bantam Book / published by arrangement with
Harper's Magazine Press*

PRINTING HISTORY

Harper's Magazine Press edition published March 1974
2nd printing........March 1974
3rd printing........March 1974
4th printing.....November 1974
Bantam edition / February 1975
2nd printing

*Grateful acknowledgment is made to the following for per-
mission to reprint excerpts from these books:*
Dodd, Mead & Company, Inc., for selections from The Insect
World of J. Henri Fabre, *selected and edited by Edwin Way
Teale;* Days Without Time *by Edwin Way Teale;* The Strange
Lives of Familiar Insects *by Edwin Way Teale.*
Methuen & Co. Ltd. for selections from Space and Sight *by
Marius von Senden.*

*Portions of this work previously appeared in the following
publications:* THE ATLANTIC, HARPER'S MAGAZINE, TRAVEL AND
LEISURE, SPORTS ILLUSTRATED, PROSE, THE CHRISTIAN SCIENCE
MONITOR, THE CAROLINA QUARTERLY, THE LIVING WILDERNESS,
COSMOPOLITAN.

Line drawing by Annie Dillard.

*Bantam Books are published by Bantam Books, Inc. Its trade-
mark, consisting of the words "Bantam Books" and the
portrayal of a bantam, is registered in the United States
Patent Office and in other countries. Marca Registrada. Bantam
Books, Inc., 666 Fifth Avenue, New York, New York 10019.*

PRINTED IN THE UNITED STATES OF AMERICA

for Richard

It ever was, and is, and shall be,
ever-living Fire, in measures being
kindled and in measures going out.

HERACLITUS

CONTENTS

CHAPTER 1

Heaven and Earth in Jest

I USED TO HAVE a cat, an old fighting tom, who would jump through the open window by my bed in the middle of the night and land on my chest. I'd half-awaken. He'd stick his skull under my nose and purr, stinking of urine and blood. Some nights he kneaded my bare chest with his front paws, powerfully, arching his back, as if sharpening his claws, or pummeling a mother for milk. And some mornings I'd wake in daylight to find my body covered with paw prints in blood; I looked as though I'd been painted with roses.

It was hot, so hot the mirror felt warm. I washed before the mirror in a daze, my twisted summer sleep still hung about me like sea kelp. What blood was this, and what roses? It could have been the rose of union, the blood of murder, or the rose of beauty bare and the blood of some unspeakable sacrifice or birth. The sign on my body could have been an emblem or a stain, the keys to the kingdom or the mark of Cain. I never knew. I never knew as I washed, and the blood streaked, faded, and finally disappeared, whether I'd purified myself or ruined the blood sign of the passover. We wake, if we ever wake at all, to mystery, rumors of death, beauty, violence. . . . "Seem like we're just set down here," a woman said to me recently, "and don't nobody know why."

These are morning matters, pictures you dream as the final wave heaves you up on the sand to the bright light and drying air. You remember pressure, and a curved sleep you rested against, soft, like a scallop in its shell. But the air hardens your skin; you stand; you leave the lighted shore to explore some dim headland, and soon you're lost in the leafy interior, intent, remembering nothing.

I still think of that old tomcat, mornings, when I wake. Things are tamer now; I sleep with the window shut. The cat and our rites are gone and my life is changed, but the memory remains of something powerful playing over me. I wake expectant, hoping to see a new thing. If I'm lucky I might be jogged awake by a strange birdcall. I dress in a hurry, imagining the yard flapping with auks, or flamingos. This morning it was a wood duck, down at the creek. It flew away.

I live by a creek, Tinker Creek, in a valley in Virginia's Blue Ridge. An anchorite's hermitage is called an anchorhold; some anchor-holds were simple sheds clamped to the side of a church like a barnacle to a rock. I think of this house clamped to the side of Tinker Creek as an anchorhold. It holds me at anchor to the rock bottom of the creek itself and it keeps me steadied in the current, as a sea anchor does, facing the stream of light pouring down. It's a good place to live; there's a lot to think about. The creeks— Tinker and Carvin's—are an active mystery, fresh every minute. Theirs is the mystery of the continuous creation and all that providence implies: the uncertainty of vision, the horror of the fixed, the dissolution of the present, the intricacy of beauty, the pressure of fecundity, the elusiveness of the free, and the flawed nature of perfection. The mountains—Tinker and Brushy, McAfee's Knob and Dead Man —are a passive mystery, the oldest of all. Theirs is the one simple mystery of creation from nothing, of matter itself, anything at all, the given. Mountains are giant, restful, absorbent. You can heave your spirit into a mountain and the mountain will keep it, folded, and not throw it back as some creeks will. The creeks are the world with all its stimulus and beauty; I live there. But the mountains are home.

The wood duck flew away. I caught only a glimpse of something like a bright torpedo that blasted the leaves where it flew. Back at the house I ate a bowl of oatmeal; much later in the day came the long slant of light that means good walking.

If the day is fine, any walk will do; it all looks good. Water in particular looks its best, reflecting blue sky in the flat, and chopping it into graveled shallows and white chute and foam in the riffles. On a dark day, or a hazy one, everything's washed-out and lack-luster but the water. It carries its own lights. I set out for the railroad tracks, for the hill the flocks fly over, for the woods where the white mare lives. But I go to the water.

Today is one of those excellent January partly cloudies in which light chooses an unexpected part of the landscape to trick out in gilt, and then shadow sweeps it away. You know you're alive. You take huge steps, trying to feel the planet's roundness arc between your feet. Kazantzakis says that when he was young he had a canary and a globe. When he freed the canary, it would perch on the globe and sing. All his life, wandering the earth, he felt as though he had a canary on top of his mind, singing.

West of the house, Tinker Creek makes a sharp loop, so that the creek is both in back of the house, south of me, and also on the other side of the road, north of me. I like to go north. There the afternoon sun hits the creek just right, deepening the reflected blue and lighting the sides of trees on the banks. Steers from the pasture across the creek come down to drink; I always flush a rabbit or two there; I sit on a fallen trunk in the shade and watch the squirrels in the sun. There are two separated wooden fences suspended from cables that cross the creek just upstream from my tree-trunk bench. They keep the steers from escaping up or down the creek when they come to drink. Squirrels, the neighborhood children, and I use the downstream fence as a swaying bridge across the creek. But the steers are there today.

I sit on the downed tree and watch the black steers slip on the creek bottom. They are all bred beef: beef heart, beef hide, beef hocks. They're a human product like rayon. They're like a field of shoes. They have cast-iron shanks and tongues like foam insoles. You can't see through to their brains as you can with other animals; they have beef fat behind their eyes, beef stew.

I cross the fence six feet above the water, walking my hands down the rusty cable and tightroping my feet along the narrow edge of the planks. When I hit the other bank and terra firma, some steers are bunched in a knot between me and the barbed-wire fence I want to cross. So I suddenly rush at them in an enthusiastic sprint, flailing my arms and hollering, "Lightning! Copperhead! Swedish meatballs!" They flee, still in a knot, stumbling across the flat pasture. I stand with the wind on my face.

When I slide under a barbed-wire fence, cross a field, and run over a sycamore trunk felled across the water, I'm on a little island shaped like a tear in the middle of Tinker Creek. On one side of the creek is a steep forested bank; the water is swift and deep on that side of the island. On the other side is the level field I walked through next to the steers' pasture; the water between the field and the island is shallow and sluggish. In summer's low water, flags and bulrushes grow along a series of shallow pools cooled by the lazy current. Water striders patrol the surface film, crayfish hump along the silt bottom eating filth, frogs shout and glare, and shiners and small bream hide among roots from the sulky green heron's eye. I come to this island every month of the year. I walk around it, stopping and staring, or I straddle the sycamore log over the creek, curling my legs out of the water in winter, trying to read. Today I sit on dry grass at the end of the island by the slower side of the creek. I'm drawn to this spot. I come to it as to an oracle; I return to it as a man years later will seek out the battlefield where he lost a leg or an arm.

A couple of summers ago I was walking along the edge of the island to see what I could see in the water, and mainly to scare frogs. Frogs have an inelegant way of taking off from invisible positions on the bank just ahead of your feet, in dire panic, emitting a froggy "Yike!" and splashing into the water. Incredibly, this amused me, and, incredibly, it amuses me still. As I walked along the grassy edge of the island, I got better and better at seeing frogs both in and out of the water. I learned to recognize, slow-ing down, the difference in texture of the light reflected from mudbank, water, grass, or frog. Frogs were flying all around me. At the end of the island I noticed a small green frog. He was exactly half in and half out of the water, looking like a schematic diagram of an amphibian, and he didn't jump.

He didn't jump; I crept closer. At last I knelt on ·the island's winterkilled grass, lost, dumbstruck, staring at the frog in the creek just four feet away. He was a very small frog with wide, dull eyes. And just as I looked at him, he slowly crumpled and began to sag. The spirit vanished from his eyes as if snuffed. His skin emptied and drooped; his very skull seemed to collapse and settle like a kicked tent. He was shrinking before my eyes like a deflating football. I watched the taut, glistening skin on his shoulders ruck, and rumple, and fall. Soon, part of his skin, formless as a pricked balloon, lay in floating folds like bright scum on top of the water: it was a monstrous and terrifying thing. I gaped bewildered, appalled. An oval shadow hung in the water behind the drained frog; then the shadow glided away. The frog skin bag started to sink.

I had read about the giant water bug, but never seen one. "Giant water bug" is really the name of the creature, which is an enormous, heavy-bodied brown beetle. It eats insects, tadpoles, fish, and frogs. Its grasping forelegs are mighty and hooked inward. It seizes a victim with these legs, hugs it tight, and paralyzes it with enzymes injected during a vicious bite. That one bite is the only bite it ever takes. Through the puncture shoot the poisons that dissolve the victim's muscles and bones and organs—all but the skin—and through it the giant water bug sucks out the victim's body, reduced to a juice. This event is quite common in warm fresh water. The frog I saw was being sucked by a giant water bug. I had been kneeling on the island grass; when the unrecognizable flap of frog skin settled on the creek bottom, swaying, I stood up and brushed the knees of my pants. I couldn't catch my breath.

Of course, many carnivorous animals devour their prey alive. The usual method seems to be to subdue the victim by downing or grasping it so it can't flee, then eating it whole or in a series of bloody bites. Frogs eat everything whole, stuffing prey into their mouths with their thumbs. People have seen frogs with their wide jaws so full of live dragonflies they couldn't close them. Ants don't even have to catch their prey: in the spring they swarm over newly hatched, featherless birds in the nest and eat them tiny bite by bite.

That it's rough out there and chancy is no surprise. Every live thing is a survivor on a kind of extended emergency bivouac. But at the same time we are also created. In the Koran, Allah asks, "The heaven and the earth and all in between, thinkest thou I made them *in jest?*" It's a good question. What do we think of the created universe, spanning an unthinkable void with an unthinkable profusion of forms? Or what do we think of nothingness, those sickening reaches of time in either direction? If the giant water bug was not made in jest, was it then made in earnest? Pascal uses a nice term to describe the notion of the creator's, once having called forth the universe, turning his back to it: *Deus Absconditus*. Is this what we think happened? Was the sense of it there, and God absconded with it, ate it, like a wolf who disappears round the edge of the house with the Thanksgiving turkey? "God is subtle," Einstein said, "but not malicious." Again, Einstein said that "nature conceals her mystery by means of her essential grandeur, not by her cunning." It could be that God has not absconded but spread, as our vision and understanding of the universe have spread, to a fabric of spirit and sense so grand and subtle, so powerful in a new way, that we can only feel blindly of its hem. In making the thick darkness a swaddling band for the sea, God "set bars and doors" and said, "Hitherto shalt thou come, but no further." But have we come even that far? Have we rowed out to the thick darkness, or are we all playing pinochle in the bottom of the boat?

Cruelty is a mystery, and the waste of pain. But if we describe a world to compass these things, a world that is a long, brute game, then we bump against another mystery: the inrush of power and light, the canary that sings on the skull. Unless all ages and races of men have been deluded by the same mass hypnotist (who?), there seems to be such a thing as beauty, a grace wholly gratuitous. About five years ago I saw a mockingbird make a straight vertical descent from the roof gutter of a four-story building. It was an act as careless and spontaneous as the curl of a stem or the kindling of a star.

The mockingbird took a single step into the air and dropped. His wings were still folded against his sides as though he were singing from a limb and not falling, accelerating thirty-two feet per second per second, through empty air. Just a breath before he would have been dashed to the ground, he unfurled his wings with exact, deliberate care, revealing the broad bars of white, spread his elegant, white-banded tail, and so floated onto the grass. I had just rounded a corner when his insouciant step caught my eye; there was no one else in sight. The fact of his free fall was like the old philosophical conundrum about the tree that falls in the forest. The answer must be, I think, that beauty and grace are performed whether or not we will or sense them. The least we can do is try to be there.

Another time I saw another wonder: sharks off the

Atlantic coast of Florida. There is a way a wave rises above the ocean horizon, a triangular wedge against the sky. If you stand where the ocean breaks on a shallow beach, you see the raised water in a wave is translucent, shot with lights. One late afternoon at low tide a hundred big sharks passed the beach near the mouth of a tidal river in a feeding frenzy. As each green wave rose from the churning water, it illuminated within itself the six- or eight-foot-long bodies of twisting sharks. The sharks disappeared as each wave rolled toward me; then a new wave would swell above the horizon, containing in it, like scorpions in amber, sharks that roiled and heaved. The sight held awesome wonders: power and beauty, grace tangled in a rapture with violence.

We don't know what's going on here. If these tremendous events are random combinations of matter run amok, the yield of millions of monkeys at millions of typewriters, then what is it in us, hammered out of those same typewriters, that they ignite? We don't know. Our life is a faint tracing on the surface of mystery, like the idle, curved tunnels of leaf miners on the face of a leaf. We must somehow take a wider view, look at the whole landscape, really see it, and describe what's going on here. Then we can at least wail the right question into the swaddling band of darkness, or, if it comes to that, choir the proper praise.

At the time of Lewis and Clark, setting the prairies on fire was a well-known signal that meant, "Come down to the water." It was an extravagant gesture, but we can't do less. If the landscape reveals one certainty, it is that the extravagant gesture is the very stuff of creation. After the one extravagant gesture of creation in the first place, the universe has continued to deal exclusively in extravagances, flinging intricacies and colossi down aeons of emptiness, heaping profusions on profligacies with ever-fresh vigor.

The whole show has been on fire from the word go. I come down to the water to cool my eyes. But everywhere I look I see fire; that which isn't flint is tinder, and the whole world sparks and flames.

I have come to the grassy island late in the day. The creek is up; icy water sweeps under the sycamore log bridge. The frog skin, of course, is utterly gone. I have stared at that one spot on the creek bottom for so long, focusing past the rush of water, that when I stand, the opposite bank seems to stretch before my eyes and flow grassily upstream. When the bank settles down I cross the sycamore log and enter again the big plowed field next to the steers' pasture.

The wind is terrific out of the west; the sun comes and goes. I can see the shadow on the field before me deepen uniformly and spread like a plague. Everything seems so dull I am amazed I can even distinguish objects. And suddenly the light runs across the land like a comber, and up the trees, and goes again in a wink: I think I've gone blind or died. When it comes again, the light, you hold your breath, and if it stays you forget about it until it goes again.

It's the most beautiful day of the year. At four o'clock the eastern sky is a dead stratus black flecked with low white clouds. The sun in the west illuminates the ground, the mountains, and especially the bare branches of trees, so that everywhere silver trees cut into the black sky like a photographer's negative of a landscape. The air and the ground are dry; the mountains are going on and off like neon signs. Clouds slide east as if pulled from the horizon, like a tablecloth whipped off a table. The hemlocks by the barbed-wire fence are flinging themselves east as though their backs would break. Purple shadows are racing east; the wind makes me face east, and again I feel the dizzying, drawn sensation I felt when the creek bank reeled.

At four-thirty the sky in the east is clear; how could that big blackness be blown? Fifteen minutes later another darkness is coming overhead from the northwest; and it's here. Everything is drained of its light as if sucked. Only at the horizon do inky black mountains give way to distant, lighted mountains—lighted not by direct illumination but rather paled by glowing sheets of mist hung before them. Now the blackness is in the east; everything is half in shadow, half in sun, every clod, tree, mountain, and hedge. I can't see Tinker Mountain through the line of hemlock, till it comes on like a streetlight, ping, *ex nihilo*. Its sandstone cliffs pink and swell. Suddenly the light goes; the cliffs recede as if pushed. The sun hits a clump of sycamores between me and the mountains; the sycamore arms light up, and *I can't see the cliffs*. They're gone. The pale network of sycamore arms, which a second ago was transparent as a screen, is suddenly opaque, glowing with light. Now the sycamore arms snuff out, the mountains come on, and there are the cliffs again.

I walk home. By five-thirty the show has pulled out. Nothing is left but an unreal blue and a few banked clouds low in the north. Some sort of carnival magician has been here, some fast-talking worker of wonders who has the act backwards. "Something in this hand," he says, "something in this hand, something up my sleeve, something behind my back . . ." and abracadabra, he snaps his fingers, and it's all gone. Only the bland, blank-faced magician remains, in his unruffled coat, barehanded, acknowledging a smattering of baffled applause. When you look again the whole show has pulled up stakes and moved on down the road. It never stops. New shows roll in from over the mountains and the magician reappears unannounced from a fold in the curtain you never dreamed was an opening. Scarves of clouds, rabbits in plain view, disappear into the black hat forever. Presto chango. The audience, if there is an audience at all, is dizzy from head-turning, dazed.

Like the bear who went over the mountain, I went out to see what I could see. And, I might as well warn you, like the bear, all that I could see was the other side of the mountain: more of same. On a good day I might catch a glimpse of another wooded ridge rolling under the sun like water, another bivouac. I propose to keep here what Thoreau called "a meteorological journal of the mind," telling some tales and describing some of the sights of this rather tamed valley, and exploring, in fear and trembling, some of the unmapped dim reaches and unholy fastnesses to which those tales and sights so dizzyingly lead.

I am no scientist. I explore the neighborhood. An infant who has just learned to hold his head up has a frank and forthright way of gazing about him in bewilderment. He hasn't the faintest clue where he is, and he aims to learn. In a couple of years, what he will have learned instead is how to fake it: he'll have the cocksure air of a squatter who has come to feel he owns the place. Some unwonted, taught pride diverts us from our original intent, which is to explore the neighborhood, view the landscape, to discover at least *where* it is that we have been so startlingly set down, if we can't learn why.

So I think about the valley. It is my leisure as well as my work, a game. It is a fierce game I have joined because it is being played anyway, a game of both skill and chance, played against an unseen adversary—the conditions of time —in which the payoffs, which may suddenly arrive in a blast of light at any moment, might as well come to me as anyone else. I stake the time I'm grateful to have, the energies I'm glad to direct. I risk getting stuck on the board, so to speak, unable to move in any direction, which happens enough, God knows; and I risk the searing, exhausting nightmares that plunder rest and force me face down all night long in some muddy ditch seething with hatching insects and crustaceans.

But if I can bear the nights, the days are a pleasure. I walk out; I see something, some event that would otherwise have been utterly missed and lost; or something sees me, some enormous power brushes me with its clean wing, and I resound like a beaten bell.

I am an explorer, then, and I am also a stalker, or the instrument of the hunt itself. Certain Indians used to carve long grooves along the wooden shafts of their arrows. They called the grooves "lightning marks," because they resembled the curved fissure lightning slices down the trunks of trees. The function of lightning marks is this: if the arrow fails to kill the game, blood from a deep wound will channel along the lightning mark, streak down the arrow shaft, and spatter to the ground, laying a trail dripped on broadleaves, on stones, that the barefoot and trembling archer can follow into whatever deep or rare wilderness it leads. I am the arrow shaft, carved along my length by unexpected lights and gashes from the very sky, and this book is the straying trail of blood.

Something pummels us, something barely sheathed. Power broods and lights. We're played on like a pipe; our breath is not our own. James Houston describes two young Eskimo girls sitting cross-legged on the ground, mouth on mouth, blowing by turns each other's throat cords, making a low, unearthly music. When I cross again the bridge that is really the steers' fence, the wind has thinned to the delicate air of twilight; it crumples the water's skin. I watch the running sheets of light raised on the creek's surface. The sight has the appeal of the purely passive, like the racing of light under clouds on a field, the beautiful dream at the moment of being dreamed. The breeze is the merest puff, but you yourself sail headlong and breathless under the gale force of the spirit.

CHAPTER 2

Seeing

WHEN I WAS SIX or seven years old, growing up in Pittsburgh, I used to take a precious penny of my own and hide it for someone else to find. It was a curious compulsion; sadly, I've never been seized by it since. For some reason I always "hid" the penny along the same stretch of sidewalk up the street. I would cradle it at the roots of a sycamore, say, or in a hole left by a chipped-off piece of sidewalk. Then I would take a piece of chalk, and, starting at either end of the block, draw huge arrows leading up to the penny from both directions. After I learned to write I labeled the arrows: SURPRISE AHEAD or MONEY THIS WAY. I was greatly excited, during all this arrow-drawing, at the thought of the first lucky passer-by who would receive in this way, regardless of merit, a free gift from the universe. But I never lurked about. I would go straight home and not give the matter another thought, until, some months later, I would be gripped again by the impulse to hide another penny.

It is still the first week in January, and I've got great plans. I've been thinking about seeing. There are lots of things to see, unwrapped gifts and free surprises. The world is fairly studded and strewn with pennies cast broadside from a generous hand. But—and this is the point—who gets excited by a mere penny? If you follow one arrow, if you crouch motionless on a bank to watch a tremulous ripple thrill on the water and are rewarded by the sight of a muskrat kit paddling from its den, will you count that sight a chip of copper only, and go your rueful way? It is dire poverty indeed when a man is so malnourished and fatigued that he won't stoop to pick up a penny. But if you cultivate a healthy poverty and simplicity, so that finding a penny will literally make your day, then, since the world is in fact planted in pennies, you have with your poverty bought a lifetime of days. It is that simple. What you see is what you get.

I used to be able to see flying insects in the air. I'd look ahead and see, not the row of hemlocks across the road, but the air in front of it. My eyes would focus along that column of air, picking out flying insects. But I lost interest, I guess, for I dropped the habit. Now I can see birds. Probably some people can look at the grass at their feet and discover all the crawling creatures. I would like to know grasses and sedges—and care. Then my least journey into the world would be a field trip, a series of happy recognitions. Thoreau, in an expansive mood, exulted, "What a rich book might be made about buds, including, perhaps, sprouts!" It would be nice to think so. I cherish mental images I have of three perfectly happy people. One collects stones. Another—an Englishman, say—watches clouds. The third lives on a coast and collects drops of seawater which he examines microscopically and mounts. But I don't see what the specialist sees, and so I cut myself off, not only from the total picture, but from the various forms of happiness.

Unfortunately, nature is very much a now-you-see-it, now-you-don't affair. A fish flashes, then dissolves in the water before my eyes like so much salt. Deer apparently ascend bodily into heaven; the brightest oriole fades into leaves. These disappearances stun me into stillness and concentration; they say of nature that it conceals with a grand nonchalance, and they say of vision that it is a deliberate gift, the revelation of a dancer who for my eyes only flings away her seven veils. For nature does reveal as well as conceal: now-you-don't-see-it, now-you-do. For a week last September migrating red-winged blackbirds were feeding heavily down by the creek at the back of the house. One day I went out to investigate the racket; I walked up to a tree, an Osage orange, and a hundred birds flew away. They simply materialized out of the tree. I saw a tree, then a whisk of color, then a tree again. I walked closer and another hundred blackbirds took flight. Not a branch, not a twig budged: the birds were apparently weightless as well as invisible. Or, it was as if the leaves of the Osage orange had been freed from a spell in the form of red-winged blackbirds; they flew from the tree, caught my eye in the sky, and vanished. When I looked again at the tree the leaves had reassembled as if nothing had happened. Finally I walked directly to the trunk of the tree and a final hundred, the real diehards, appeared, spread, and vanished. How could so many hide in the tree without my seeing them? The Osage orange, unruffled, looked just as it had looked from the house, when three hundred red-winged blackbirds cried from its crown.

I looked downstream where they flew, and they were gone. Searching, I couldn't spot one. I wandered downstream to force them to play their hand, but they'd crossed the creek and scattered. One show to a customer. These appearances catch at my throat; they are the free gifts, the bright coppers at the roots of trees.

It's all a matter of keeping my eyes open. Nature is like one of those line drawings of a tree that are puzzles for children: Can you find hidden in the leaves a duck, a house, a boy, a bucket, a zebra, and a boot? Specialists can find the most incredibly well-hidden things. A book I read when I was young recommended an easy way to find caterpillars to rear: you simply find some fresh caterpillar droppings, look up, and there's your caterpillar. More recently an author advised me to set my mind at ease about those piles of cut stems on the ground in grassy fields. Field mice make them; they cut the grass down by degrees to reach the seeds at the head. It seems that when the grass is tightly packed, as in a field of ripe grain, the blade won't topple at a single cut through the stem; instead, the cut stem simply drops vertically, held in the crush of grain. The mouse severs the bottom again and again, the stem keeps dropping an inch at a time, and finally the head is low enough for the mouse to reach the seeds. Meanwhile, the mouse is positively littering the field with its little piles of cut stems into which, presumably, the author of the book is constantly stumbling.

If I can't see these minutiae, I still try to keep my eyes open. I'm always on the lookout for antlion traps in sandy soil, monarch pupae near milkweed, skipper larvae in locust leaves. These things are utterly common, and I've not seen one. I bang on hollow trees near water, but so far no flying squirrels have appeared. In flat country I watch every sunset in hopes of seeing the green ray. The green ray is a seldom-seen streak of light that rises from the sun like a spurting fountain at the moment of sunset; it throbs into the sky for two seconds and disappears. One more reason to keep my eyes open. A photography professor at the University of Florida just happened to see a bird die in midflight; it jerked, died, dropped, and smashed on the ground. I squint at the wind because I read Stewart Edward White: "I have always maintained that if you looked closely enough you could *see* the wind—the dim, hardly-made-out, fine débris fleeing high in the air." White was an excellent observer, and devoted an entire chapter of *The Mountains* to the subject of seeing deer: "As soon as you can forget the naturally obvious and construct an artificial obvious, then you too will see deer."

But the artificial obvious is hard to see. My eyes account for less than one percent of the weight of my head; I'm bony and dense; I see what I expect. I once spent a full three minutes looking at a bullfrog that was so unexpectedly large I couldn't see it even though a dozen enthusiastic campers were shouting directions. Finally I asked, "What color am I looking for?" and a fellow said, "Green." When at last I picked out the frog, I saw what painters are up against: the thing wasn't green at all, but the color of wet hickory bark.

The lover can see, and the knowledgeable. I visited an aunt and uncle at a quarter-horse ranch in Cody, Wyoming. I couldn't do much of anything useful, but I could, I thought, draw. So, as we all sat around the kitchen table after supper, I produced a sheet of paper and drew a horse. "That's one lame horse," my aunt volunteered. The rest of the family joined in: "Only place to saddle that one is his neck"; "Looks like we better shoot the poor thing, on account of those terrible growths." Meekly, I slid the pencil and paper down the table. Everyone in that family, including my three young cousins, could draw a horse. Beautifully. When the paper came back it looked as though five shining, real quarter horses had been corraled by mistake with a papier-mâché moose; the real horses seemed to gaze at the monster with a steady, puzzled air. I stay away from horses now, but I can do a creditable goldfish. The point is that I just don't know what the lover knows; I just can't see the artificial obvious that those in the know construct. The herpetologist asks the native, "Are there snakes in that ravine?" "Nosir." And the herpetologist comes home with, yessir, three bags full. Are there butterflies on that mountain? Are the bluets in bloom, are there arrowheads here, or fossil shells in the shale?

Peeping through my keyhole I see within the range of only about thirty percent of the light that comes from the sun; the rest is infrared and some little ultraviolet, perfectly apparent to many animals, but invisible to me. A nightmare network of ganglia, charged and firing without my knowledge, cuts and splices what I do see, editing it for my brain. Donald E. Carr points out that the sense impressions of one-celled animals are *not* edited for the brain: "This is philosophically interesting in a rather mournful way, since it means that only the simplest animals perceive the universe as it is."

A fog that won't burn away drifts and flows across my field of vision. When you see fog move against a backdrop of deep pines, you don't see the fog itself, but streaks of clearness floating across the air in dark shreds. So I see only tatters of clearness through a pervading obscurity. I can't distinguish the fog from the overcast sky; I can't be sure if the light is direct or reflected. Everywhere darkness and the presence of the unseen appalls. We estimate now that only one atom dances alone in every cubic meter of intergalactic space. I blink and squint. What planet or power yanks Halley's Comet out of orbit? We haven't seen that force yet; it's a question of distance, density, and the pallor of reflected light. We rock, cradled in the swaddling band of darkness. Even the simple darkness of night whispers suggestions to the mind. Last summer, in August, I stayed at the creek too late.

Where Tinker Creek flows under the sycamore log bridge to the tear-shaped island, it is slow and shallow, fringed thinly in cattail marsh. At this spot an astonishing bloom of life supports vast breeding populations of insects, fish, reptiles, birds, and mammals. On windless summer evenings I stalk along the creek bank or straddle the sycamore log in absolute stillness, watching for muskrats. The night I stayed too late I was hunched on the log staring spellbound at spreading, reflected stains of lilac on the water. A cloud in the sky suddenly lighted as if turned on by a switch; its reflection just as suddenly materialized on the water upstream, flat and floating, so that I couldn't see the creek bottom, or life in the water under the cloud. Downstream, away from the cloud on the water, water turtles smooth as beans were gliding down with the current in a series of easy, weightless push-offs, as men bound on the moon. I didn't know whether to trace the progress of one turtle I was sure of, risking sticking my face in one of the bridge's spider webs made invisible by the gathering dark, or take a chance on seeing the carp, or scan the mudbank in hope of seeing a muskrat, or follow the last of the swallows who caught at my heart and trailed it after them like streamers as they appeared from directly below, under the log, flying upstream with their tails forked, so fast.

But shadows spread, and deepened, and stayed. After thousands of years we're still strangers to darkness, fearful aliens in an enemy camp with our arms crossed over our chests. I stirred. A land turtle on the bank, startled, hissed

the air from its lungs and withdrew into its shell. An un-
easy pink here, an unfathomable blue there, gave great suggestion of lurking beings. Things were going on. I couldn't
see whether that sere rustle I heard was a distant rattlesnake, slit-eyed, or a nearby sparrow kicking in the dry
flood debris slung at the foot of a willow. Tremendous action roiled the water everywhere I looked, big action, inexplicable. A tremor welled up beside a gaping muskrat
burrow in the bank and I caught my breath, but no muskrat
appeared. The ripples continued to fan upstream with a
steady, powerful thrust. Night was knitting over my face an
eyeless mask, and I still sat transfixed. A distant airplane, a
delta wing out of nightmare, made a gliding shadow on the
creek's bottom that looked like a stingray cruising upstream.
At once a black fin slit the pink cloud on the water, shearing it in two. The two halves merged together and seemed
to dissolve before my eyes. Darkness pooled in the cleft of
the creek and rose, as water collects in a well. Untamed,
dreaming lights flickered over the sky. I saw hints of hulk-
ing underwater shadows, two pale splashes out of the water,
and round ripples rolling close together from a blackened
center.

At last I stared upstream where only the deepest violet
remained of the cloud, a cloud so high its underbelly still
glowed feeble color reflected from a hidden sky lighted in
turn by a sun halfway to China. And out of that violet, a
sudden enormous black body arced over the water. I saw
only a cylindrical sleekness. Head and tail, if there was a
head and tail, were both submerged in cloud. I saw only
one ebony fling, a headlong dive to darkness; then the
waters closed, and the lights went out.

I walked home in a shivering daze, up hill and down.
Later I lay open-mouthed in bed, my arms flung wide at
my sides to steady the whirling darkness. At this latitude

I'm spinning 836 miles an hour round the earth's axis; I often fancy I feel my sweeping fall as a breakneck arc like the dive of dolphins, and the hollow rushing of wind raises hair on my neck and the side of my face. In orbit around the sun I'm moving 64,800 miles an hour. The solar system as a whole, like a merry-go-round unhinged, spins, bobs, and blinks at the speed of 43,200 miles an hour along a course set east of Hercules. Someone has piped, and we are dancing a tarantella until the sweat pours. I open my eyes and I see dark, muscled forms curl out of water, with flapping gills and flattened eyes. I close my eyes and I see stars, deep stars giving way to deeper stars, deeper stars bowing to deepest stars at the crown of an infinite cone.

"Still," wrote van Gogh in a letter, "a great deal of light falls on everything." If we are blinded by darkness, we are also blinded by light. When too much light falls on everything, a special terror results. Peter Freuchen describes the notorious kayak sickness to which Greenland Eskimos are prone. "The Greenland fjords are peculiar for the spells of completely quiet weather, when there is not enough wind to blow out a match and the water is like a sheet of glass. The kayak hunter must sit in his boat without stirring a finger so as not to scare the shy seals away. . . . The sun, low in the sky, sends a glare into his eyes, and the landscape around moves into the realm of the unreal. The reflex from the mirror-like water hypnotizes him, he seems to be unable to move, and all of a sudden it is as if he were floating in a bottomless void, sinking, sinking, and sinking. . . . Horror-stricken, he tries to stir, to cry out, but he cannot, he is completely paralyzed, he just falls and falls." Some hunters are especially cursed with this panic, and bring ruin and sometimes starvation to their families.

Sometimes here in Virginia at sunset low clouds on the southern or northern horizon are completely invisible in the lighted sky. I only know one is there because I can see its reflection in still water. The first time I discovered this mystery I looked from cloud to no-cloud in bewilderment, checking my bearings over and over, thinking maybe the ark of the covenant was just passing by south of Dead Man Mountain. Only much later did I read the explanation: polarized light from the sky is very much weakened by reflection, but the light in clouds isn't polarized. So invisible clouds pass among visible clouds, till all slide over the mountains; so a greater light extinguishes a lesser as though it didn't exist.

In the great meteor shower of August, the Perseid, I wail all day for the shooting stars I miss. They're out there showering down, committing hara-kiri in a flame of fatal attraction, and hissing perhaps at last into the ocean. But at dawn what looks like a blue dome clamps down over me like a lid on a pot. The stars and planets could smash and I'd never know. Only a piece of ashen moon occasionally climbs up or down the inside of the dome, and our local star without surcease explodes on our heads. We have really only that one light, one source for all power, and yet we must turn away from it by universal decree. Nobody here on the planet seems aware of this strange, powerful taboo, that we all walk about carefully averting our faces, this way and that, lest our eyes be blasted forever.

Darkness appalls and light dazzles; the scrap of visible light that doesn't hurt my eyes hurts my brain. What I see sets me swaying. Size and distance and the sudden swelling of meanings confuse me, bowl me over. I straddle the sycamore log bridge over Tinker Creek in the summer. I look at the lighted creek bottom: snail tracks tunnel the mud in quavering curves. A crayfish jerks, but by the time I absorb what has happened, he's gone in a billowing smokescreen of silt. I look at the water: minnows and shiners. If I'm thinking minnows, a carp will fill my brain till I scream. I look at the water's surface: skaters, bubbles, and leaves sliding down. Suddenly, my own face, reflected, startles me witless. Those snails have been tracking my face! Finally, with a shuddering wrench of the will, I see clouds, cirrus clouds. I'm dizzy, I fall in. This looking business is risky.

Once I stood on a humped rock on nearby Purgatory Mountain, watching through binoculars the great autumn hawk migration below, until I discovered that I was in danger of joining the hawks on a vertical migration of my own. I was used to binoculars, but not, apparently, to balancing on humped rocks while looking through them. I staggered. Everything advanced and receded by turns; the world was full of unexplained foreshortenings and depths. A distant huge tan object, a hawk the size of an elephant, turned out to be the browned bough of a nearby loblolly pine. I followed a sharp-shinned hawk against a featureless sky, rotating my head unawares as it flew, and when I lowered the glass a glimpse of my own looming shoulder sent me staggering. What prevents the men on Palomar from falling, voiceless and blinded, from their tiny, vaulted chairs?

I reel in confusion; I don't understand what I see. With the naked eye I can see two million light-years to the Andromeda galaxy. Often I slop some creek water in a jar and when I get home I dump it in a white china bowl. After the silt settles I return and see tracings of minute snails on the bottom, a planarian or two winding round the rim of water, roundworms shimmying frantically, and finally, when my eyes have adjusted to these dimensions, amoebae. At first the amoebae look like muscae volitantes, those curled moving spots you seem to see in your eyes when you stare at a distant wall. Then I see the amoebae as drops of water congealed, bluish, translucent, like chips of sky in the bowl. At length I choose one individual and give my-self over to its idea of an evening. I see it dribble a grainy foot before it on its wet, unfathomable way. Do its unedited sense impressions include the fierce focus of my eyes? Shall I take it outside and show it Andromeda, and blow its little endoplasm? I stir the water with a finger, in case it's run-ning out of oxygen. Maybe I should get a tropical aquarium with motorized bubblers and lights, and keep this one for a pet. Yes, it would tell its fissioned descendants, the universe is two feet by five, and if you listen closely you can hear the buzzing music of the spheres.

Oh, it's mysterious lamplit evenings, here in the galaxy, one after the other. It's one of those nights when I wander from window to window, looking for a sign. But I can't see. Terror and a beauty insoluble are a ribband of blue woven into the fringes of garments of things both great and small. No culture explains, no bivouac offers real haven or rest. But it could be that we are not seeing some-thing. Galileo thought comets were an optical illusion. This is fertile ground: since we are certain that they're not, we can look at what our scientists have been saying with fresh hope. What if there are *really* gleaming, castellated cities hung upside-down over the desert sand? What limpid lakes and cool date palms have our caravans always passed untried? Until, one by one, by the blindest of leaps, we light on the road to these places, we must stumble in dark-ness and hunger. I turn from the window. I'm blind as a bat, sensing only from every direction the echo of my own thin cries.

I chanced on a wonderful book by Marius von Senden, called *Space and Sight*. When Western surgeons discovered how to perform safe cataract operations, they ranged across Europe and America operating on dozens of men and

women of all ages who had been blinded by cataracts since
birth. Von Senden collected accounts of such cases; the histories are fascinating. Many doctors had tested their patients' sense perceptions and ideas of space both before and
after the operations. The vast majority of patients, of both
sexes and all ages, had, in von Senden's opinion, no idea of
space whatsoever. Form, distance, and size were so many
meaningless syllables. A patient "had no idea of depth,
confusing it with roundness." Before the operation a doctor
would give a blind patient a cube and a sphere; the patient
would tongue it or feel it with his hands, and name it cor-
rectly. After the operation the doctor would show the same
objects to the patient without letting him touch them; now
he had no clue whatsoever what he was seeing. One patient
called lemonade "square" because it pricked on his tongue
as a square shape pricked on the touch of his hands. Of
another postoperative patient, the doctor writes, "I have
found in her no notion of size, for example, not even
within the narrow limits which she might have encom-
passed with the aid of touch. Thus when I asked her to
show me how big her mother was, she did not stretch out
her hands, but set her two index-fingers a few inches
apart." Other doctors reported their patients' own state-
ments to similar effect. "The room he was in . . . he knew
to be but part of the house, yet he could not conceive that
the whole house could look bigger"; "Those who are blind
from birth . . . have no real conception of height or distance. A house that is a mile away is thought of as nearby,
but requiring the taking of a lot of steps. . . . The elevator
that whizzes him up and down gives no more sense of vertical distance than does the train of horizontal."

For the newly sighted, vision is pure sensation unen-
cumbered by meaning: "The girl went through the experience that we all go through and forget, the moment we are

born. She saw, but it did not mean anything but a lot of different kinds of brightness." Again, "I asked the patient what he could see; he answered that he saw an extensive field of light, in which everything appeared dull, confused, and in motion. He could not distinguish objects." Another patient saw "nothing but a confusion of forms and colours." When a newly sighted girl saw photographs and paintings, she asked, " 'Why do they put those dark marks all over them?' 'Those aren't dark marks,' her mother explained, 'those are shadows. That is one of the ways the eye knows that things have shape. If it were not for shadows many things would look flat.' 'Well, that's how things do look,' Joan answered. 'Everything looks flat with dark patches.' "

But it is the patients' concepts of space that are most revealing. One patient, according to his doctor, "practiced his vision in a strange fashion; thus he takes off one of his boots, throws it some way off in front of him, and then attempts to gauge the distance at which it lies; he takes a few steps towards the boot and tries to grasp it; on failing to reach it, he moves on a step or two and gropes for the boot until he finally gets hold of it." "But even at this stage, after three weeks' experience of seeing," von Senden goes on, " 'space,' as he conceives it, ends with visual space, i.e., with colour-patches that happen to bound his view. He does not yet have the notion that a larger object (a chair) can mask a smaller one (a dog), or that the latter can still be present even though it is not directly seen."

In general the newly sighted see the world as a dazzle of color-patches. They are pleased by the sensation of color, and learn quickly to name the colors, but the rest of seeing is tormentingly difficult. Soon after his operation a patient "generally bumps into one of these colour-patches and observes them to be substantial, since they resist him as tactual objects do. In walking about it also strikes him—or can if he pays attention—that he is continually passing in between the colours he sees, that he can go past a visual object, that a part of it then steadily disappears from view; and that in spite of this, however he twists and turns—whether entering the room from the door, for example, or returning back to it—he always has a visual space in front of him. Thus he gradually comes to realize that there is also a space behind him, which he does not see."

The mental effort involved in these reasonings proves overwhelming for many patients. It oppresses them to realize, if they ever do at all, the tremendous size of the world, which they had previously conceived of as something touchingly manageable. It oppresses them to realize that they have been visible to people all along, perhaps unattractively so, without their knowledge or consent. A disheartening number of them refuse to use their new vision, continuing to go over objects with their tongues, and lapsing into apathy and despair. "The child can see, but will not make use of his sight. Only when pressed can he with difficulty be brought to look at objects in his neighbourhood; but more than a foot away it is impossible to bestir him to the necessary effort." Of a twenty-one-year-old girl, the doctor relates, "Her unfortunate father, who had hoped for so much from this operation, wrote that his daughter carefully shuts her eyes whenever she wishes to go about the house, especially when she comes to a staircase, and that she is never happier or more at ease than when, by closing her eyelids, she relapses into her former state of total blindness." A fifteen-year-old boy, who was also in love with a girl at the asylum for the blind, finally blurted out, "No, really, I can't stand it any more; I want to be sent back to the asylum again. If things aren't altered, I'll tear my eyes out."

Some do learn to see, especially the young ones. But it

changes their lives. One doctor comments on "the rapid and complete loss of that striking and wonderful serenity which is characteristic only of those who have never yet seen." A blind man who learns to see is ashamed of his old habits. He dresses up, grooms himself, and tries to make a good impression. While he was blind he was indifferent to objects unless they were edible; now, "a sifting of values sets in . . . his thoughts and wishes are mightily stirred and some few of the patients are thereby led into dissimulation, envy, theft and fraud."

On the other hand, many newly sighted people speak well of the world, and teach us how dull is our own vision. To one patient, a human hand, unrecognized, is "something bright and then holes." Shown a bunch of grapes, a boy calls out, "It is dark, blue and shiny. . . . It isn't smooth, it has bumps and hollows." A little girl visits a garden. "She is greatly astonished, and can scarcely be persuaded to answer, stands speechless in front of the tree, which she only names on taking hold of it, and then as 'the tree with the lights in it.' " Some delight in their sight and give themselves over to the visual world. Of a patient just after her bandages were removed, her doctor writes, "The first things to attract her attention were her own hands; she looked at them very closely, moved them repeatedly to and fro, bent and stretched the fingers, and seemed greatly astonished at the sight." One girl was eager to tell her blind friend that "men do not really look like trees at all," and astounded to discover that her every visitor had an utterly different face. Finally, a twenty-two-year-old girl was dazzled by the world's brightness and kept her eyes shut for two weeks. When at the end of that time she opened her eyes again, she did not recognize any objects, but, "the more she now directed her gaze upon everything about her, the more it could be seen how an expression of gratification and astonishment overspread her features; she repeatedly exclaimed: 'Oh God! How beautiful!' "

I saw color-patches for weeks after I read this wonderful book. It was summer; the peaches were ripe in the valley orchards. When I woke in the morning, color-patches wrapped round my eyes, intricately, leaving not one un-filled spot. All day long I walked among shifting color-patches that parted before me like the Red Sea and closed again in silence, transfigured, wherever I looked back. Some patches swelled and loomed, while others vanished utterly, and dark marks flitted at random over the whole dazzling sweep. But I couldn't sustain the illusion of flat-ness. I've been around for too long. Form is condemned to an eternal danse macabre with meaning: I couldn't unpeach the peaches. Nor can I remember ever having seen without understanding; the color-patches of infancy are lost. My brain then must have been smooth as any balloon. I'm told I reached for the moon; many babies do. But the color-patches of infancy swelled as meaning filled them; they arrayed themselves in solemn ranks down distances which unrolled and stretched before me like a plain. The moon rocketed away. I live now in a world of shadows that shape and distance color, a world where space makes a kind of terrible sense. What gnosticism is this, and what physics? The fluttering patch I saw in my nursery window—silver and green and shape-shifting blue—is gone; a row of Lombardy poplars takes its place, mute, across the distant lawn. That humming oblong creature pale as light that stole along the walls of my room at night, stretching exhilarat-ingly around the corners, is gone, too, gone the night I ate of the bittersweet fruit, put two and two together and puckered forever my brain. Martin Buber tells this tale: "Rabbi Mendel once boasted to his teacher Rabbi Elimelekh

that evenings he saw the angel who rolls away the light before the darkness, and mornings the angel who rolls away
the darkness before the light. 'Yes,' said Rabbi Elimelekh,
'in my youth I saw that too. Later on you don't see these
things any more.' "

Why didn't someone hand those newly sighted people
paints and brushes from the start, when they still didn't
know what anything was? Then maybe we all could see
color-patches too, the world unraveled from reason, Eden
before Adam gave names. The scales would drop from my
eyes; I'd see trees like men walking; I'd run down the road
against all orders, hallooing and leaping.

Seeing is of course very much a matter of verbalization.
Unless I call my attention to what passes before my eyes,
I simply won't see it. It is, as Ruskin says, "not merely
unnoticed, but in the full, clear sense of the word, unseen."
My eyes alone can't solve analogy tests using figures, the
ones which show, with increasing elaborations, a big square,
then a small square in a big square, then a big triangle, and
expect me to find a small triangle in a big triangle. I have
to say the words, describe what I'm seeing. If Tinker
Mountain erupted, I'd be likely to notice. But if I want to
notice the lesser cataclysms of valley life, I have to maintain
in my head a running description of the present. It's not
that I'm observant; it's just that I talk too much. Otherwise, especially in a strange place, I'll never know what's
happening. Like a blind man at the ball game, I need a
radio.

When I see this way I analyze and pry. I hurl over logs
and roll away stones; I study the bank a square foot at a
time, probing and tilting my head. Some days when a mist
covers the mountains, when the muskrats won't show and
the microscope's mirror shatters, I want to climb up the

blank blue dome as a man would storm the inside of a circus tent, wildly, dangling, and with a steel knife claw a rent in the top, peep, and, if I must, fall.

But there is another kind of seeing that involves a letting go. When I see this way I sway transfixed and emptied. The difference between the two ways of seeing is the difference between walking with and without a camera. When I walk with a camera, I walk from shot to shot, reading the light on a calibrated meter. When I walk without a camera, my own shutter opens, and the moment's light prints on my own silver gut. When I see this second way I am above all an unscrupulous observer.

It was sunny one evening last summer at Tinker Creek; the sun was low in the sky, upstream. I was sitting on the sycamore log bridge with the sunset at my back, watching the shiners the size of minnows who were feeding over the muddy sand in skittery schools. Again and again, one fish, then another, turned for a split second across the current and flash! the sun shot out from its silver side. I couldn't watch for it. It was always just happening somewhere else, and it drew my vision just as it disappeared: flash, like a sudden dazzle of the thinnest blade, a sparking over a dun and olive ground at chance intervals from every direction. Then I noticed white specks, some sort of pale petals, small, floating from under my feet on the creek's surface, very slow and steady. So I blurred my eyes and gazed towards the brim of my hat and saw a new world. I saw the pale white circles roll up, roll up, like the world's turning, mute and perfect, and I saw the linear flashes, gleaming silver, like stars being born at random down a rolling scroll of time. Something broke and something opened. I filled up like a new wineskin. I breathed an air like light; I saw a light like water. I was the lip of a fountain the creek filled forever; I was ether, the leaf in the zephyr; I was flesh-flake, feather, bone.

When I see this way I see truly. As Thoreau says, I return to my senses. I am the man who watches the baseball game in silence in an empty stadium. I see the game purely; I'm abstracted and dazed. When it's all over and the white-suited players lope off the green field to their shadowed dugouts, I leap to my feet; I cheer and cheer.

But I can't go out and try to see this way. I'll fail, I'll go mad. All I can do is try to gag the commentator, to hush the noise of useless interior babble that keeps me from seeing just as surely as a newspaper dangled before my eyes. The effort is really a discipline requiring a lifetime of dedicated struggle; it marks the literature of saints and monks of every order East and West, under every rule and no rule, discalced and shod. The world's spiritual geniuses seem to discover universally that the mind's muddy river, this ceaseless flow of trivia and trash, cannot be dammed, and that trying to dam it is a waste of effort that might lead to madness. Instead you must allow the muddy river to flow unheeded in the dim channels of consciousness; you raise your sights; you look along it, mildly, acknowledging its presence without interest and gazing beyond it into the realm of the real where subjects and objects act and rest purely, without utterance. "Launch into the deep," says Jacques Ellul, "and you shall see."

The secret of seeing is, then, the pearl of great price. If I thought he could teach me to find it and keep it forever I would stagger barefoot across a hundred deserts after any lunatic at all. But although the pearl may be found, it may not be sought. The literature of illumination reveals this above all: although it comes to those who wait for it, it is always, even to the most practiced and adept, a gift and a total surprise. I return from one walk knowing where the killdeer nests in the field by the creek and the hour the laurel blooms. I return from the same walk a day later scarcely knowing my own name. Litanies hum in my ears; my tongue flaps in my mouth Ailinon, alleluia! I cannot cause light; the most I can do is try to put myself in the path of its beam. It is possible, in deep space, to sail on solar wind. Light, be it particle or wave, has force: you rig a giant sail and go. The secret of seeing is to sail on solar wind. Hone and spread your spirit till you yourself are a sail, whetted, translucent, broadside to the merest puff.

When her doctor took her bandages off and led her into the garden, the girl who was no longer blind saw "the tree with the lights in it." It was for this tree I searched through the peach orchards of summer, in the forests of fall and down winter and spring for years. Then one day I was walking along Tinker Creek thinking of nothing at all and I saw the tree with the lights in it. I saw the backyard cedar where the mourning doves roost charged and transfigured, each cell buzzing with flame. I stood on the grass with the lights in it, grass that was wholly fire, utterly focused and utterly dreamed. It was less like seeing than like being for the first time seen, knocked breathless by a powerful glance. The flood of fire abated, but I'm still spending the power. Gradually the lights went out in the cedar, the colors died, the cells unflamed and disappeared. I was still ringing. I had been my whole life a bell, and never knew it until at that moment I was lifted and struck. I have since only very rarely seen the tree with the lights in it. The vision comes and goes, mostly goes, but I live for it, for the moment when the mountains open and a new light roars in spate through the crack, and the mountains slam.

CHAPTER 3

Winter

I

IT IS THE FIRST OF FEBRUARY, and everyone is talking about starlings. Starlings came to this country on a passenger liner from Europe. One hundred of them were deliberately released in Central Park, and from those hundred descended all of our countless millions of starlings today. According to Edwin Way Teale, "Their coming was the result of one man's fancy. That man was Eugene Schieffelin, a wealthy New York drug manufacturer. His curious hobby was the introduction into America of all the birds mentioned in William Shakespeare." The birds adapted to their new country splendidly.

When John Cowper Powys lived in the United States, he wrote about chickadees stealing crumbs from his favorite

flock of starlings. Around here they're not so popular. Instead of quietly curling for sleep, one by one, here and
there in dense shrubbery, as many birds do, starlings roost
all together in vast hordes and droves. They have favorite
roosting sites to which they return winter after winter; apparently southwest Virginia is their idea of Miami Beach.
In Waynesboro, where the starlings roost in the woods near
the Coyner Springs area, residents can't go outside for any
length of time, or even just to hang laundry, because of the
stink—"will knock you over"—the droppings, and the lice.

Starlings are notoriously difficult to "control." The story
is told of a man who was bothered by starlings roosting in
a large sycamore near his house. He said he tried everything to get rid of them and finally took a shotgun to three
of them and killed them. When asked if that discouraged
the birds, he reflected a minute, leaned forward, and said
confidentially, "Those three it did."

Radford, Virginia, had a little stink of its own a few
years ago. Radford had starlings the way a horse has flies,
and in similarly unapproachable spots. Wildlife biologists
estimated the Radford figure at one hundred fifty thousand
starlings. The people complained of the noise, the stench,
the inevitable whitewash effect, and the possibility of an
epidemic of an exotic, dust-borne virus disease. Finally, in
January, 1972, various officials and biologists got together
and decided that something needed to be done. After studying
the feasibility of various methods, they decided to kill the
starlings with foam. The idea was to shoot a special deter-
gent foam through hoses at the roosting starlings on a night
when weathermen predicted a sudden drop in temperature.
The foam would penetrate the birds' waterproof feathers
and soak their skins. Then when the temperature dropped,
the birds would drop too, having quietly died of exposure.

Meanwhile, before anything actually happened, the

papers were having a field day. Every crazy up and down every mountain had his shrill say. The local bird societies screamed for blood—the starlings' blood. Starlings, after all, compete with native birds for food and nesting sites. Other people challenged the mayor of Radford, the Virginia Tech Wildlife Bureau, the newspaper's editors and all its readers in Radford and everywhere else, to tell how THEY would like to freeze to death inside a bunch of bubbles.

The Wildlife Bureau went ahead with its plan. The needed equipment was expensive, and no one was quite sure if it would work. Sure enough, on the night they sprayed the roosts the temperature didn't drop far enough. Out of the hundred and fifty thousand starlings they hoped to exterminate, they got only three thousand. Somebody figured out that the whole show had cost citizens two dollars per dead starling.

That is, in effect, the story of the Radford starlings. The people didn't give up at once, however. They mulled and fussed, giving the starlings a brief reprieve, and then came up with a new plan. Soon, one day when the birds returned at sunset to their roost, the wildlife managers were ready for them. They fired shotguns loaded with multiple, high-powered explosives into the air. BANG, went the guns; the birds settled down to sleep. The experts went back to their desks and fretted and fumed some more. At last they brought out the ultimate weapon: recordings of starling distress calls. Failure. YIKE OUCH HELP went the recordings; snore went the birds. That, *in toto*, is the story of the Radford starlings. They still thrive.

Our valley starlings thrive, too. They plod morosely around the grass under the feeder. Other people apparently go to great lengths to avoid feeding them. Starlings are early to bed and late to rise, so people sneak out with grain and suet before dawn, for early rising birds, and whisk it away at the first whiff of a starling; after sunset, when the starlings are safely to roost bothering somebody else, they spread out the suet and grain once again. I don't care what eats the stuff.

It is winter proper; the cold weather, such as it is, has come to stay. I bloom indoors in the winter like a forced forsythia; I come in to come out. At night I read and write, and things I have never understood become clear; I reap the harvest of the rest of the year's planting.

Outside, everything has opened up. Winter clear-cuts and reseeds the easy way. Everywhere paths unclog; in late fall and winter, and only then, can I scale the cliff to the Lucas orchard, circle the forested quarry pond, or follow the left-hand bank of Tinker Creek downstream. The woods are acres of sticks; I could walk to the Gulf of Mexico in a straight line. When the leaves fall the strip-tease is over; things stand mute and revealed. Everywhere skies extend, vistas deepen, walls become windows, doors open. Now I can see the house where the Whites and the Garretts lived on the hill under oaks. The thickly grown banks of Carvin's Creek where it edges the road have long since thinned to a twiggy haze, and I can see Maren and Sandy in blue jackets out running the dogs. The mountains' bones poke through, all shoulder and knob and shin. All that summer conceals, winter reveals. Here are the birds' nests hid in the hedge, and squirrels' nests splotched all over the walnuts and elms.

Today a gibbous moon marked the eastern sky like a smudge of chalk. The shadows of its features had the same blue tone and light value as the sky itself, so it looked transparent in its depths, or softly frayed, like the heel of a sock. Not too long ago, according to Edwin Way Teale, the people of Europe believed that geese and swans wintered there, on the moon's pale seas. Now it is sunset. The mountains warm in tone as the day chills, and a hot blush deepens over the land. "Observe," said da Vinci, "observe in the streets at twilight, when the day is cloudy, the loveliness and tenderness spread on the faces of men and women." I have seen those faces, when the day is cloudy, and I have seen at sunset on a clear winter day houses, ordinary houses, whose bricks were coals and windows flame.

At dusk every evening an extended flock of starlings appears out of the northern sky and winds toward the setting sun. It is the winter day's major event. Late yesterday, I climbed across the creek, through the steers' pasture, beyond the grassy island where I had seen the giant water bug sip a frog, and up a high hill. Curiously, the best vantage point on the hill was occupied by a pile of burnt books. I opened some of them carefully: they were good cloth- and leather-bound novels, a complete, charred set of encyclopedias decades old, and old, watercolor-illustrated children's books. They flaked in my hands like pieces of pie. Today I learned that the owners of the house behind the books had suffered a fire. But I didn't know that then; I thought they'd suffered a terrible fit of pique. I crouched beside the books and looked over the valley.

On my right a woods thickly overgrown with creeper descended the hill's slope to Tinker Creek. On my left was a planting of large shade trees on the ridge of the hill. Before me the grassy hill pitched abruptly and gave way to a large, level field fringed in trees where it bordered the creek. Beyond the creek I could see with effort the vertical sliced rock where men had long ago quarried the mountain under the forest. Beyond that I saw Hollins Pond and all its woods and pastures; then I saw in a blue haze all the world poured flat and pale between the mountains.

Out of the dimming sky a speck appeared, then another, and another. It was the starlings going to roost. They gathered deep in the distance, flock sifting into flock, and strayed towards me, transparent and whirling, like smoke. They seemed to unravel as they flew, lengthening in curves, like a loosened skein. I didn't move; they flew directly over my head for half an hour. The flight extended like a fluttering banner, an unfurled oriflamme, in either direction as far as I could see. Each individual bird bobbed and knitted up and down in the flight at apparent random, for no known reason except that that's how starlings fly, yet all remained perfectly spaced. The flocks each tapered at either end from a rounded middle, like an eye. Over my head I heard a sound of beaten air, like a million shook rugs, a muffled whuff. Into the woods they sifted without shifting a twig, right through the crowns of trees, intricate and rushing, like wind.

After half an hour, the last of the stragglers had vanished into the trees. I stood with difficulty, bashed by the unexpectedness of this beauty, and my spread lungs roared. My eyes pricked from the effort of trying to trace a feathered dot's passage through a weft of limbs. Could tiny birds be sifting through me right now, birds winging through the gaps between my cells, touching nothing, but quickening in my tissues, fleet?

Some weather's coming; you can taste on the sides of your tongue a quince tang in the air. This fall everyone looked to the bands on a woolly bear caterpillar, and predicted as usual the direst of dire winters. This routine always calls to mind the Angiers' story about the trappers in the far north. They approached an Indian whose ancestors had dwelled from time immemorial in those fir forests, and asked him about the severity of the coming winter. The Indian

cast a canny eye over the landscape and pronounced, "Bad
winter." The others asked him how he knew. The Indian
replied unhesitatingly, "The white man makes a big woodpile." Here the woodpile is an exercise doggedly, exhaustedly
maintained despite what must be great temptation. The
other day I saw a store displaying a neatly stacked quarter-
cord of fireplace logs manufactured of rolled, pressed paper.
On the wrapper of each "log" was printed in huge letters
the beguiling slogan, "The ROMANCE Without The HEART-
ACHE."

I lay a cherry log fire and settle in. I'm getting used to
this planet and to this curious human culture which is as
cheerfully enthusiastic as it is cheerfully cruel. I never cease
to marvel at the newspapers. In my life I've seen one million pictures of a duck that has adopted a kitten, or a cat
that has adopted a duckling, or a sow and a puppy, a mare
and a muskrat. And for the one millionth time I'm fascinated. I wish I lived near them, in Corpus Christi or
Damariscotta; I wish I had the wonderful pair before me,
mooning about the yard. It's all beginning to smack of
home. The winter pictures that come in over the wire from
every spot on the continent are getting to be as familiar as
my own hearth. I wait for the annual aerial photograph of
an enterprising fellow who has stamped in the snow a giant
Valentine for his girl. Here's the annual chickadee-trying-
to-drink-from-a-frozen-birdbath picture, captioned, "Sorry,
Wait Till Spring," and the shot of an utterly bundled child
crying piteously on a sled at the top of a snowy hill, labeled,
"Needs a Push." How can an old world be so innocent?

Finally I see tonight a picture of a friendly member of
the Forest Service in Wisconsin, who is freeing a duck
frozen onto the ice by chopping out its feet with a hand ax.
It calls to mind the spare, cruel story Thomas McGonigle
told me about herring gulls frozen on ice off Long Island.

When his father was young, he used to walk out on Great South Bay, which had frozen over, and frozen the gulls to it. Some of the gulls were already dead. He would take a hunk of driftwood and brain the living gulls; then, with a steel knife he hacked them free below the body and rammed them into a burlap sack. The family ate herring gull all winter, close around a lighted table in a steamy room. And out on the Bay, the ice was studded with paired, red stumps.

Winter knives. With their broad snow knives, Eskimos used to cut blocks of snow to spiral into domed igloos for temporary shelter. They sharpened their flensing knives by licking a thin coat of ice on the blade. Sometimes an Eskimo would catch a wolf with a knife. He slathered the knife with blubber and buried the hilt in snow or ice. A hungry wolf would scent the blubber, find the knife, and lick it compulsively with numbed tongue, until he sliced his tongue to ribbons, and bled to death.

This is the sort of stuff I read all winter. The books I read are like the stone men built by the Eskimos of the great desolate tundras west of Hudson's Bay. They still build them today, according to Farley Mowat. An Eskimo traveling alone in flat barrens will heap round stones to the height of a man, travel till he can no longer see the beacon, and build another. So I travel mute among these books, these eyeless men and women that people the empty plain. I wake up thinking: What am I reading? What will I read next? I'm terrified that I'll run out, that I will read through all I want to, and be forced to learn wildflowers at last, to keep awake. In the meantime I lose myself in a liturgy of names. The names of the men are Knud Rasmussen, Sir John Franklin, Peter Freuchen, Scott, Peary, and Byrd; Jedediah Smith, Peter Skene Ogden, and Milton Sublette; or Daniel Boone singing on his blanket in the Green River country. The names of waters are Baffin Bay, Repulse Bay, Coronation Gulf, and the Ross Sea; the Coppermine River, the Judith, the Snake, and the Musselshell; the Pelly, the Dease, the Tanana, and Telegraph Creek. Beaver plews, zero degrees latitude, and gold. I like the clean urgency of these tales, the sense of being set out in a wilderness with a jackknife and a length of twine. If I can get up a pinochle game, a little three-hand cutthroat for half a penny a point and a bottle of wine, fine; if not I'll spend these southern nights caught in the pack off Franz Josef Land, or casting for arctic char.

II

It snowed. It snowed all yesterday and never emptied the sky, although the clouds looked so low and heavy they might drop all at once with a thud. The light is diffuse and hueless, like the light on paper inside a pewter bowl. The snow looks light and the sky dark, but in fact the sky is lighter than the snow. Obviously the thing illuminated cannot be lighter than its illuminator. The classical demonstration of this point involves simply laying a mirror flat on the snow so that it reflects in its surface the sky, and comparing by sight this value to that of the snow. This is all very well, even conclusive, but the illusion persists. The dark is overhead and the light at my feet; I'm walking upside-down in the sky.

Yesterday I watched a curious nightfall. The cloud ceiling took on a warm tone, deepened, and departed as if drawn on a leash. I could no longer see the fat snow flying against the sky; I could see it only as it fell before dark objects. Any object at a distance—like the dead, ivy-covered walnut I see from the bay window—looked like a black-

and-white frontispiece seen through the sheet of white tissue. It was like dying, this watching the world recede into deeper and deeper blues while the snow piled; silence swelled and extended, distance dissolved, and soon only concentration at the largest shadows let me make out the movement of falling snow, and that too failed. The snow on the yard was blue as ink, faintly luminous; the sky violet. The bay window betrayed me, and started giving me back the room's lamps. It was like dying, that growing dimmer and deeper and then going out.

Today I went out for a look around. The snow had stopped, and a couple of inches lay on the ground. I walked through the yard to the creek; everything was slate-blue and gunmetal and white, except for the hemlocks and cedars, which showed a brittle, secret green if I looked for it under the snow.

Lo and behold, here in the creek was a silly-looking coot. It looked like a black and gray duck, but its head was smaller; its clunky white bill sloped straight from the curve of its skull like a cone from its base. I had read somewhere that coots were shy. They were liable to take umbrage at a footfall, skitter terrified along the water, and take to the air. But I wanted a good look. So when the coot tipped tail and dove, I raced towards it across the snow and hid behind a cedar trunk. As it popped up again its neck was as rigid and eyes as blank as a rubber duck's in the bathtub. It paddled downstream, away from me. I waited until it submerged again, then made a break for the trunk of the Osage orange. But up it came all at once, as though the child in the tub had held the rubber duck under water with both hands, and suddenly released it. I froze stock-still, thinking that after all I really was, actually and at bottom, a tree, a dead tree perhaps, even a wobbly one, but a treeish creature nonetheless. The coot wouldn't notice that a tree hadn't grown in that spot the moment before; what did it know? It was new to the area, a mere dude. As tree I allowed myself only the luxury of keeping a wary eye on the coot's eye. Nothing; it didn't suspect a thing—unless, of course, it was just leading me on, beguiling me into scratching my nose, when the jig would be up once and for all, and I'd be left unmasked, untreed, with no itch and an empty creek. So.

At its next dive I made the Osage orange and looked around its trunk while the coot fed from the pool behind the riffles. From there I ran downstream to the sycamore, getting treed in open ground again—and so forth for forty minutes, until it gradually began to light in my leafy brain that maybe the coot wasn't shy after all. That all this subterfuge was unnecessary, that the bird was singularly stupid, or at least not of an analytical turn of mind, and that in fact I'd been making a perfect idiot of myself all alone in the snow. So from behind the trunk of a black walnut, which was my present blind, I stepped boldly into the open. Nothing. The coot floated just across the creek from me, absolutely serene. Could it possibly be that I'd been flirting all afternoon with a *decoy*? No, decoys don't dive. I walked back to the sycamore, actually moving in plain sight not ten yards from the creature, which gave no sign of alarm or flight. I stopped; I raised my arm and waved. Nothing. In its beak hung a long, wet strand of some shore plant; it sucked it at length down its throat and dove again. I'll kill it. I'll hit the thing with a snowball, I really will; I'll make a mud-hen hash.

But I didn't even make a snowball. I wandered upstream, along smooth banks under trees. I had gotten, after all, a very good look at the coot. Now here were its tracks in the snow, three-toed and very close together. The wide, slow place in the creek by the road bridge was frozen over. From this bank at this spot in summer I can always see tadpoles, fat-bodied, scraping brown algae from a sort of shallow underwater ledge. Now I couldn't see the ledge under the ice. Most of the tadpoles were now frogs, and the frogs were buried alive in the mud at the bottom of the creek. They went to all that trouble to get out of the water and breathe air, only to hop back in before the first killing frost. The frogs of Tinker Creek are slathered in mud, mud at their eyes and mud at their nostrils; their damp skins absorb a muddy oxygen, and so they pass the dreaming winter.

Also from this bank at this spot in summer I can often see turtles by crouching low to catch the triangular poke of their heads out of water. Now snow smothered the ice; if it stays cold, I thought, and the neighborhood kids get busy with brooms, they can skate. Meanwhile, a turtle in the creek under the ice is getting oxygen by an almost incredible arrangement. It sucks water posteriorly into its large cloacal opening, where sensitive tissues filter the oxygen directly into the blood, as a gill does. Then the turtle discharges the water and gives another suck. The neighborhood kids can skate right over this curious rush of small waters.

Under the ice the bluegills and carp are still alive; this far south the ice never stays on the water long enough that fish metabolize all the oxygen and die. Farther north, fish sometimes die in this way and float up to the ice, which thickens around their bodies and holds them fast, open-eyed, until the thaw. Some worms are still burrowing in the silt, dragonfly larvae are active on the bottom, some algae carry on a dim photosynthesis, and that's about it. Everything else is dead, killed by the cold, or mutely alive in any of various still forms: egg, seed, pupa, spore. Water snakes are hibernating as dense balls, water striders hibernate as adults along the bank, and mourning cloak butterflies secret themselves in the bark of trees: all of these emerge groggily in winter thaws, to slink, skitter, and flit about in one afternoon's sunshine, and then at dusk to seek shelter, chill, fold, and forget.

The muskrats are out: they can feed under the ice, where the silver trail of bubbles that rises from their fur catches and freezes in streaming, glittering globes. What else? The birds, of course, are fine. Cold is no problem for warm-blooded animals, so long as they have food for fuel. Birds migrate for food, not for warmth as such. That is why, when so many people all over the country started feeding stations, southern birds like the mockingbird easily extended their ranges north. Some of our local birds go south, like the female robin; other birds, like the coot, consider *this* south. Mountain birds come down to the valley in a vertical migration; some of them, like the chickadees, eat not only seeds but such tiny fare as aphid eggs hid near winter buds and the ends of twigs. This afternoon I watched a chickadee swooping and dangling high in a tulip tree. It seemed astonishingly heated and congealed, as though a giant pair of hands had scooped a skyful of molecules and squeezed it like a snowball to produce this fireball, this feeding, flying, warm solid bit.

Other interesting things are going on wherever there is shelter. Slugs, of all creatures, hibernate, inside a waterproof sac. All the bumblebees and paper wasps are dead except the queens, who sleep a fat, numbed sleep, unless a mouse finds one and eats her alive. Honeybees have their own honey for fuel, so they can overwinter as adults, according to Edwin Way Teale, by buzzing together in a tightly packed, living sphere. Their shimmying activity heats the hive; they switch positions from time to time so that each bee gets its chance in the cozy middle and its turn on the cold outside. Ants hibernate en masse; the woolly bear hibernates alone in a bristling ball. Ladybugs hibernate under shelter in huge orange clusters sometimes the size of basketballs. Out West, people hunt for these overwintering masses in the mountains. They take them down to warehouses in the valleys, which pay handsomely. Then, according to Will Barker, the mail-order houses ship them to people who want them to eat garden aphids. They're mailed in the cool of night in boxes of old pine cones. It's a clever device: How do you pack a hundred living ladybugs? The insects naturally crawl deep into the depths of the pine cones; the sturdy "branches" of the opened cones protect them through all the bumpings of transit.

I crossed the bridge invigorated and came to a favorite spot. It is the spit of land enclosed in the oxbow of Tinker Creek. A few years ago I called these few acres the weed-field; they grew mostly sassafras, ivy, and poke. Now I call it the woods by the creek; young tulip grows there, and locust and oak. The snow on the wide path through the woods was unbroken. I stood in a little clearing beside the dry ditch that the creek cuts, bisecting the land, in high water. Here I ate a late lunch of ham sandwiches and wished I'd brought water and left more fat on the ham.

There was something new in the woods today—a bunch of sodden, hand-lettered signs tied to the trees all along the winding path. They said "SLOW," "SLIPPERY WHEN WET," "STOP," "PIT ROW," "ESSO," and "BUMP!!" These signs indicated an awful lot of excitement over a little snow. When I saw the first one, "SLOW," I thought, sure, I'll go slow; I won't screech around on the unbroken path in the woods by the creek under snow. What was going on here? The other signs made it clear. Under "BUMP!!" lay, sure enough, a bump. I scraped away the smooth snow. Hand-fashioned of red clay, and now frozen, the bump was about six inches high and eighteen inches across. The slope, such as it was, was gentle; tread marks stitched the clay. On the way out I saw that I'd missed the key sign, which had fallen: "WELCOME TO MARTINSVILLE SPEEDWAY." So my "woods by the creek" was a motorbike trail to the local boys, their "Martinsville Speedway." I had always wondered why they bothered to take a tractor-mower to these woods all summer long, keeping the many paths open; it was a great convenience to me.

Now the speedway was a stillnessway. Next to me in a sapling, a bird's nest cradled aloft a newborn burden of snow. From a crab apple tree hung a single frozen apple with blistered and shiny skin; it was heavy and hard as a stone. Everywhere through the trees I saw the creek run blue under the ledge of ice from the banks; it made a thin, metallic sound like foil beating foil.

When I left the woods I stepped into a yellow light. The sun behind a uniform layer of gray had the diffuse shine of a very much rubbed and burnished metal boss. On the mountains the wan light slanted over the snow and gouged out shallow depressions and intricacies in the mountains' sides I never knew were there. I walked home. No school today. The motorbike boys were nowhere in sight; they were probably skidding on sleds down the very steep hill and out onto the road. Here my neighbor's small children were rolling a snowman. The noon sun had dampened the snow; it caught in slabs, leaving green, irregular tracks on the yard. I just now discovered the most extraordinary essay, a treatise on making a snowman. ". . . By all means use what is ready to hand. In a fuel-oil burning area, for instance, it is inconceivable that fathers should sacrifice their days hunting downtown for lumps of coal for their children's snowmen's eyes. Charcoal briquettes from the barbecue are an unwieldy substitute, and fuel-oil itself is of course out of the question. Use pieces of rock, brick, or dark sticks; use bits of tire tread or even dark fallen leaves rolled tightly, cigarwise, and deeply inserted into sockets formed by a finger." Why, why in the blue-green world write this sort of thing? Funny written culture, I guess; we pass things on.

There are seven or eight categories of phenomena in the world that are worth talking about, and one of them is the weather. Any time you care to get in your car and drive across the country and over the mountains, come into our valley, cross Tinker Creek, drive up the road to the house, walk across the yard, knock on the door and ask to come in and talk about the weather, you'd be welcome. If you came tonight from up north, you'd have a terrific tailwind; between Tinker and Dead Man you'd chute through the orchardy pass like an iceboat. When I let you in, we might not be able to close the door. The wind shrieks and hisses down the valley, sonant and surd, drying the puddles and dismantling the nests from the trees.

Inside the house, my single goldfish, Ellery Channing, whips around and around the sides of his bowl. Can he feel a glassy vibration, a ripple out of the north that urges him to swim for deeper, warmer waters? Saint-Exupéry says that when flocks of wild geese migrate high over a barnyard, the cocks and even the dim, fatted chickens fling themselves a foot or so into the air and flap for the south. Eskimo sled dogs feed all summer on famished salmon flung to them from creeks. I have often wondered if those dogs feel a wistful downhill drift in the fall, or an upstream yank, an urge to leap ladders, in the spring. To what hail do you hark, Ellery?—what sunny bottom under chill waters, what Chinese emperor's petaled pond? Even the spiders are restless under this wind, roving about alert-eyed over their fluff in every corner.

I allow the spiders the run of the house. I figure that any predator that hopes to make a living on whatever smaller creatures might blunder into a four-inch square bit of space in the corner of the bathroom where the tub meets the floor, needs every bit of my support. They catch flies and even field crickets in those webs. Large spiders in barns have been known to trap, wrap, and suck hummingbirds, but there's no danger of that here. I tolerate the webs, only occasionally sweeping away the very dirtiest of them after the spider itself has scrambled to safety. I'm always leaving a bath towel draped over the tub so that the big, haired spiders, who are constantly getting trapped by the tub's smooth sides, can use its rough surface as an exit ramp. Inside the house the spiders have only given me one mild surprise. I washed some dishes and set them to dry over a plastic drainer. Then I wanted a cup of coffee, so I picked from the drainer my mug, which was still warm from the hot rinse water, and across the rim of the mug, strand after strand, was a spider web.

Outside in summer I watch the orb-weavers, the spiders at their wheels. Last summer I watched one spin her web, which was especially interesting because the light just happened to be such that I couldn't see the web at all. I had read that spiders lay their major straight lines with fluid that isn't sticky, and then lay a nonsticky spiral. Then they walk along that safe road and lay a sticky spiral going the other way. It seems to be very much a matter of concentration. The spider I watched was a matter of mystery: she seemed to be scrambling up, down, and across the air. There was a small white mass of silk visible at the center of the orb, and she returned to this hub after each frenzied foray between air and air. It was a sort of Tinker Creek to her, from which she bore lightly in every direction an invisible news. She had a nice ability to make hairpin turns at the most acute angles in the air, all at topmost speed. I understand that you can lure an orb-weaver spider, if you want one, by vibrating or twirling a blade of grass against the web, as a flying insect would struggle if caught. This little ruse has never worked for me; I need a tuning fork; I leave the webs on the bushes bristling with grass.

Things are well in their place. Last week I found a brown, cocoonlike object, light and dry, and pocketed it in an outside, unlined pocket where it wouldn't warm and come alive. Then I saw on the ground another one, slightly torn open, so I split it further with my fingers, and saw a pale froth. I held it closer; the froth took on intricacy. I held it next to my eye and saw a tiny spider, yellowish but so infinitesimal it was translucent, waving each of its eight legs in what was clearly threat behavior. It was one of hundreds of spiders, already alive, all squirming in a tangled orgy of legs. Not on me they won't; I emptied that pocket fast. Things out of place are ill. Tonight I hear outside a sound of going in the tops of the mulberry trees; I stay in to do battle with—what? Once I looked into a little wooden birdhouse hung from a tree; it had a pointed roof like an Alpine cottage, a peg perch, and a neat round door. Inside, watching me, was a coiled snake. I used to kill insects with carbon tetrachloride—cleaning fluid vapor—and pin them in cigar boxes, labeled, in neat rows. That was many years ago: I quit when one day I opened a cigar-box lid and saw a carrion beetle, staked down high between its wing covers, trying to crawl, swimming on its pin. It was dancing with its own shadow, untouching, and had been for days. If I go downstairs now will I see a possum just rounding a corner, trailing its scaled pink tail? I know that one night, in just this sort of rattling wind, I will go to the kitchen for milk and find on the back of the stove a sudden stew I never fixed, bubbling, with a deer leg sticking out.

In a dry wind like this, snow and ice can pass directly into the air as a gas without having first melted to water. This process is called sublimation; tonight the snow in the yard and the ice in the creek sublime. A breeze buffets my palm held a foot from the wall. A wind like this does my breathing for me; it engenders something quick and kicking in my lungs. Pliny believed the mares of the Portuguese used to raise their tails to the wind, "and turn them full against it, and so conceive that genital air instead of natural seed: in such sort, as they become great withal, and quicken in their time, and bring forth foals as swift as the wind, but they live not above three years." Does the white mare Itch in the dell in the Adams' woods up the road turn tail to this wind with white-lashed, lidded eyes? A single cell quivers at a windy embrace; it swells and splits, it bubbles into a raspberry; a dark clot starts to throb. Soon something perfect is born. Something wholly new rides the wind, something fleet and fleeting I'm likely to miss.

To sleep, spiders and fish; the wind won't stop, but the house will hold. To shelter, starlings and coot; bow to the wind.

CHAPTER 4

The Fixed

I

I HAVE JUST LEARNED to see praying mantis egg cases. Suddenly I see them everywhere; a tan oval of light catches my eye, or I notice a blob of thickness in a patch of slender weeds. As I write I can see the one I tied to the mock orange hedge outside my study window. It is over an inch long and shaped like a bell, or like the northern hemisphere of an egg cut through its equator. The full length of one of its long sides is affixed to a twig; the side that catches the light is perfectly flat. It has a dead straw, deadweed color, and a curious brittle texture, hard as varnish, but pitted minutely, like frozen foam. I carried it home this afternoon, holding it carefully by the twig, along with several others—they were light as air. I dropped one without missing it until I got home and made a count.

Within the week I've seen thirty or so of these egg cases in a rose-grown field on Tinker Mountain, and another thirty in weeds along Carvin's Creek. One was on a twig of tiny dogwood on the mud lawn of a newly built house. I think the mail-order houses sell them to gardeners at a dollar apiece. It beats spraying, because each case contains between one hundred twenty-five and three hundred fifty eggs. If the eggs survive ants, woodpeckers, and mice—and most do—then you get the fun of seeing the new mantises hatch, and the smug feeling of knowing, all summer long, that they're out there in your garden devouring gruesome numbers of fellow insects all nice and organically. When a mantis has crunched up the last shred of its victim, it cleans its smooth green face like a cat.

In late summer I often see a winged adult stalking the insects that swarm about my porch light. Its body is a clear, warm green; its naked, triangular head can revolve uncannily, so that I often see one twist its head to gaze at me as it were over its shoulder. When it strikes, it jerks so suddenly and with such a fearful clatter of raised wings, that even a hardened entomologist like J. Henri Fabre confessed to being startled witless every time.

Adult mantises eat more or less everything that breathes and is small enough to capture. They eat honeybees and butterflies, including monarch butterflies. People have actually seen them seize and devour garter snakes, mice, and even *hummingbirds*. Newly hatched mantises, on the other hand, eat small creatures like aphids and each other. When I was in elementary school, one of the teachers brought in a mantis egg case in a Mason jar. I watched the newly hatched mantises emerge and shed their skins; they were spidery and translucent, all over joints. They trailed from the egg case to the base of the Mason jar in a living bridge that looked like Arabic calligraphy, some baffling text from the Koran inscribed down the air by a fine hand. Over a period of several hours, during which time the teacher never summoned the nerve or the sense to release them, they ate each other until only two were left. Tiny legs were still kicking from the mouths of both. The two survivors grappled and sawed in the Mason jar; finally both died of injuries. I felt as though I myself should swallow the corpses, shutting my eyes and washing them down like jagged pills, so all that life wouldn't be lost.

When mantises hatch in the wild, however, they straggle about prettily, dodging ants, till all are lost in the grass. So it was in hopes of seeing an eventual hatch that I pocketed my jackknife this afternoon before I set out to walk. Now that I can see the egg cases, I'm embarrassed to realize how many I must have missed all along. I walked east through the Adams' woods to the cornfield, cutting three undamaged egg cases I found at the edge of the field. It was a clear, picturesque day, a February day without clouds, without emotion or spirit, like a beautiful woman with an empty face. In my fingers I carried the thorny stems from which the egg cases hung like roses; I switched the bouquet from hand to hand, warming the free hand in a pocket. Passing the house again, deciding not to fetch gloves, I walked north to the hill by the place where the steers come to drink from Tinker Creek. There in the weeds on the hill I found another eight egg cases. I was stunned—I cross this hill several times a week, and I always look for egg cases here, because it was here that I had once seen a mantis laying her eggs.

It was several years ago that I witnessed this extraordinary procedure, but I remember, and confess, an inescapable feeling that I was watching something not real and present, but a horrible nature movie, a "secrets-of-nature" short, beautifully photographed in full color, that I had to sit through unable to look anywhere else but at the dimly lighted EXIT signs along the walls, and that behind the scenes some amateur moviemaker was congratulating himself on having stumbled across this little wonder, or even on having contrived so natural a setting, as though the whole scene had been shot very carefully in a terrarium in someone's greenhouse.

I was ambling across this hill that day when I noticed a speck of pure white. The hill is eroded; the slope is a rutted wreck of red clay broken by grassy hillocks and low wild roses whose roots clasp a pittance of topsoil. I leaned to examine the white thing and saw a mass of bubbles like spittle. Then I saw something dark like an engorged leech rummaging over the spittle, and then I saw the praying mantis.

She was upside-down, clinging to a horizontal stem of wild rose by her feet which pointed to heaven. Her head was deep in dried grass. Her abdomen was swollen like a smashed finger; it tapered to a fleshy tip out of which bubbled a wet, whipped froth. I couldn't believe my eyes. I lay on the hill this way and that, my knees in thorns and my cheeks in clay, trying to see as well as I could. I poked near the female's head with a grass; she was clearly undisturbed, so I settled my nose an inch from that pulsing abdomen. It puffed like a concertina, it throbbed like a bellows; it roved, pumping, over the glistening, clabbered surface of the egg case testing and patting, thrusting and smoothing. It seemed to act so independently that I forgot the panting brown stick at the other end. The bubble creature seemed to have two eyes, a frantic little brain, and two busy, soft hands. It looked like a hideous, harried mother slicking up a fat daughter for a beauty pageant, touching her up, slobbering over her, patting and hemming and brushing and stroking.

The male was nowhere in sight. The female had probably eaten him. Fabre says that, at least in captivity, the female will mate with and devour up to seven males, whether she has laid her egg cases or not. The mating rites of mantises are well known: a chemical produced in the head of the male insect says, in effect, "No, don't go near her, you fool, she'll eat you alive." At the same time a chemical in his abdomen says, "Yes, by all means, now and forever yes."

While the male is making up what passes for his mind, the female tips the balance in her favor by eating his head. He mounts her. Fabre describes the mating, which sometimes lasts six hours, as follows: "The male, absorbed in the performance of his vital functions, holds the female in a tight embrace. But the wretch has no head; he has no neck; he has hardly a body. The other, with her muzzle turned over her shoulder continues very placidly to gnaw what remains of the gentle swain. And, all the time, that masculine stump, holding on firmly, goes on with the business! . . . I have seen it done with my own eyes and have not yet recovered from my astonishment."

I watched the egg-laying for over an hour. When I returned the next day, the mantis was gone. The white foam had hardened and browned to a dirty suds; then, and on subsequent days, I had trouble pinpointing the case, which was only an inch or so off the ground. I checked on it every week all winter long. In the spring the ants discovered it;

every week I saw dozens of ants scrambling over the sides, unable to chew a way in. Later in the spring I climbed the hill every day, hoping to catch the hatch. The leaves of the trees had long since unfolded, the butterflies were out, and the robins' first broods were fledged; still the egg case hung silent and full on the stem. I read that I should wait for June, but still I visited the case every day. One morning at the beginning of June everything was gone. I couldn't find the lower thorn in the clump of three to which the egg case was fixed. I couldn't find the clump of three. Tracks ridged the clay, and I saw the lopped stems: somehow my neighbor had contrived to run a tractor-mower over that steep clay hill on which there grew nothing to mow but a few stubby thorns.

So. Today from this same hill I cut another three un-damaged cases and carried them home with the others by their twigs. I also collected a suspiciously light cynthia moth cocoon. My fingers were stiff and red with cold, and my nose ran. I had forgotten the Law of the Wild, which is, "Carry Kleenex." At home I tied the twigs with their egg cases to various sunny bushes and trees in the yard. They're easy to find because I used white string; at any rate, I'm unlikely to mow my own trees. I hope the woodpeckers that come to the feeder don't find them, but I don't see how they'd get a purchase on them if they did.

Night is rising in the valley; the creek has been extin-guished for an hour, and now only the naked tips of trees fire tapers into the sky like trails of sparks. The scene that was in the back of my brain all afternoon, obscurely, is be-ginning to rise from night's lagoon. It really has nothing to do with praying mantises. But this afternoon I threw tiny string lashings and hitches with frozen hands, gingerly, fearing to touch the egg cases even for a minute because I remembered the Polyphemus moth.

I have no intention of inflicting all my childhood memories on anyone. Far less do I want to excoriate my old teachers who, in their bungling, unforgettable way, exposed me to the natural world, a world covered in chitin, where implacable realities hold sway. The Polyphemus moth never made it to the past; it crawls in that crowded, pellucid pool at the lip of the great waterfall. It is as present as this blue desk and brazen lamp, as this blackened window before me in which I can no longer see even the white string that binds the egg case to the hedge, but only my own pale, astonished face.

Once, when I was ten or eleven years old, my friend Judy brought in a Polyphemus moth cocoon. It was January; there were doily snowflakes taped to the schoolroom panes. The teacher kept the cocoon in her desk all morning and brought it out when we were getting restless before recess. In a book we found what the adult moth would look like; it would be beautiful. With a wingspread of up to six inches, the Polyphemus is one of the few huge American silk moths, much larger than, say, a giant or tiger swallowtail butterfly. The moth's enormous wings are velveted in a rich, warm brown, and edged in bands of blue and pink delicate as a watercolor wash. A startling "eyespot," immense, and deep blue melding to an almost translucent yellow, luxuriates in the center of each hind wing. The effect is one of a masculine splendor foreign to the butterflies, a fragility unfurled to strength. The Polyphemus moth in the picture looked like a mighty wraith, a beating essence of the hardwood forest, alien-skinned and brown, with spread, blind eyes. This was the giant moth packed in the faded cocoon. We closed the book and turned to the cocoon. It was an oak leaf sewn into a plump oval bundle; Judy had found it loose in a pile of frozen leaves.

We passed the cocoon around; it was heavy. As we held it in our hands, the creature within warmed and squirmed. We were delighted, and wrapped it tighter in our fists. The pupa began to jerk violently, in heart-stopping knocks. Who's there? I can still feel those thumps, urgent through a muffling of spun silk and leaf, urgent through the swaddling of many years, against the curve of my palm. We kept passing it around. When it came to me again it was hot as a bun; it jumped half out of my hand. The teacher intervened. She put it, still heaving and banging, in the ubiquitous Mason jar.

It was coming. There was no stopping it now, January or not. One end of the cocoon dampened and gradually frayed in a furious battle. The whole cocoon twisted and slapped around in the bottom of the jar. The teacher fades, the classmates fade, I fade: I don't remember anything but that thing's struggle to be a moth or die trying. It emerged at last, a sodden crumple. It was a male; his long antennae were thickly plumed, as wide as his fat abdomen. His body was very thick, over an inch long, and deeply furred. A gray, furlike plush covered his head; a long, tan furlike hair hung from his wide thorax over his brown-furred, segmented abdomen. His multijointed legs, pale and powerful, were shaggy as a bear's. He stood still, but he breathed.

He couldn't spread his wings. There was no room. The chemical that coated his wings like varnish, stiffening them permanently, dried, and hardened his wings as they were. He was a monster in a Mason jar. Those huge wings stuck on his back in a torture of random pleats and folds, wrinkled as a dirty tissue, rigid as leather. They made a single nightmare clump still wracked with useless, frantic convulsions.

The next thing I remember, it was recess. The school was in Shadyside, a busy residential part of Pittsburgh. Everyone was playing dodgeball in the fenced playground or racing around the concrete schoolyard by the swings. Next to the playground a long delivery drive sloped downhill to the sidewalk and street. Someone—it must have been the teacher—had let the moth out. I was standing in the driveway, alone, stock-still, but shivering. Someone had given the Polyphemus moth his freedom, and he was walking away.

He heaved himself down the asphalt driveway by infinite degrees, unwavering. His hideous crumpled wings lay glued and rucked on his back, perfectly still now, like a collapsed tent. The bell rang twice; I had to go. The moth was receding down the driveway, dragging on. I went; I ran inside. The Polyphemus moth is still crawling down the driveway, crawling down the driveway hunched, crawling down the driveway on six furred feet, forever.

Shading the glass with a hand, I can see how shadow has pooled in the valley. It washes up the sandstone cliffs on Tinker Mountain and obliterates them in a deluge; freshets of shadow leak into the sky. I am exhausted. In Pliny I read about the invention of clay modeling. A Sicyonian potter came to Corinth. There his daughter fell in love with a young man who had to make frequent long journeys away from the city. When he sat with her at home, she used to trace the outline of his shadow that a candle's light cast on the wall. Then, in his absence she worked over the profile, deepening it, so that she might enjoy his face, and remember. One day the father slapped some potter's clay over the gouged plaster; when the clay hardened he removed it, baked it, and "showed it abroad." The story ends here. Did the boy come back? What did the girl think of her father's dragging her lover all over town by the hair? What I really want to know is this: Is the shadow still there? If I went back and found the shadow of that face there on the wall by the fireplace, I'd rip down the house with my hands for that hunk.

The shadow's the thing. Outside shadows are blue, I read, because they are lighted by the blue sky and not the yellow sun. Their blueness bespeaks infinitesimal particles scattered down inestimable distance. Muslims, whose religion bans representational art as idolatrous, don't observe the rule strictly; but they do forbid sculpture, because it casts a shadow. So shadows define the real. If I no longer see shadows as "dark marks," as do the newly sighted, then I see them as making some sort of sense of the light. They give the light distance; they put it in its place. They inform my eyes of my location here, here O Israel, here in the world's flawed sculpture, here in the flickering shade of the nothingness between me and the light.

Now that shadow has dissolved the heavens' blue dome, I can see Andromeda again; I stand pressed to the window, rapt and shrunk in the galaxy's chill glare. "Nostalgia of the Infinite," di Chirico: cast shadows stream across the sunlit courtyard, gouging canyons. There is a sense in which shadows are actually cast, hurled with a power, cast as Ishmael was cast, *out*, with a flinging force. This is the blue strip running through creation, the icy roadside stream on whose banks the mantis mates, in whose unweighed waters the giant water bug sips frogs. Shadow Creek is the blue subterranean stream that chills Carvin's Creek and Tinker Creek; it cuts like ice under the ribs of the mountains, Tinker and Dead Man. Shadow Creek storms through limestone vaults under forests, or surfaces anywhere, damp, on the underside of a leaf. I wring it from rocks; it seeps into my cup. Chasms open at the glance of an eye; the ground parts like a wind-rent cloud over stars. Shadow Creek: on my least walk to the mailbox I may find myself knee-deep in its sucking, frigid pools. I must either wear rubber boots, or dance to keep warm.

II

Fish gotta swim and bird gotta fly; insects, it seems, gotta do one horrible thing after another. I never ask why of a vulture or shark, but I ask why of almost every insect I see. More than one insect—the possibility of fertile reproduction—is an assault on all human value, all hope of a reasonable god. Even that devout Frenchman, J. Henri Fabre, who devoted his entire life to the study of insects, cannot restrain a feeling of unholy revulsion. He describes a bee-eating wasp, the Philanthus, who has killed a honeybee. If the bee is heavy with honey, the wasp squeezes its crop "so as to make her disgorge the delicious syrup, which she drinks by licking the tongue which her unfortunate victim, in her death-agony, sticks out of her mouth at full length. . . . At the moment of some such horrible banquet, I have seen the Wasp, with her prey, seized by the Mantis: the bandit was rifled by another bandit. And here is an awful detail: while the Mantis held her transfixed under the points of the double saw and was already munching her belly, the Wasp continued to lick the honey of her Bee, unable to relinquish the delicious food even amid the terrors of death. Let us hasten to cast a veil over these horrors."

The remarkable thing about the world of insects, however, is precisely that there is no veil cast over these horrors. These are mysteries performed in broad daylight before our very eyes; we can see every detail, and yet they are still mysteries. If, as Heraclitus suggests, god, like an oracle, neither "declares nor hides, but sets forth by signs," then clearly I had better be scrying the signs. The earth devotes an overwhelming proportion of its energy to these buzzings and leaps in the grass, to these brittle gnawings and crawlings about. Theirs is the biggest wedge of the pie: Why? I ought to keep a giant water bug in an aquarium on my dresser, so I can think about it. We have brass candlesticks in our houses now; we ought to display praying mantises in our churches. Why do we turn from the insects in loathing? Our competitors are not only cold-blooded, and green- and yellow-blooded, but are also cased in a clacking horn. They lack the grace to go about as we do, softside-out to the wind and thorns. They have rigid eyes and brains strung down their backs. But they make up the bulk of our comrades-at-life, so I look to them for a glimmer of companionship.

When a grasshopper landed on my study window last summer, I looked at it for a long time. Its hard wing covers were short; its body was a dead waxen yellow, with black-green, indecipherable marks. Like all large insects, it gave me pause, plenty pause, with its hideous horizontal, multi-jointed mouthparts and intricate, mechanical-looking feet, all cups and spikes. I looked at its tapered, chitin-covered abdomen, plated and barred as a tank tread, and was about to turn away when I saw it breathe, puff puff, and I grew sympathetic. Yeah, I said, puff puff, isn't it? It jerked away with a buzz like a rasping file, audible through the pane, and continued to puff in the grass. So puff it is, and that's all there is; though I'm partial to honey myself.

Nature is, above all, profligate. Don't believe them when they tell you how economical and thrifty nature is, whose leaves return to the soil. Wouldn't it be cheaper to leave them on the tree in the first place? This deciduous business alone is a radical scheme, the brainchild of a deranged manic-depressive with limitless capital. Extravagance! Nature will try anything once. This is what the sign of the insects says. No form is too gruesome, no behavior too grotesque. If you're dealing with organic compounds, then let them combine. If it works, if it quickens, set it clacking in the grass; there's always room for one more; you ain't so handsome yourself. This is a spendthrift economy; though nothing is lost, all is spent.

That the insects have adapted is obvious. Their failures to adapt, however, are dazzling. It is hard to believe that nature is partial to such dim-wittedness. Howard Ensign Evans tells of dragonflies trying to lay eggs on the shining hoods of cars. Other dragonflies seem to test a surface, to learn if it's really water, by dipping the tips of their abdomens in it. At the Los Angeles La Brea tar pits, they dip their abdomens into the reeking tar and get stuck. If by tremendous effort a dragonfly frees itself, Evans reports, it is apt to repeat the maneuver. Sometimes the tar pits glitter with the dry bodies of dead dragonflies.

J. Henri Fabre's pine processionaries speak to the same point. Although the new studies show that some insects can on occasion strike out into new territory, leaving instinct behind, still a blindered and blinkered enslavement to instinct is the rule, as the pine processionaries show. Pine processionaries are moth caterpillars with shiny black heads, who travel about at night in pine trees along a silken road of their own making. They straddle the road in a tight file, head to rear touching, and each caterpillar adds its thread to the original track first laid by the one who happens to lead the procession. Fabre interferes; he catches them on a daytime exploration approaching a circular track, the rim of a wide palm vase in his greenhouse. When the leader of the insect train completes a full circle, Fabre removes the caterpillars still climbing the vase and brushes away all extraneous silken tracks. Now he has a closed circuit of caterpillars, leaderless, trudging round his vase on a never-ending track. He wants to see how long it will take them to catch on. To his horror, they march not just an hour or so, but all day. When Fabre leaves the greenhouse at night, they are still tracing that wearying circle, although night is the time they usually feed.

In the chill of the next morning they are deadly still; when they rouse themselves, however, they resume what Fabre calls their "imbecility." They slog along all day, head to tail. The next night is bitterly cold; in the morning Fabre finds them slumped on the vase rim in two distinct clumps. When they line up again, they have two leaders, and the leaders in nature often explore to the sides of an already laid track. But the two ranks meet, and the entranced circle winds on. Fabre can't believe his eyes. The creatures have had neither water nor food nor rest; they are shelterless all day and all night long. Again the next night a hard frost numbs the caterpillars, who huddle in heaps. By chance the first one to wake is off the track; it strikes out in a new direction, and encounters the soil in the pot. Six others follow his track. Now the ones on the vase have a leader, because there is a gap in the rim. But they drag on stubbornly around their circle of hell. Soon the seven rebels, unable to eat the palm in the vase, follow their trail back to the rim of the pot and join the doomed march. The circle often breaks as starved or exhausted caterpillars stagger to a halt; but they soon breach the gap they leave, and no leaders emerge.

The next day a heat spell hits. The caterpillars lean far over the rim of the vase, exploring. At last one veers from the track. Followed by four others it explores down the long side of the vase; there, next to the vase, Fabre has placed some pine needles for them to feed on. They ramble within nine inches of the pine needles, but, incredibly, wander upward to the rim and rejoin the dismal parade. For two more days the processionaries stagger on; at last they try the path laid down the vase by the last group. They venture out to new ground; they straggle at last to their nest. It has been seven days. Fabre himself, "already familiar with the abysmal stupidity of insects as a class whenever the least accident occurs," is nevertheless clearly oppressed by this new confirmation that the caterpillars lack "any gleam of intelligence in their benighted minds." "The caterpillars in distress," he concludes, "starved, shelterless, chilled with cold at night, cling obstinately to the silk ribbon covered hundreds of times, because they lack the rudimentary glimmers of reason which would advise them to abandon it."

I want out of this still air. What street-corner vendor wound the key on the backs of tin soldiers and abandoned them to the sidewalk, and crashings over the curb? Elijah mocked the prophets of Baal, who laid a bullock on a woodpile and begged Baal to consume it: "Cry aloud: for he is a god; either he is talking, or he is pursuing, or he is in a journey, or peradventure he sleepeth, and must be awaked." Cry aloud. It is the fixed that horrifies us, the fixed that assails us with the tremendous force of its mindlessness. The fixed is a Mason jar, and we can't beat it open. The prophets of Baal gashed themselves with knives and lancets, and the wood stayed wood. The fixed is the world without fire—dead flint, dead tinder, and nowhere a spark. It is motion without direction, force without power, the aimless procession of caterpillars round the rim of a vase, and I hate it because at any moment I myself might step to that charmed and glistening thread. Last spring in the flood I saw a brown cattail bob in the high muddy water of Carvin's Creek, up and down, side to side, a jerk a second.

I went back the next day and nothing had changed; that empty twitching beat on in an endless, sickening tattoo. What geomancy reads what the windblown sand writes on the desert rock? I read there that all things live by a generous power and dance to a mighty tune; or I read there that all things are scattered and hurled, that our every arabesque and grand jeté is a frantic variation on our one free fall.

Two weeks ago, in the dark of night, I bundled up and quit the house for Tinker Creek. Long before I could actually see the creek, I heard it shooting the sandstone riffles with a chilled rush and splash. It has always been a happy thought to me that the creek runs on all night, new every minute, whether I wish it or know it or care, as a closed book on a shelf continues to whisper to itself its own inexhaustible tale. So many things have been shown me on these banks, so much light has illumined me by reflection here where the water comes down, that I can hardly believe that this grace never flags, that the pouring from ever-renewable sources is endless, impartial, and free. But that night Tinker Creek had vanished, usurped, and Shadow Creek blocked its banks. The night-cold pulsed in my bones. I stood on the frozen grass under the Osage orange. The night was moonless; the mountains loomed over the stars. By half looking away I could barely make out the gray line of foam at the riffles; the skin tightened over the corners of my mouth, and I blinked in the cold. That night the fact of the creek's running on in the dark—from high on the unseen side of Tinker Mountain, miles away—smacked sinister. Where was the old exhilaration? This dumb dead drop over rocks was a hideous parody of real natural life, warm and willful. It was senseless and horrifying; I turned away. The damned thing was flowing because it was *pushed*.

That was two weeks ago; tonight I don't know. Tonight the moon is full, and I wonder. I'm pleased with my day's "work," with the cocoon and egg cases hung on the hedge. Van Gogh found nerve to call this world "a study that didn't come off," but I'm not so sure. Where do I get my standards that I fancy the fixed world of insects doesn't meet? I'm tired of reading; I pick up a book and learn that "pieces of the leech's body can also swim." Take a deep breath, Elijah: light your pile. Van Gogh is utterly dead; the world may be fixed, but it never was broken. And shadow itself may resolve into beauty.

Once, when Tinker Creek had frozen inches thick at a wide part near the bridge, I found a pileated woodpecker in the sky by its giant shadow flapping blue on the white ice below. It flew under the neighborhood children's skates; it soared whole and wholly wild though they sliced its wings. I'd like a chunk of that shadow, a pane of fresh-water ice to lug with me everywhere, fluttering huge under my arm, to use as the Eskimos did for a window on the world. Shadow is the blue patch where the light doesn't hit. It is mystery itself, and mystery is the ancients' ultima Thule, the modern explorers' Point of Relative Inaccessibility, that boreal point most distant from all known lands. There the twin oceans of beauty and horror meet. The great glaciers are calving. Ice that sifted to earth as snow in the time of Christ shears from the pack with a roar and crumbles to water. It could be that our instruments have not looked deeply enough. The RNA deep in the mantis's jaw is a beautiful ribbon. Did the crawling Polyphemus have in its watery heart one cell, and in that cell one special molecule, and in that molecule one hydrogen atom, and round that atom's nucleus one wild, distant electron that, spilt, showed a forest, swaying?

In lieu of a pinochle game, I'll walk a step before bed. No hesitation about gloves now; I swath myself in wool and down from head to foot, and step into the night.

The air bites my nose like pepper. I walk down the road, leap a ditch, and mount the hill where today I clipped the egg cases, where years ago I watched the female mantis frothing out foam. The rutted clay is frozen tonight in shards; its scarps loom in the slanting light like pressure ridges in ice under aurora. The light from the moon is awesome, full and wan. It's not the lustre of noonday it gives, but the lustre of elf-light, utterly lambent and utterly dreamed. I crash over clumps of brittle, hand-blown grass —and I stop still. The frozen twigs of the huge tulip poplar next to the hill clack in the cold like tinsnips.

I look to the sky. What do I know of deep space with its red giants and white dwarfs? I think of our own solar system, of the five mute moons of Uranus—Ariel, Umbriel, Titania, Oberon, Miranda—spinning in their fixed sleep of thralldom. These our actors, as I foretold you, were all spirits. At last I look to the moon; it hangs fixed and full in the east, enormously scrubbed and simple. Our own hometown ultima moon. It must have been a wonderful sight from there, when the olive continents cracked and spread, and the white ice rolled down and up like a window blind. My eyes feel cold when I blink; this is enough of a walk tonight. I lack the apparatus to feel a warmth that few have felt—but it's there. According to Arthur Koestler, Kepler felt the focused warmth when he was experimenting on something entirely different, using concave mirrors. Kepler wrote, "I was engaged in other experiments with mirrors, without thinking of the warmth; I involuntarily turned around to see whether somebody was breathing on my hand." It was warmth from the moon.

CHAPTER 5

Untying the Knot

YESTERDAY I SET OUT to catch the new season, and instead I found an old snakeskin. I was in the sunny February woods by the quarry; the snakeskin was lying in a heap of leaves right next to an aquarium someone had thrown away. I don't know why that someone hauled the aquarium deep into the woods to get rid of it; it had only one broken glass side. The snake found it handy, I imagine; snakes like to rub against something rigid to help them out of their skins, and the broken aquarium looked like the nearest likely object. Together the snakeskin and the aquarium made an interesting scene on the forest floor. It looked like an exhibit at a trial—circumstantial evidence—of a wild scene, as though a snake had burst through the broken side of the aquarium, burst through his ugly old skin, and dis-

73

appeared, perhaps straight up in the air, in a rush of freedom and beauty.

The snakeskin had unkeeled scales, so it belonged to a nonpoisonous snake. It was roughly five feet long by the yardstick, but I'm not sure because it was very wrinkled and dry, and every time I tried to stretch it flat it broke. I ended up with seven or eight pieces of it all over the kitchen table in a fine film of forest dust.

The point I want to make about the snakeskin is that, when I found it, it was whole and tied in a knot. Now there have been stories told, even by reputable scientists, of snakes that have deliberately tied themselves in a knot to prevent larger snakes from trying to swallow them—but I couldn't imagine any way that throwing itself into a half hitch would help a snake trying to escape its skin. Still, ever cautious, I figured that one of the neighborhood boys could possibly have tied it in a knot in the fall, for some whimsical boyish reason, and left it there, where it dried and gathered dust. So I carried the skin along thoughtlessly as I walked, snagging it sure enough on a low branch and ripping it in two for the first of many times. I saw that thick ice still lay on the quarry pond and that the skunk cabbage was already out in the clearings, and then I came home and looked at the skin and its knot.

The knot had no beginning. Idly I turned it around in my hand, searching for a place to untie; I came to with a start when I realized I must have turned the thing around fully ten times. Intently, then, I traced the knot's lump around with a finger: it was continuous. I couldn't untie it any more than I could untie a doughnut; it was a loop without beginning or end. These snakes *are* magic, I thought for a second, and then of course I reasoned what must have happened. The skin had been pulled inside-out like a peeled sock for several inches; then an inch or so of the inside-out part—a piece whose length was coincidentally equal to the diameter of the skin—had somehow been turned right-side out again, making a thick lump whose edges were lost in wrinkles, looking exactly like a knot.

So. I have been thinking about the change of seasons. I don't want to miss spring this year. I want to distinguish the last winter frost from the out-of-season one, the frost of spring. I want to be there on the spot the moment the grass turns green. I always miss this radical revolution; I see it the next day from a window, the yard so suddenly green and lush I could envy Nebuchadnezzar down on all fours eating grass. This year I want to stick a net into time and say "now," as men plant flags on the ice and snow and say, "here." But it occurred to me that I could no more catch spring by the tip of the tail than I could untie the apparent knot in the snakeskin; there are no edges to grasp. Both are continuous loops.

I wonder how long it would take you to notice the regular recurrence of the seasons if you were the first man on earth. What would it be like to live in open-ended time broken only by days and nights? You could say, "it's cold again; it was cold before," but you couldn't make the key connection and say, "it was cold this time last year," because the notion of "year" is precisely the one you lack. Assuming that you hadn't yet noticed any orderly progression of heavenly bodies, how long would you have to live on earth before you could feel with any assurance that any one particular long period of cold would, in fact, end? "While the earth remaineth, seedtime and harvest, and cold and heat, and summer and winter, and day and night shall not cease": God makes this guarantee very early in Genesis to a people whose fears on this point had perhaps not been completely allayed.

It must have been fantastically important, at the real beginnings of human culture, to conserve and relay this vital seasonal information, so that the people could anticipate dry or cold seasons, and not huddle on some November rock hoping pathetically that spring was just around the corner. We still very much stress the simple fact of four seasons to schoolchildren; even the most modern of modern new teachers, who don't seem to care if their charges can read or write or name two products of Peru, will still muster some seasonal chitchat and set the kids to making paper pumpkins, or tulips, for the walls. "The people," wrote Van Gogh in a letter, "are very sensitive to the changing seasons." That we are "very sensitive to the changing seasons" is, incidentally, one of the few good reasons to shun travel. If I stay at home I preserve the illusion that what is happening on Tinker Creek is the very newest thing, that I'm at the very vanguard and cutting edge of each new season. I don't want the same season twice in a row; I don't want to know I'm getting last week's weather, used weather, weather broadcast up and down the coast, old-hat weather.

But there's always unseasonable weather. What we think of the weather and behavior of life on the planet at any given season is really all a matter of statistical probabilities; at any given point, anything might happen. There is a bit of every season in each season. Green plants—deciduous green leaves—grow everywhere, all winter long, and small shoots come up pale and new in every season. Leaves die on the tree in May, turn brown, and fall into the creek. The calendar, the weather, and the behavior of wild creatures have the slimmest of connections. Everything overlaps smoothly for only a few weeks each season, and then it all tangles up again. The temperature, of course, lags far behind the calendar seasons, since the earth absorbs and releases heat slowly, like a leviathan breathing. Migrating birds head south in what appears to be dire panic, leaving mild weather and fields full of insects and seeds; they reappear as if in all eagerness in January, and poke about morosely in the snow. Several years ago our October woods would have made a dismal colored photograph for a sadist's calendar: a killing frost came before the leaves had even begun to brown; they drooped from every tree like crepe, blackened and limp. It's all a chancy, jumbled affair at best, as things seem to be below the stars.

Time is the continuous loop, the snakeskin with scales endlessly overlapping without beginning or end, or time is an ascending spiral if you will, like a child's toy Slinky. Of course we have no idea which arc on the loop is our time, let alone where the loop itself is, so to speak, or down whose lofty flight of stairs the Slinky so uncannily walks.

The power we seek, too, seems to be a continuous loop. I have always been sympathetic with the early notion of a divine power that exists in a particular place, or that travels about over the face of the earth as a man might wander— and when he is "there" he is surely not here. You can shake the hand of a man you meet in the woods; but the spirit seems to roll along like the mythical hoop snake with its tail in its mouth. There are no hands to shake or edges to untie. It rolls along the mountain ridges like a fireball, shooting off a spray of sparks at random, and will not be trapped, slowed, grasped, fetched, peeled, or aimed. "As for the wheels, it was cried unto them in my hearing, O wheel." This is the hoop of flame that shoots the rapids in the creek or spins across the dizzy meadows; this is the arsonist of the sunny woods: catch it if you can.

CHAPTER 6

The Present

I

CATCH IT IF YOU CAN.

It is early March. I am dazed from a long day of interstate driving homeward; I pull in at a gas station in Nowhere, Virginia, north of Lexington. The young boy in charge ("Chick 'at oll?") is offering a free cup of coffee with every gas purchase. We talk in the glass-walled office while my coffee cools enough to drink. He tells me, among other things, that the rival gas station down the road, whose FREE COFFEE sign is visible from the interstate, charges you fifteen cents if you want your coffee in a Styrofoam cup, as opposed, I guess, to your bare hands.

All the time we talk, the boy's new beagle puppy is skidding around the office, sniffing impartially at my shoes and

at the wire rack of folded maps. The cheerful human conversation wakes me, recalls me, not to a normal consciousness, but to a kind of energetic readiness. I step outside,
followed by the puppy.

I am absolutely alone. There are no other customers. The
road is vacant, the interstate is out of sight and earshot. I
have hazarded into a new corner of the world, an unknown
spot, a Brigadoon. Before me extends a low hill trembling
in yellow brome, and behind the hill, filling the sky, rises
an enormous mountain ridge, forested, alive and awesome
with brilliant blown lights. I have never seen anything so
tremulous and live. Overhead, great strips and chunks of
cloud dash to the northwest in a gold rush. At my back the
sun is setting—how can I not have noticed before that the
sun is setting? My mind has been a blank slab of black
asphalt for hours, but that doesn't stop the sun's wild wheel.
I set my coffee beside me on the curb; I smell loam on the
wind; I pat the puppy; I watch the mountain.

My hand works automatically over the puppy's fur, following the line of hair under his ears, down his neck, inside
his forelegs, along his hot-skinned belly.

Shadows lope along the mountain's rumpled flanks; they
elongate like root tips, like lobes of spilling water, faster
and faster. A warm purple pigment pools in each ruck and
tuck of the rock; it deepens and spreads, boring crevasses,
canyons. As the purple vaults and slides, it tricks out the
unleafed forest and rumpled rock in gilt, in shape-shifting
patches of glow. These gold lights veer and retract, shatter
and glide in a series of dazzling splashes, shrinking, leaking, exploding. The ridge's bosses and hummocks sprout
bulging from its side; the whole mountain looms miles
closer; the light warms and reddens; the bare forest folds
and pleats itself like living protoplasm before my eyes, like
a running chart, a wildly scrawling oscillograph on the

present moment. The air cools; the puppy's skin is hot. I am more alive than all the world.

This is it, I think, this is it, right now, the present, this empty gas station, here, this western wind, this tang of coffee on the tongue, and I am patting the puppy, I am watching the mountain. And the second I verbalize this awareness in my brain, I cease to see the mountain or feel the puppy. I am opaque, so much black asphalt. But at the same second, the second I know I've lost it, I also realize that the puppy is still squirming on his back under my hand. Nothing has changed for him. He draws his legs down to stretch the skin taut so he feels every fingertip's stroke along his furred and arching side, his flank, his flung-back throat.

I sip my coffee. I look at the mountain, which is still doing its tricks, as you look at a still-beautiful face belonging to a person who was once your lover in another country years ago: with fond nostalgia, and recognition, but no real feeling save a secret astonishment that you are now strangers. Thanks. For the memories. It is ironic that the one thing that all religions recognize as separating us from our creator—our very self-consciousness—is also the one thing that divides us from our fellow creatures. It was a bitter birthday present from evolution, cutting us off at both ends. I get in the car and drive home.

Catch it if you can. The present is an invisible electron; its lightning path traced faintly on a blackened screen is fleet, and fleeing, and gone.

That I ended this experience prematurely for myself— that I drew scales over my eyes between me and the mountain and gloved my hand between me and the puppy—is not the only point. After all, it would have ended anyway. I've never seen a sunset or felt a wind that didn't. The levitating saints came down at last, and their two feet bore real weight. No, the point is that not only does time fly and do we die, but that in these reckless conditions we live at all, and are vouchsafed, for the duration of certain inexplicable moments, to know it.

Stephen Graham startled me by describing this same gift in his antique and elegant book, *The Gentle Art of Tramping*. He wrote, "And as you sit on the hillside, or lie prone under the trees of the forest, or sprawl wet-legged on the shingly beach of a mountain stream, the great door, that does not look like a door, opens." That great door opens on the present, illuminates it as with a multitude of flashing torches.

I had thought, because I had seen the tree with the lights in it, that the great door, by definition, opens on eternity. Now that I have "patted the puppy"—now that I have experienced the present purely through my senses—I discover that, although the door to the tree with the lights in it was opened *from* eternity, as it were, and shone on that tree eternal lights, it nevertheless opened on the real and present cedar. It opened on time: Where else? That Christ's incarnation occurred improbably, ridiculously, at such-and-such a time, into such-and-such a place, is referred to— with great sincerity even among believers—as "the scandal of particularity." Well, the "scandal of particularity" is the only world that I, in particular, know. What use has eternity for light? We're all up to our necks in this particular scandal. Why, we might as well ask, not a plane tree, instead of a bo? I never saw a tree that was no tree in particular; I never met a man, not the greatest theologian, who filled infinity, or even whose hand, say, was undifferentiated, fingerless, like a griddlecake, and not lobed and split just so with the incursions of time.

I don't want to stress this too much. Seeing the tree with

the lights in it was an experience vastly different in quality as well as in import from patting the puppy. On that cedar tree shone, however briefly, the steady, inward flames of eternity; across the mountain by the gas station raced the familiar flames of the falling sun. But on both occasions I thought, with rising exultation, this is it, this is it; praise the lord; praise the land. Experiencing the present purely is being emptied and hollow; you catch grace as a man fills his cup under a waterfall.

Consciousness itself does not hinder living in the present. In fact, it is only to a heightened awareness that the great door to the present opens at all. Even a certain amount of interior verbalization is helpful to enforce the memory of whatever it is that is taking place. The gas station beagle puppy, after all, may have experienced those same moments more purely than I did, but he brought fewer instruments to bear on the same material, he had no data for comparison, and he profited only in the grossest of ways, by having an assortment of itches scratched.

Self-consciousness, however, does hinder the experience of the present. It is the one instrument that unplugs all the rest. So long as I lose myself in a tree, say, I can scent its leafy breath or estimate its board feet of lumber, I can draw its fruits or boil tea on its branches, and the tree stays tree. But the second I become aware of myself at any of these activities—looking over my own shoulder, as it were—the tree vanishes, uprooted from the spot and flung out of sight as if it had never grown. And time, which had flowed down into the tree bearing new revelations like floating leaves at every moment, ceases. It dams, stills, stagnates.

Self-consciousness is the curse of the city and all that sophistication implies. It is the glimpse of oneself in a storefront window, the unbidden awareness of reactions on the faces of other people—the novelist's world, not the poet's. I've lived there. I remember what the city has to offer: human companionship, major-league baseball, and a clatter of quickening stimulus like a rush from strong drugs that leaves you drained. I remember how you bide your time in the city, and think, if you stop to think, "next year . . . I'll start living; next year . . . I'll start my life." Innocence is a better world.

Innocence sees that this is it, and finds it world enough, and time. Innocence is not the prerogative of infants and puppies, and far less of mountains and fixed stars, which have no prerogatives at all. It is not lost to us; the world is a better place than that. Like any other of the spirit's good gifts, it is there if you want it, free for the asking, as has been stressed by stronger words than mine. It is possible to pursue innocence as hounds pursue hares: single-mindedly, driven by a kind of love, crashing over creeks, keening and lost in field and forests, circling, vaulting over hedges and hills wide-eyed, giving loud tongue all unawares to the deepest, most incomprehensible longing, a root-flame in the heart, and that warbling chorus resounding back from the mountains, hurling itself from ridge to ridge over the valley, now faint, now clear, ringing the air through which the hounds tear, open-mouthed, the echoes of their own wails dimly knocking in their lungs.

What I call innocence is the spirit's unself-conscious state at any moment of pure devotion to any object. It is at once a receptiveness and total concentration. One needn't be, shouldn't be, reduced to a puppy. If you wish to tell me that the city offers galleries, I'll pour you a drink and enjoy your company while it lasts; but I'll bear with me to my grave those pure moments at the Tate (was it the Tate?) where I stood planted, open-mouthed, born, before that one particular canvas, that river, up to my neck, gasping, lost, receding into watercolor depth and depth to the vanishing point, buoyant, awed, and had to be literally hauled away. These are our few live seasons. Let us live them as purely as we can, in the present.

The color-patches of vision part, shift, and reform as I move through space in time. The present is the object of vision, and what I see before me at any given second is a full field of color-patches scattered just so. The configuration will never be repeated. Living is moving; time is a live creek bearing changing lights. As I move, or as the world moves around me, the fullness of what I see shatters. This second of shattering is an *augenblick*, a particular configuration, a slant of light shot in the open eye. Goethe's Faust risks all if he should cry to the moment, the *augenblick*, *"Verweile doch!"* "Last forever!" Who hasn't prayed that prayer? But the *augenblick* isn't going to *verweile*. You were lucky to get it in the first place. The present is a freely given canvas. That it is constantly being ripped apart and washed downstream goes without saying; it is a canvas, nevertheless.

I like the slants of light; I'm a collector. That's a good one, I say, that bit of bank there, the snakeskin and the aquarium, that patch of light from the creek on bark. Sometimes I spread my fingers into a viewfinder; more often I peek through a tiny square or rectangle—a frame of shadow—formed by the tips of index fingers and thumbs held directly before my eye. Speaking of the development of *papier collé* in late Cubism, Picasso said, "We tried to get rid of *trompe-l'oeil* to find a *trompe-l'esprit*." Trompe-l'esprit! I don't know why the world didn't latch on to the phrase. Our whole life is a stroll—or a forced march— through a gallery hung in trompes-l'esprit.

Once I visited a great university and wandered, a stranger, into the subterranean halls of its famous biology

department. I saw a sign on a door: ichthyology department.
The door was open a crack, and as I walked past I glanced
in. I saw just a flash. There were two white-coated men
seated opposite each other on high lab stools at a hard-
surfaced table. They bent over identical white enamel trays.
On one side, one man, with a lancet, was just cutting into
an enormous preserved fish he'd taken from a jar. On the
other side, the other man, with a silver spoon, was eating a
grapefruit. I laughed all the way back to Virginia.

Michael Goldman wrote in a poem, "When the Muse
comes She doesn't tell you to write;/ She says get up for a
minute, I've something to show you, stand here." What
made me look up at that roadside tree?

The road to Grundy, Virginia, is, as you might expect, a
narrow scrawl scribbled all over the most improbably
peaked and hunched mountains you ever saw. The few
people who live along the road also seem peaked and
hunched. But what on earth—? It was hot, sunny summer.
The road was just bending off sharply to the right. I hadn't
seen a house in miles, and none was in sight. At the apogee
of the road's curve grew an enormous oak, a massive bur
oak two hundred years old, one hundred and fifty feet high,
an oak whose lowest limb was beyond the span of the
highest ladder. I looked up: there were clothes spread all
over the tree. Red shirts, blue trousers, black pants, little
baby smocks—they weren't hung from branches. They were
outside, carefully spread, splayed as if to dry, on the outer
leaves of the great oak's crown. Were there pillowcases,
blankets? I can't remember. There was a gay assortment of
cotton underwear, yellow dresses, children's green sweaters,
plaid skirts. . . . You know roads. A bend comes and you
take it, thoughtlessly, moving on. I looked behind me for
another split second, astonished; both sides of the tree's
canopy, clear to the top, bore clothes. Trompe!

But there is more to the present than a series of snapshots. We are not merely sensitized film; we have feelings, a memory for information and an eidetic memory for the imagery of our own pasts.

Our layered consciousness is a tiered track for an unmatched assortment of concentrically wound reels. Each one plays out for all of life its dazzle and blur of translucent shadow-pictures; each one hums at every moment its own secret melody in its own unique key. We tune in and out. But moments are not lost. Time out of mind is time nevertheless, cumulative, informing the present. From even the deepest slumber you wake with a jolt—older, closer to death, and wiser, grateful for breath. You quit your seat in a darkened movie theatre, walk past the empty lobby, out the double glass doors, and step like Orpheus into the street. And the cumulative force of the present you've forgotten sets you reeling, staggering, as if you'd been struck broadside by a plank. It all floods back to you. Yes, you say, as if you'd been asleep a hundred years, this is it, this is the real weather, the lavender light fading, the full moisture in your lungs, the heat from the pavement on your lips and palms—not the dry orange dust from horses' hooves, the salt sea, the sour Coke—but this solid air, the blood pumping up your thighs again, your fingers alive. And on the way home you drive exhilarated, energized, under scented, silhouetted trees.

II

I am sitting under a sycamore by Tinker Creek. It is early spring, the day after I patted the puppy. I have come to the creek—the backyard stretch of the creek—in the middle of the day, to feel the delicate gathering of heat, real sun's heat, in the air, and to watch new water come down the creek. Don't expect more than this, and a mental ramble. I'm in the market for some present tense; I'm on the lookout, shopping around, more so every year. It's a seller's market—do you think I won't sell all that I have to buy it? Thomas Merton wrote, in a light passage in one of his Gethsemane journals: "Suggested emendation in the Lord's Prayer: Take out 'Thy Kingdom come' and substitute 'Give us time!'" But time is the one thing we have been given, and we have been given to time. Time gives us a whirl. We keep waking from a dream we can't recall, looking around in surprise, and lapsing back, for years on end. All I want to do is stay awake, keep my head up, prop my eyes open, with toothpicks, with trees.

Before me the creek is seventeen feet wide, splashing over random sandstone outcroppings and scattered rocks. I'm lucky; the creek is loud here, because of the rocks, and wild. In the low water of summer and fall I can cross to the opposite bank by leaping from stone to stone. Upstream is a wall of light split into planks by smooth sandstone ledges that cross the creek evenly, like steps. Downstream the live water before me stills, dies suddenly as if extinguished, and vanishes around a bend shaded summer and winter by overarching tulips, locusts, and Osage orange. Everywhere I look are creekside trees whose ascending boles against water and grass accent the vertical thrust of the land in this spot. The creek rests the eye, a haven, a breast; the two steep banks vault from the creek like wings. Not even the sycamore's crown can peek over the land in any direction.

My friend Rosanne Coggeshall, the poet, says that "sycamore" is the most intrinsically beautiful word in English. This sycamore is old; its lower bark is always dusty from years of floodwaters lapping up its trunk. Like many sycamores, too, it is quirky, given to flights and excursions. Its trunk lists over the creek at a dizzying angle, and from that trunk extends a long, skinny limb that spurts high over the opposite bank without branching. The creek reflects the speckled surface of this limb, pale even against the highest clouds, and that image pales whiter and thins as it crosses the creek, shatters in the riffles and melds together, quivering and mottled, like some enormous primeval reptile under the water.

I want to think about trees. Trees have a curious relationship to the subject of the present moment. There are many created things in the universe that outlive us, that outlive the sun, even, but I can't think about them. I live with trees. There are creatures under our feet, creatures that live over our heads, but trees live quite convincingly in the same filament of air we inhabit, and, in addition, they extend impressively in both directions, up and down, shearing rock and fanning air, doing their real business just out of reach. A blind man's idea of hugeness is a tree. They have their sturdy bodies and special skills; they garner fresh water; they abide. This sycamore above me, below me, by Tinker Creek, is a case in point; the sight of it crowds my brain with an assortment of diverting thoughts, all as present to me as these slivers of pressure from grass on my elbow's skin. I want to come at the subject of the present by showing how consciousness dashes and ambles around the labyrinthine tracks of the mind, returning again and again, however briefly, to the senses: "If there were but one erect and solid standing tree in the woods, all creatures would go to rub against it and make sure of their footing." But so long as I stay in my thoughts, my foot slides under trees; I fall, or I dance.

Sycamores are among the last trees to go into leaf; in the fall, they are the first to shed. They make sweet food in

green broadleaves for a while—leaves wide as plates—and
then go wild and wave their long white arms. In ancient
Rome men honored the sycamore—in the form of its
cousin, the Oriental plane—by watering its roots with wine.
Xerxes, I read, "halted his unwieldy army for days that he
might contemplate to his satisfaction" the beauty of a single
sycamore.

You are Xerxes in Persia. Your army spreads on a vast
and arid peneplain . . . you call to you all your sad captains,
and give the order to halt. You have seen the tree with the
lights in it, haven't you? You must have. Xerxes buffeted on
a plain, ambition drained in a puff. That fusillade halts any
army in its tracks. Your men are bewildered; they lean on
their spears, sucking the rinds of gourds. There is nothing
to catch the eye in this flatness, nothing but a hollow, ham-
mering sky, a waste of sedge in the lee of wind-blown
rocks, a meagre ribbon of scrub willow tracing a slumbering
watercourse . . . and that sycamore. You saw it; you still
stand rapt and mute, exalted, remembering or not remembering over a period of days to shade your head with your
robe.

"He had its form wrought upon a medal of gold to help
him remember it the rest of his life." Your teeth are chatter-
ing; it is just before dawn and you have started briefly from
your daze. "Goldsmith!" The goldsmith is sodden with
sleep, surly. He lights his forge, he unrolls the dusty cotton
wrapping from his half-forgotten stylus and tongs, he waits
for the sun. We all ought to have a goldsmith following
us around. But it goes without saying, doesn't it, Xerxes,
that no gold medal worn around your neck will bring back
the glad hour, keep those lights kindled so long as you live,
forever present? Pascal saw it. He grabbed pen and paper;
he managed to scrawl the one word, FEU; he wore that scrap

of paper sewn in his shirt the rest of his life. I don't know what Pascal saw. I saw a cedar. Xerxes saw a sycamore.

These trees stir me. The past inserts a finger into a slit in the skin of the present, and pulls. I remember how sycamores grew—and presumably still grow—in the city, in Pittsburgh, even along the busiest streets. I used to spend hours in the backyard, thinking God knows what, and peeling the mottled bark of a sycamore, idly, littering the grass with dried lappets and strips, leaving the tree's trunk at eye level moist, thin-skinned and yellow—until someone would catch me at it from the kitchen window, and I would awake, and look at my work in astonishment, and think oh no, this time I've killed the sycamore for sure.

Here in Virginia the trees reach enormous proportions, especially in the lowlands on banksides. It is hard to understand how the same tree could thrive both choking along Pittsburgh's Penn Avenue and slogging knee-deep in Tinker Creek. Of course, come to think of it, I've done the same thing myself. Because a sycamore's primitive bark is not elastic but frangible, it sheds continuously as it grows; seen from a distance, a sycamore seems to grow in pallor and vulnerability as it grows in height; the bare uppermost branches are white against the sky.

The sky is deep and distant, laced with sycamore limbs like a hatching of crossed swords. I can scarcely see it; I'm not looking. I don't come to the creek for sky unmediated, but for shelter. My back rests on a steep bank under the sycamore; before me shines the creek—the creek which is about all the light I can stand—and beyond it rises the other bank, also steep, and planted in trees.

I have never understood why so many mystics of all creeds experience the presence of God on mountaintops. Aren't they afraid of being blown away? God said to Moses on Sinai that even the priests, who have access to the Lord, must hallow themselves, for fear that the Lord may break out against them. This is *the* fear. It often feels best to lie low, inconspicuous, instead of waving your spirit around from high places like a lightning rod. For if God is in one sense the igniter, a fireball that spins over the ground of continents, God is also in another sense the destroyer, lightning, blind power, impartial as the atmosphere. Or God is one "G." You get a comforting sense, in a curved, hollow place, of being vulnerable to only a relatively narrow column of God as air.

In the open, anything might happen. Dorothy Dunnett, the great medievalist, states categorically: "There is no reply, in clear terrain, to an archer in cover." Any copperhead anywhere is an archer in cover; how much more so is God! Invisibility is the all-time great "cover"; and that the one infinite power deals so extravagantly and unfathomably in death—death morning, noon, and night, all manner of death—makes that power an archer, there is no getting around it. And we the people are so vulnerable. Our bodies are shot with mortality. Our legs are fear and our arms are time. These chill humors seep through our capillaries, weighting each cell with an icy dab of nonbeing, and that dab grows and swells and sucks the cell dry. That is why physical courage is so important—it fills, as it were, the holes—and why it is so invigorating. The least brave act, chance taken and passage won, makes you feel loud as a child.

But it gets harder. The courage of children and beasts is a function of innocence. We let our bodies go the way of our fears. A teen-aged boy, king of the world, will spend weeks in front of a mirror perfecting some difficult trick with a lighter, a muscle, a tennis ball, a coin. Why do we lose interest in physical mastery? If I feel like turning cartwheels—and I do—why don't I learn to turn cartwheels, instead of regretting that I never learned as a child? We could all be aerialists like squirrels, divers like seals; we could be purely patient, perfectly fleet, walking on our hands even, if our living or stature required it. We can't even sit straight, or support our weary heads.

When we lose our innocence—when we start feeling the weight of the atmosphere and learn that there's death in the pot—we take leave of our senses. Only children can hear the song of the male house mouse. Only children keep their eyes open. The only thing they *have* got is sense; they have highly developed "input systems," admitting all data indiscriminately. Matt Spireng has collected thousands of arrowheads and spearheads; he says that if you really want to find arrowheads, you must walk with a child—a child will pick up *everything*. All my adult life I have wished to see the cemented case of a caddisfly larva. It took Sally Moore, the young daughter of friends, to find one on the pebbled bottom of a shallow stream on whose bank we sat side by side. "What's this?" she asked. That, I wanted to say as I recognized the prize she held, is a memento mori for people who read too much.

We found other caddisfly cases that day, Sally and I, after I had learned to focus so fine, and I saved one. It is a hollow cylinder three quarters of an inch long, a little masterpiece of masonry consisting entirely of cemented grains of coarse sand only one layer thick. Some of the sand grains are red, and it was by searching for this red that I learned to spot the cases. The caddisfly larva will use any bits it can find to fashion its house; in fact, entomologists have amused themselves by placing a naked larva in an aquarium furnished only with, say, red sand. When the larva has laid around its body several rows of red sand, the entomologist transfers it to another aquarium in which only white bits are available. The larva busily adds rows of white to the red wall, and then here comes the entomologist again, with a third and final aquarium full of blue sand. At any rate, the point I want to make is that this tiny immature creature responds to an instinct to put something between its flesh and a jagged world. If you give a "masonry mosaic" kind of caddisfly larva only large decayed leaves, that larva, confronted by something utterly novel, will nevertheless bite the leaves into shreds and rig those shreds into a case.

The general rule in nature is that live things are soft within and rigid without. We vertebrates are living danger-ously, and we vertebrates are positively piteous, like so many peeled trees. This oft was thought, but ne'er so well expressed as by Pliny, who writes of nature, "To all the rest, given she hath sufficient to clad them everyone accord-ing to their kind: as namely, shells, cods, hard hides, pricks, shags, bristles, hair, down feathers, quills, scales, and fleeces of wool. The very trunks and stems of trees and plants, she hath defended with bark and rind, yea and the same some-times double, against the injuries both of heat and cold: man alone, poor wretch, she hath laid all naked upon the bare earth, even on his birthday, to cry and wraule presently from the very first hour that he is born into the world."

I am sitting under a sycamore tree: I am soft-shell and peeled to the least puff of wind or smack of grit. The pres-ent of our life looks different under trees. Trees have dominion. I never killed that backyard sycamore; even its frailest inner bark was a shield. Trees do not accumulate life, but deadwood, like a thickening coat of mail. Their odds actually improve as they age. Some trees, like giant sequoias, are, practically speaking, immortal, vulnerable only to another ice age. They are not even susceptible to fire. Sequoia wood barely burns, and the bark is "nearly as fireproof as asbestos. The top of one sequoia, struck by lightning a few years ago during a July thunderstorm, smoldered quietly, without apparently damaging the tree, until it was put out by a snowstorm in October." Some trees sink taproots to rock; some spread wide mats of roots clutching at acres. They will not be blown. We run around under these obelisk-creatures, teetering on our soft, small feet. We are out on a jaunt, picnicking, fattening like puppies for our deaths. Shall I carve a name on this trunk? What if *I* fell in a forest: Would a tree hear?

I am sitting under a bankside sycamore; my mind is a slope. Arthur Koestler wrote, "In his review of the literature on the psychological present, Woodrow found that its maximum span is estimated to lie between 2.3 and 12 seconds." How did anyone measure that slide? As soon as you are conscious of it, it is gone. I repeat a phrase: the thin tops of mountains. Soon the thin tops of mountains erupt, as if volcanically, from my brain's core. I can see them; they are, surprisingly, serrate—scalloped like the blade of a kitchen knife—and brown as leaves. The serrated edges are so thin they are translucent; through the top of one side of the brown ridge I can see, in silhouette, a circling sharp-shinned hawk; through another, deep tenuous veins of metallic ore. This isn't Tinker Creek. Where do I live, anyway? I lose myself, I float. . . . I am in Persia, trying to order a watermelon in German. It's insane. The engineer has abandoned the control room, and an idiot is splicing the reels. What could I contribute to the "literature on the psychological present?" If I could remember to press the knob on the stopwatch, I wouldn't be in Persia. Before they invented the unit of the second, people used to time the lapse of short events on their pulses. Oh, but what about that heave in the wrist when I saw the tree with the lights in it, and my heart ceased, but I am still there?

Scenes drift across the screen from nowhere. I can never discover the connection between any one scene and what I am more consciously thinking, nor can I ever conjure the scene back in full vividness. It is like a ghost, in full-dress regalia, that wafts across the stage set unnoticed by the principal characters. It appears complete, in full color, wordless, though already receding: the tennis courts on Fifth Avenue in Pittsburgh, an equestrian statue in a Washington park, a basement dress shop in New York city—scenes that I thought meant nothing to me. These aren't still shots; the camera is always moving. And the scene is always just slipping out of sight, as if in spite of myself I were always just descending a hill, rounding a corner, stepping into the street with a companion who urges me on, while I look back over my shoulder at the sight which recedes, vanishes. The present of my consciousness is itself a mystery which is also always just rounding a bend like a floating branch borne by a flood. Where am I? But I'm not. "I will overturn, overturn, overturn, it: and it shall be no more. . . ."

All right then. Pull yourself together. Is this where I'm spending my life, in the "reptile brain," this lamp at the top of the spine like a lighthouse flipping mad beams indiscriminately into the darkness, into the furred thoraxes of moths, onto the backs of leaping fishes and the wrecks of schooners? Come up a level; surface.

I am sitting under a sycamore by Tinker Creek. I am really here, alive on the intricate earth under trees. But under me, directly under the weight of my body on the grass, are other creatures, just as real, for whom also this moment, this tree, is "it." Take just the top inch of soil, the world squirming right under my palms. In the top inch of forest soil, biologists found "an average of 1,356 living creatures present in each square foot, including 865 mites, 265 springtails, 22 millipedes, 19 adult beetles and various numbers of 12 other forms. . . . Had an estimate also been made of the microscopic population, it might have ranged up to two billion bacteria and many millions of fungi, protozoa and algae—in a mere *teaspoonful* of soil." The chrysalids of butterflies linger here too, folded, rigid, and dreamless. I might as well include these creatures in this moment, as best I can. My ignoring them won't strip them of their reality, and admitting them, one by one, into my consciousness might heighten mine, might add their dim awareness to my human consciousness, such as it is, and set up a buzz, a vibration like the beating ripples a submerged muskrat makes on the water, from this particular moment, this tree. Hasidism has a tradition that one of man's purposes is to assist God in the work of redemption by "hallowing" the things of creation. By a tremendous heave of his spirit, the devout man frees the divine sparks trapped in the mute things of time; he uplifts the forms and moments of creation, bearing them aloft into that rare air and hallowing fire in which all clays must shatter and burst. Keeping the subsoil world under trees in mind, in intelligence, is the *least* I can do.

Earthworms in staggering processions lurch through the grit underfoot, gobbling downed leaves and spewing forth castings by the ton. Moles mine intricate tunnels in networks; there are often so many of these mole tunnels here by the creek that when I walk, every step is a letdown. A mole is almost entirely loose inside its skin, and enormously mighty. If you can catch a mole, it will, in addition to biting you memorably, leap from your hand in a single convulsive contraction and be gone as soon as you have it. You are never really able to see it; you only feel its surge and thrust against your palm, as if you held a beating heart in a paper bag. What could I not do if I had the power and will of a mole! But the mole churns earth.

Last summer some muskrats had a den under this tree's roots on the bank; I think they are still there now. Muskrats' wet fur rounds the domed clay walls of the den and slicks them smooth as any igloo. They strew the floor with plant husks and seeds, rut in repeated bursts, and sleep humped and soaking, huddled in balls. These, too, are part of what Buber calls "the infinite ethos of the moment."

I am not here yet; I can't shake that day on the interstate. My mind branches and shoots like a tree.

Under my spine, the sycamore roots suck watery salts. Root tips thrust and squirm between particles of soil, probing minutely; from their roving, burgeoning tissues spring infinitesimal root hairs, transparent and hollow, which affix themselves to specks of grit and sip. These runnels run silent and deep; the whole earth trembles, rent and fissured, hurled and drained. I wonder what happens to root systems when trees die. Do those spread blind networks starve, starve in the midst of plently, and dessicate, clawing at specks?

Under the world's conifers—under the creekside cedar behind where I sit—a mantle of fungus wraps the soil in a weft, shooting out blind thread after frail thread of palest dissolved white. From root tip to root tip, root hair to root hair, these filaments loop and wind; the thought of them always reminds me of Rimbaud's "I have stretched cords from steeple to steeple, garlands from window to window, chains of gold from star to star, and I dance." King David leaped and danced naked before the ark of the Lord in a barren desert. Here the very looped soil is an intricate throng of praise. Make connections; let rip; and dance where you can.

The insects and earthworms, moles, muskrats, roots and fungal strands are not all. An even frailer, dimmer movement, a pavane, is being performed deep under me now. The nymphs of cicadas are alive. You see their split skins, an inch long, brown, and translucent, curved and segmented like shrimp, stuck arching on the trunks of trees. And you see the adults occasionally, large and sturdy, with glittering black and green bodies, veined transparent wings folded over their backs, and artificial-looking, bright red eyes. But you never see the living nymphs. They are underground, clasping roots and sucking the sweet sap of trees.

In the South, the periodical cicada has a breeding cycle of thirteen years, instead of seventeen years as in the North. That a live creature spends thirteen consecutive years scrabbling around in the root systems of trees in the dark and damp—thirteen years!—is amply boggling for me. Four more years—or four less—wouldn't alter the picture a jot. In the dark of an April night the nymphs emerge, all at once, as many as eighty-four of them digging into the air from every square foot of ground. They inch up trees and bushes, shed their skins, and begin that hollow, shrill grind that lasts all summer. I guess as nymphs they never see the sun. Adults lay eggs in slits along twig bark; the hatched nymphs drop to the ground and burrow, vanish from the face of the earth, biding their time, for thirteen years. How many are under me now, wishing what? What would I think about for thirteen years? They curl, crawl, clutch at roots and suck, suck blinded, suck trees, rain or shine, heat or frost, year after groping year.

And under the cicadas, deeper down than the longest taproot, between and beneath the rounded black rocks and slanting slabs of sandstone in the earth, ground water is creeping. Ground water seeps and slides, across and down, across and down, leaking from here to there minutely, at the rate of a mile a year. What a tug of waters goes on! There are flings and pulls in every direction at every moment. The world is a wild wrestle under the grass: earth shall be moved.

What else is going on right this minute while ground water creeps under my feet? The galaxy is careening in a slow, muffled widening. If a million solar systems are born every hour, then surely hundreds burst into being as I shift my weight to the other elbow. The sun's surface is now exploding; other stars implode and vanish, heavy and black, out of sight. Meteorites are arcing to earth invisibly all day long. On the planet the winds are blowing: the polar easterlies, the westerlies, the northeast and southeast trades. Somewhere, someone under full sail is becalmed, in the horse latitudes, in the doldrums; in the northland, a trapper is maddened, crazed, by the eerie scent of the chinook, the snow-eater, a wind that can melt two feet of snow in a day. The pampero blows, and the tramontane, and the Boro, sirocco, levanter, mistral. Lick a finger: feel the now.

Spring is seeping north, towards me and away from me, at sixteen miles a day. Caribou straggle across the tundra from the spruce-fir forests of the south, first the pregnant does, hurried, then the old and unmated does, then suddenly a massing of bucks, and finally the diseased and injured, one by one. Somewhere, people in airplanes are watching the sun set and peering down at clustered houselights, stricken. In the montana in Peru, on the rain-forested slopes of the Andes, a woman kneels in a dust clearing before a dark shelter of overlapping broadleaves; between her breasts hangs a cross of smooth sticks she peeled with her teeth and lashed with twistings of vine. Along estuary banks of tidal rivers all over the world, snails in black clusters like currants are gliding up and down the stems of reed and sedge, migrating every moment with the dip and swing of tides. Behind me, Tinker Mountain, and to my left, Dead Man Mountain, are eroding one thousandth of an inch a year.

The tomcat that used to wake me is dead; he was long since grist for an earthworm's casting, and is now the clear sap of a Pittsburgh sycamore, or the honeydew of aphids sucked from that sycamore's high twigs and sprayed in sticky drops on a stranger's car. A steer across the road stumbles into the creek to drink; he blinks; he laps; a floating leaf in the current catches against his hock and wrenches away. The giant water bug I saw is dead, long dead, and its moist gut and rigid casing are both, like the empty skin of the frog it sucked, dissolved, spread, still spreading right now, in the steer's capillaries, in the windblown smatter of clouds overhead, in the Sargasso Sea. The mockingbird that dropped furled from a roof . . . but this is no time to count my dead. That is nightwork. The dead are staring, underground, their sleeping heels in the air.

The sharks I saw are roving up and down the coast. If the sharks cease roving, if they still their twist and rest for a moment, they die. They need new water pushed into their gills; they need dance. Somewhere east of me, on another continent, it is sunset, and starlings in breathtaking bands are winding high in the sky to their evening roost. Under the water just around the bend downstream, the coot feels with its foot in the creek, rolling its round red eyes. In the house a spider slumbers at her wheel like a spinster curled in a corner all day long. The mantis egg cases are tied to the mock-orange hedge; within each case, within each egg, cells elongate, narrow, and split; cells bubble and curve inward, align, harden or hollow or stretch. The Polyphemus moth, its wings crushed to its back, crawls down the driveway, crawls down the driveway, crawls. . . . The snake whose skin I tossed away, whose homemade, personal skin is now tangled at the county dump—that snake in the woods by the quarry stirs now, quickens now, prodded under the leafmold by sunlight, by the probing root of May apple, the bud of bloodroot. And where are you now?

I stand. All the blood in my body crashes to my feet and instantly heaves to my head, so I blind and blush, as a tree blasts into leaf spouting water hurled up from roots. What happens to me? I stand before the sycamore dazed; I gaze at its giant trunk.

Big trees stir memories. You stand in their dimness, where the very light is blue, staring unfocused at the thickest part of the trunk as though it were a long, dim tunnel—: the Squirrel Hill tunnel. You're gone. The egg-shaped patch of light at the end of the blackened tunnel swells and looms; the sing of tire tread over brick reaches an ear-splitting crescendo; the light breaks over the hood, smack, and full on your face. You have achieved the past.

Eskimo shamans bound with sealskin thongs on the igloo floor used to leave their bodies, their skins, and swim "muscle-naked" like a flensed seal through the rock of continents, in order to placate an old woman who lived on the sea floor and sent or withheld game. When he fulfilled this excruciating mission, the Eskimo shaman would awake, returned to his skin exhausted from the dark ardors of flailing peeled through rock, and find himself in a lighted igloo, at a sort of party, among dear faces.

In the same way, having bored through a sycamore trunk and tunneled beneath a Pennsylvania mountain, I blink, awed by the yellow light, and find myself in a shady side of town, in a stripped dining room, dancing, years ago. There is a din of trumpets, upbeat and indistinct, like some movie score for a love scene played on a city balcony; there is an immeasurably distant light glowing from half-remembered faces. . . . I stir. The heave of my shoulders returns me to the present, to the tree, the sycamore, and I yank myself away, shove off and moving, seeking live water.

III

Live water heals memories. I look up the creek and here it comes, the future, being borne aloft as on a winding succession of laden trays. You may wake and look from the window and breathe the real air, and say, with satisfaction or with longing, "This is it." But if you look up the creek, if you look up the creek in any weather, your spirit fills, and you are saying, with an exulting rise of the lungs, "Here it comes!"

Here it comes. In the far distance I can see the concrete bridge where the road crosses the creek. Under that bridge and beyond it the water is flat and silent, blued by distance and stilled by depth. It is so much sky, a fallen shred caught in the cleft of banks. But it pours. The channel here is straight as an arrow; grace itself is an archer. Between the dangling wands of bankside willows, beneath the overarching limbs of tulip, walnut, and Osage orange, I see the creek pour down. It spills toward me streaming over a series of sandstone tiers, down, and down, and down. I feel as though I stand at the foot of an infinitely high staircase, down which some exuberant spirit is flinging tennis ball after tennis ball, eternally, and the one thing I want in the world is a tennis ball.

There must be something wrong with a creekside person who, all things being equal, chooses to face downstream. It's like fouling your own nest. For this and a leather couch they pay fifty dollars an hour? Tinker Creek doesn't back up, pushed up its own craw, from the Roanoke River; it flows down, easing, from the northern, unseen side of Tinker Mountain. "Gravity, to Copernicus, is the nostalgia of things to become spheres." This is a curious, tugged version of the great chain of being. Ease is the way of perfection, letting fall. But, as in the classic version of the great chain, the pure trickle that leaks from the unfathomable heart of Tinker Mountain, this Tinker Creek, widens, taking shape and cleaving banks, weighted with the live and intricate impurities of time, as it descends to me, to where I happen to find myself, in this intermediate spot, halfway between here and there. Look upstream. Just simply turn around; have you no will? The future is a spirit, or a distillation of *the* spirit, heading my way. It is north. The future is the light on the water; it comes, mediated, only on the skin of the real and present creek. My eyes can stand no brighter light than this; nor can they see without it, if only the undersides of leaves.

Trees are tough. They last, taproot and bark, and we soften at their feet. "For we are strangers before thee, and sojourners, as were all our fathers: our days on the earth are as a shadow, and there is none abiding." We can't take the lightning, the scourge of high places and rare airs. But we can take the light, the reflected light that shines up the valleys on creeks. Trees stir memories; live waters heal them. The creek is the mediator, benevolent, impartial, subsuming my shabbiest evils and dissolving them, transforming them into live moles, and shiners, and sycamore leaves. It is a place even my faithlessness hasn't offended; it still flashes for me, now and tomorrow, that intricate, innocent face. It waters an undeserving world, saturating cells with lodes of light. I stand by the creek over rock under trees.

It is sheer coincidence that my hunk of the creek is strewn with boulders. I never merited this grace, that when I face upstream I scent the virgin breath of mountains, I feel a spray of mist on my cheeks and lips, I hear a ceaseless splash and susurrus, a sound of water not merely poured smoothly down air to fill a steady pool, but tumbling live about, over, under, around, between, through an intricate speckling of rock. It is sheer coincidence that upstream from me the creek's bed is ridged in horizontal croppings of sandstone. I never merited this grace, that when I face upstream I see the light on the water careening towards me, inevitably, freely, down a graded series of terraces like the balanced winged platforms on an infinite, inexhaustible font. "Ho, if you are thirsty, come down to the water; ho, if you are hungry, come and sit and eat." This is the present, at last. I can pat the puppy any time I want. This is the now, this flickering, broken light, this air that the wind of the future presses down my throat, pumping me buoyant and giddy with praise.

My God, I look at the creek. It is the answer to Merton's prayer, "Give us time!" It never stops. If I seek the senses and skill of children, the information of a thousand books, the innocence of puppies, even the insights of my own city past, I do so only, solely, and entirely that I might look well at the creek. You don't run down the present, pursue it with baited hooks and nets. You wait for it, empty-handed, and you are filled. You'll have fish left over. The creek is the one great giver. It is, by definition, Christmas, the incarnation. This old rock planet gets the present for a present on its birthday every day.

Here is the word from a subatomic physicist: "Everything

that has already happened is particles, everything in the future is waves." Let me twist his meaning. Here it comes. The particles are broken; the waves are translucent, laving, roiling with beauty like sharks. The present is the wave that explodes over my head, flinging the air with particles at the height of its breathless unroll; it is the live water and light that bears from undisclosed sources the freshest news, renewed and renewing, world without end.

CHAPTER 7

Spring

I

WHEN I WAS QUITE YOUNG I fondly imagined that all foreign languages were codes for English. I thought that "hat," say, was the real and actual name of the thing, but that people in other countries, who obstinately persisted in speaking the code of their forefathers, might use the word "ibu," say, to designate not merely the concept hat, but the English *word* "hat." I knew only one foreign word, "oui," and since it had three letters as did the word for which it was a code, it seemed, touchingly enough, to confirm my theory. Each foreign language was a different code, I figured, and at school I would eventually be given the keys to unlock some of the most important codes' systems. Of course I knew that it might take years before I became so fluent in another language that I could code and decode easily in my head, and make of gibberish a nimble sense. On the first day of my first French course, however, things rapidly took on an entirely unexpected shape. I realized that I was going to have to learn speech all over again, word by word, one word at a time—and my dismay knew no bounds.

The birds have started singing in the valley. Their February squawks and naked chirps are fully fledged now, and long lyrics fly in the air. Birdsong catches in the mountains' rim and pools in the valley; it threads through forests, it slides down creeks. At the house a wonderful thing happens. The mockingbird that nests each year in the front-yard spruce strikes up his chant in high places, and one of those high places is my chimney. When he sings there, the hollow chimney acts as a soundbox, like the careful emptiness inside a cello or violin, and the notes of the song gather fullness and reverberate through the house. He sings a phrase and repeats it exactly; then he sings another and repeats that, then another. The mockingbird's invention is limitless; he strews newness about as casually as a god. He is tireless, too; toward June he will begin his daily marathon at two in the morning and scarcely pause for breath until eleven at night. I don't know when he sleeps.

When I lose interest in a given bird, I try to renew it by looking at the bird in either of two ways. I imagine neutrinos passing through its feathers and into its heart and lungs, or I reverse its evolution and imagine it as a lizard. I see its scaled legs and that naked ring around a shiny eye; I shrink and deplume its feathers to lizard scales, unhorn its lipless mouth, and set it stalking dragonflies, cool-eyed, under a palmetto. Then I reverse the process once again, quickly; its forelegs unfurl, its scales hatch feathers

and soften. It takes to the air seeking cool forests; it sings
songs. This is what I have on my chimney; it might as well
keep me awake out of wonder as rage.

Some reputable scientists, even today, are not wholly satis-
fied with the notion that the song of birds is strictly and
solely a territorial claim. It's an important point. We've
been on earth all these years and we still don't know for
certain why birds sing. We need someone to unlock the code
to this foreign language and give us the key; we need a new
Rosetta stone. Or should we learn, as I had to, each new
word one by one? It could be that a bird sings I am sparrow, sparrow, sparrow, as Gerard Manley Hopkins suggests: "myself it speaks and spells, Crying *What I do is
me*: *for that I came*." Sometimes birdsong seems just like
the garbled speech of infants. There is a certain age at
which a child looks at you in all earnestness and delivers
a long, pleased speech in all the true inflections of spoken
English, but with not one recognizable syllable. There is
no way you can tell the child that if language had been a
melody, he had mastered it and done well, but that since it
was in fact a sense, he had botched it utterly.

Today I watched and heard a wren, a sparrow, and the
mockingbird singing. My brain started to trill why why
why, what is the meaning meaning meaning? It's not that
they know something we don't; we know much more than
they do, and surely they don't even know why they sing. No;
we have been as usual asking the wrong question. It does not
matter a hoot what the mockingbird on the chimney is singing. If the mockingbird were chirping to give us the long-
sought formulae for a unified field theory, the point would
be only slightly less irrelevant. The real and proper question
is: Why is it beautiful? I hesitate to use the word so baldly,
but the question is there. The question is there since I take
it as given, as I have said, that beauty is something objec-

tively performed—the tree that falls in the forest—having being externally, stumbled across or missed, as real and present as both sides of the moon. This modified lizard's song welling out of the fireplace has a wild, utterly foreign music; it becomes more and more beautiful as it becomes more and more familiar. If the lyric is simply "mine mine mine," then why the extravagance of the score? It has the liquid, intricate sound of every creek's tumble over every configuration of rock creek-bottom in the country. Who, telegraphing a message, would trouble to transmit a five-act play, or Coleridge's "Kubla Khan," and who, receiving the message, could understand it? Beauty itself is the language to which we have no key; it is the mute cipher, the cryptogram, the uncracked, unbroken code. And it could be that for beauty, as it turned out to be for French, that there is no key, that "oui" will never make sense in our language but only in its own, and that we need to start all over again, on a new continent, learning the strange syllables one by one.

It is spring. I plan to try to control myself this year, to watch the progress of the season in a calm and orderly fashion. In spring I am prone to wretched excess. I abandon myself to flights and compulsions; I veer into various states of physical disarray. For the duration of one entire spring I played pinochle; another spring I played second base. One spring I missed because I had lobar pneumonia; one softball season I missed with bursitis; and every spring at just about the time the leaves first blur on the willows, I stop eating and pale, like a silver eel about to migrate. My mind wanders. Second base is a Broadway, a Hollywood and Vine; but oh, if I'm out in right field they can kiss me goodbye. As the sun sets, sundogs, which are mock suns—chunks of rainbow on either side of the sun but often very distant from it—appear over the pasture by Carvin's Creek. Wes Hillman is up in his biplane; the little Waco lords it over the stillness, cutting a fine silhouette. It might rain tomorrow, if those ice crystals find business. I have no idea how many outs there are; I luck through the left-handers, staring at rainbows. The field looks to me as it must look to Wes Hillman up in the biplane: everyone is running, and I can't hear a sound. The players look so thin on the green, and the shadows so long, and the ball a mystic thing, pale to invisibility. . . . I'm better off in the infield.

In April I walked to the Adams' woods. The grass had greened one morning when I blinked; I missed it again. As I left the house I checked the praying mantis egg case. I had given all but one of the cases to friends for their gardens; now I saw that small black ants had discovered the one that was left, the one tied to the mock-orange hedge by my study window. One side of the case was chewed away, either by ants or by something else, revealing a rigid froth slit by narrow cells. Over this protective layer the ants scrambled in a frenzy, unable to eat; the actual mantis eggs lay secure and unseen, waiting, deeper in.

The morning woods were utterly new. A strong yellow light pooled between the trees; my shadow appeared and vanished on the path, since a third of the trees I walked under were still bare, a third spread a luminous haze wherever they grew, and another third blocked the sun with new, whole leaves. The snakes were out—I saw a bright, smashed one on the path—and the butterflies were vaulting and furling about; the phlox was at its peak, and even the evergreens looked greener, newly created and washed.

Long racemes of white flowers hung from the locust trees. Last summer I heard a Cherokee legend about the locust tree and the moon. The moon goddess starts out with a big ball, the full moon, and she hurls it across the sky. She spends all day retrieving it; then she shaves a slice from it and hurls it again, retrieving, shaving, hurling, and so on. She uses up a moon a month, all year. Then, the way Park Service geologist Bill Wellman tells it, " 'long about spring of course she's knee-deep in moon-shavings," so she finds her favorite tree, the locust, and hangs the slender shavings from its boughs. And there they were, the locust flowers, pale and clustered in crescents.

The newts were back. In the small forest pond they swam bright and quivering, or hung alertly near the water's surface. I discovered that if I poked my finger into the water and wagged it slowly, a newt would investigate; then if I held my finger still, it would nibble at my skin, softly, the way my goldfish does—and, also like my goldfish, it would swim off as if in disgust at a bad job. This is salamander metropolis. If you want to find a species wholly new to science and have your name inscribed Latinly in some secular version of an eternal rollbook, then your best bet is to come to the southern Appalachians, climb some obscure and snakey mountain where, as the saying goes, "the hand of man has never set foot," and start turning over rocks. The mountains act as islands; evolution does the rest, and there are scores of different salamanders all around. The Peaks of Otter on the Blue Ridge Parkway produce their own unique species, black and spotted in dark gold; the rangers there keep a live one handy by sticking it in a Baggie and stowing it in the refrigerator, like a piece of cheese.

Newts are the most common of salamanders. Their skin is a lighted green, like water in a sunlit pond, and rows of very bright red dots line their backs. They have gills as larvae; as they grow they turn a luminescent red, lose their gills, and walk out of the water to spend a few years padding around in damp places on the forest floor. Their feet look like fingered baby hands, and they walk in the same leg patterns as all four-footed creatures—dogs, mules, and, for that matter, lesser pandas. When they mature fully, they turn green again and stream to the water in droves. A newt can scent its way home from as far as eight miles away. They are altogether excellent creatures, if somewhat moist, but no one pays the least attention to them, except children.

Once I was camped "alone" at Douthat State Park in the Allegheny Mountains near here, and spent the greater part of one afternoon watching children and newts. There were many times more red-spotted newts at the edge of the lake than there were children; the supply exceeded even that very heavy demand. One child was collecting them in a Thermos mug to take home to Lancaster, Pennsylvania, to feed an ailing cayman. Other children ran to their mothers with squirming fistfuls. One boy was mistreating the newts spectacularly: he squeezed them by their tails and threw them at a shoreline stone, one by one. I tried to reason with him, but nothing worked. Finally he asked me, "Is this one a male?" and in a fit of inspiration I said, "No, it's a baby." He cried, "Oh, isn't he *cute*!" and cradled the newt carefully back into the water.

No one but me disturbed the newts here in the Adams' woods. They hung in the water as if suspended from strings. Their specific gravity put them just a jot below the water's surface, and they could apparently relax just as well with lowered heads as lowered tails; their tiny limbs hung limp in the water. One newt was sunning on a stick in such an extravagant posture I thought she was dead. She was half out of water, her front legs grasping the stick, her nose tilted back to the zenith and then some. The concave arch of her spine stretched her neck past believing; the thin ventral skin was a bright taut yellow. I should not have nudged her—it made her relax the angle of repose—but I had to see if she was dead. Medieval Europeans believed that salamanders were so cold they could put out fires and not be burned themselves; ancient Romans thought that the poison of salamanders was so cold that if anyone ate the fruit of a tree that a salamander had merely touched, that person would die of a terrible coldness. But I survived these mild encounters—my being nibbled and my poking the salamander's neck—and stood up.

The woods were flush with flowers. The redbud trees were in flower, and the sassafras, dully; so also were the tulip trees, catawbas, and the weird pawpaw. On the floor of the little woods, hepatica and dogtooth violet had come and gone; now I saw the pink spring beauty here and there, and Solomon's seal with its pendant flowers, bloodroot, violets, trillium, and May apple in luxuriant stands. The mountains would be brilliant in mountain laurel, rhododendron, and flame azalea, and the Appalachian Trail was probably packed with picnickers. I had seen in the steers' pasture daisies, henbits, and yellow-flowering oxalis; sow thistle and sneezeweed shot up by the barbed-wire fence. Does anything eat flowers? I couldn't recall ever having seen anything actually eat a flower—are they nature's privileged pets?

But I was much more interested in the leafing of trees. By the path I discovered a wonderful tulip-tree sapling three feet tall. From its tip grew two thin slips of green tissue shaped like two tears; they enclosed, like cupped palms sheltering a flame, a tiny tulip leaf that was curled upon itself and bowed neatly at the middle. The leaf was so thin and etiolated it was translucent, but at the same time it was lambent, minutely, with a kind of pale and sufficient light. It was not wet, nor even damp, but it was clearly moist inside; the wrinkle where it folded in half looked less like a crease than a dimple, like the liquid dip a skater's leg makes on the surface film of still water. A barely concealed, powerful juice swelled its cells, and the leaf was uncurling and rising between the green slips of tissue. I looked around for more leaves like it—that part of the Adams' woods seems to be almost solely tulip trees—but all the other leaves had just lately unfurled, and were waving on pale stalks like new small hands.

The tulip-tree leaf reminded me of a newborn mammal I'd seen the other day, one of the neighborhood children's gerbils. It was less than an inch long, with a piggish snout, clenched eyes, and swollen white knobs where its ears would grow. Its skin was hairless except for an infinitesimal set of whiskers; the skin seemed as thin as the membrane on an onion, tightly packed as a sausage casing, and bulging roundly with wet, bloody meat. It seemed near to bursting with possibilities, like the taut gum over a coming tooth. This three-foot sapling was going somewhere, too; it meant business.

There's a real power here. It is amazing that trees can turn gravel and bitter salts into these soft-lipped lobes, as if I were to bite down on a granite slab and start to swell, bud, and flower. Trees seem to do their feats so effortlessly. Every year a given tree creates absolutely from scratch ninety-nine percent of its living parts. Water lifting up tree trunks can climb one hundred and fifty feet an hour; in full summer a tree can, and does, heave a ton of water every day. A big elm in a single season might make as many as *six million* leaves, wholly intricate, without budging an inch; I couldn't make one. A tree stands there, accumulating deadwood, mute and rigid as an obelisk, but secretly it seethes; it splits, sucks, and stretches; it heaves up tons and hurls them out in a green, fringed fling. No person taps this free power; the dynamo in the tulip tree pumps out ever more tulip tree, and it runs on rain and air.

John Cowper Powys said, "We have no reason for denying to the world of plants a certain slow, dim, vague, large,
leisurely semiconsciousness." He may not be right, but I like
his adjectives. The patch of bluets in the grass may not be
long on brains, but it might be, at least in a very small way,
awake. The trees especially seem to bespeak a generosity of
spirit. I suspect that the real moral thinkers end up, wherever they may start, in botany. We know nothing for certain, but we seem to see that the world turns upon growing,
grows towards growing, and growing green and clean.

I looked away from the tulip leaf at the tip of the
sapling, and I looked back. I was trying to determine if I
could actually see the bent leaf tip rise and shove against
the enclosing flaps. I couldn't tell whether I was seeing or
merely imagining progress, but I knew the leaf would be
fully erect within the hour. I couldn't wait.

I left the woods, spreading silence before me in a wave,
as though I'd stepped not through the forest, but on it. I left
the wood silent, but I myself was stirred and quickened. I'll
go to the Northwest Territories, I thought, Finland.

"Why leap ye, ye high hills?" The earth was an egg,
freshened and splitting; a new pulse struck, and I resounded. Pliny, who, you remember, came up with the
Portuguese wind-foals, must have kept his daughters in on
windy days, for he also believed that plants conceive in the
spring of the western wind Flavonius. In February the
plants go into rut; the wind impregnates them, and their
buds swell and burst in their time, bringing forth flowers
and leaves and fruit. I could smell the loamy force in the
wind. I'll go to Alaska, Greenland. I saw hundreds of holes
in the ground everywhere I looked; all kinds of creatures
were popping out of the dim earth, some for the first time,
to be lighted and warmed directly by the sun. It is a fact that
the men and women all over the northern hemisphere who

dream up new plans for a perpetual motion machine conceive their best ideas in the spring. If I swallowed a seed and some soil, could I grow grapes in my mouth? Once I dug a hole to plant a pine, and found an old gold coin on a stone. Little America, the Yukon. . . . "Why leap ye, ye high hills?"

On my way home, every bird I saw had something in its mouth. A male English sparrow, his mouth stuffed, was hopping in and out of an old nest in a bare tree, and sloshing around in its bottom. A robin on red alert in the grass, trailing half a worm from its bill, bobbed three steps and straightened up, performing unawares the universal robin trick. A mockingbird flew by with a red berry in its beak; the berry flashed in the sun and glowed like a coal from some forge or cauldron of the gods.

Finally I saw some very small children playing with a striped orange kitten, and overheard their mysterious conversation, which has since been ringing in my brain like a gong. The kitten ran into a garden, and the girl called after it, "Sweet Dreams! Sweet Dreams! Where are you?" And the boy said to her crossly, "Don't call Sweet Dreams '*you*'!"

II

Now it is May. The walrus are migrating; Diomede Island Eskimos follow them in boats through the Bering Strait. The Netsilik Eskimos hunt seal. According to Asen Balikci, a seal basks in the sun all day and slips into the water at midnight, to return at dawn to emerge from the same hole. In spring the sun, too, slips below the horizon for only a brief period, and the sky still glows. All the Netsilik hunter has to do in spring is go out at midnight,

watch a seal disappear into a given hole, and wait there
quietly in the brief twilight, on a spread piece of bearskin.
The seal will be up soon, with the sun. The glaciers are
calving; brash ice and grease ice clog the bays. From land
you can see the widening of open leads on the distant
pack ice by watching the "water sky"—the dark patches
and streaks on the glaring cloud cover that are breaks in the
light reflected from the pack.

You might think the Eskimos would welcome the spring
and the coming of summer; they did, but they looked forward more to the coming of winter. I'm talking as usual
about the various Eskimo cultures as they were before
modernization. Some Eskimos used to greet the sun on its
first appearance at the horizon in stunned silence, and with
raised arms. But in summer, they well knew, they would
have to eat lean fish and birds. Winter's snow would melt
to water and soak the thin thawed ground down to the
permafrost; the water couldn't drain away, and it would
turn the earth into a sop of puddles. Then the mosquitos
would come, the mosquitos that could easily drive migrating
caribou to a mad frenzy so that they trampled their newborn
calves, the famous arctic mosquitos of which it is said, "If
there were any more of them, they'd have to be smaller."

In winter the Eskimos could trav 1 with dog sleds and
visit; with the coming of warm weather, their pathways, like
mine in Virginia, closed. In interior Alaska and northern
Canada, breakup is the big event. Old-timers and chee-
chakos alike lay wagers on the exact day and hour it will
occur. For the ice on rivers there does not just simply melt;
it rips out in a general holocaust. Upstream, thin ice breaks
from its banks and races downriver. Where it rams solid
ice it punches it free and shoots it downstream, buckling
and shearing: ice adds to ice, exploding a Juggernaut into
motion. A grate and roar blast the air, the ice machine

razes bridges and fences and trees, and the whole year's ice rushes out like a train in an hour. Breakup: I'd give anything to see it. Now for the people in the bush the waterways are open to navigation but closed to snowmobile and snowshoe, and it's harder for them, too, to get around.

Here in the May valley, fullness is at a peak. All the plants are fully leafed, but intensive insect damage hasn't begun. The leaves are fresh, whole, and perfect. Light in the sky is clear, unfiltered by haze, and the sun hasn't yet withered the grass.

Now the plants are closing in on me. The neighborhood children are growing up; they aren't keeping all the paths open. I feel like buying them all motorbikes. The woods are a clog of green, and I have to follow the manner of the North, or of the past, and take to the waterways to get around. But maybe I think things are more difficult than they are, because once, after I had waded and slogged in tennis shoes a quarter of a mile upstream in Tinker Creek, a boy hailed me from the tangled bank. He had followed me just to pass the time of day, and he was barefoot.

When I'm up to my knees in honeysuckle, I beat a retreat, and visit the duck pond. The duck pond is a small eutrophic pond on cleared land near Carvin's Creek. It is choked with algae and seething with frogs; when I see it, I always remember Jean White's horse.

Several years ago, Jean White's old mare, Nancy, died. It died on private property where it was pastured, and Jean couldn't get permission to bury the horse there. It was just as well, because we were in the middle of a July drought, and the clay ground was fired hard as rock. Anyway, the problem remained: What do you do with a dead horse? Another friend once tried to burn a dead horse, an experiment he never repeated. Jean White made phone calls and enlisted friends who made more phone calls. All experts offered the same suggestion: try the fox farm. The fox farm is south of here; it raises various animals to make into coats. It turned out that the fox farm readily accepts dead horses from far and wide to use as "fresh" meat for the foxes. But it also turned out, oddly enough, that the fox farm was up to its hem in dead horses already, and had room for no more.

It was, as I say, July, and the problem of the dead mare's final resting place was gathering urgency. Finally someone suggested that Jean try the landfill down where the new interstate highway was being built. Certain key phone calls were made, and, to everybody's amazement, government officials accepted the dead horse. They even welcomed the dead horse, needed the dead horse, for its bulk, which, incidentally, was becoming greater each passing hour. A local dairy farmer donated his time; a crane hauled the dead horse into the farmer's truck, and he drove south. With precious little ceremony he dumped the mare into the landfill on which the new highway would rest—and that was the end of Jean White's horse. If you ever drive through Virginia on the new interstate highway between Christiansburg and Salem, and you feel a slight dip in the paving under your wheels, then loose thy shoe from off thy foot, for the place whereon thou drivest is Jean White's horse.

All this comes to mind at the duck pond, because the duck pond is rapidly turning into a landfill of its own, a landfill paved in frogs. There are a million frogs here, bullfrogs hopping all over each other on tangled mats of algae. And the pond is filling up. Small ponds don't live very long, especially in the South. Decaying matter piles up on the bottom, depleting oxygen, and the shore plants march to the middle. In another couple of centuries, if no one interferes, the duck pond will be a hickory forest.

On an evening in late May, a moist wind from Carvin's Cove shoots down the gap between Tinker and Brushy mountains, tears along Carvin's Creek valley, and buffets my face as I stand by the duck pond. The surface of the duck pond doesn't budge. The algal layer is a rigid plating; if the wind blew hard enough, I imagine it might audibly creak. On warm days in February the primitive plants start creeping over the pond, filamentous green and blue-green algae in sopping strands. From a sunlit shallow edge they green and spread, thickening throughout the water like bright gelatin. When they smother the whole pond they block sunlight, strangle respiration, and snarl creatures in hopeless tangles. Dragonfly nymphs, for instance, are easily able to shed a leg or two to escape a tight spot, but even dragonfly nymphs get stuck in the algae strands and starve.

Several times I've seen a frog trapped under the algae. I would be staring at the pond when the green muck by my feet would suddenly leap into the air and then subside. It looked as though it had been jabbed from underneath by a broom handle. Then it would leap again, somewhere else, a jumping green flare, absolutely silently—this is a very disconcerting way to spend an evening. The frog would always find an open place at last, and break successfully onto the top of the heap, trailing long green slime from its back, and emitting a hollow sound like a pipe thrown into a cavern. Tonight I walked around the pond scaring frogs; a couple of them jumped off, going, in effect, eek, and most grunted, and the pond was still. But one big frog, bright green like a poster-paint frog, didn't jump, so I waved my arm and stamped to scare it, and it jumped suddenly, and I jumped, and then everything in the pond jumped, and I laughed and laughed.

There is a muscular energy in sunlight corresponding to the spiritual energy of wind. On a sunny day, sun's energy on a square acre of land or pond can equal 4500 horse-power. These "horses" heave in every direction, like slaves building pyramids, and fashion, from the bottom up, a new and sturdy world.

The pond is popping with life. Midges are swarming over the center, and the edges are clotted with the jellied egg masses of snails. One spring I saw a snapping turtle lumber from the pond to lay her eggs. Now a green heron picks around in the pondweed and bladderwort; two musk-rats at the shallow end are stockpiling cattails. Diatoms, which are algae that look under a microscope like crystals, multiply so fast you can practically watch a submersed green leaf transform into a brown fuzz. In the plankton, single-cell algae, screw fungi, bacteria, and water mold abound. Insect larvae and nymphs carry on their eating business everywhere in the pond. Stillwater caddises, alderfly larvae, and damselfly and dragonfly nymphs stalk on the bottom debris; mayfly nymphs hide in the weeds, mosquito larvae wriggle near the surface, and red-tailed maggots stick their breathing tubes up from between decayed leaves along the shore. Also at the pond's muddy edges it is easy to see the tiny red tubifex worms and bloodworms; the convulsive jerking of hundreds and hundreds together catches my eye.

Once, when the pond was younger and the algae had not yet taken over, I saw an amazing creature. At first all I saw was a slender motion. Then I saw that it was a wormlike creature swimming in the water with a strong, whiplike thrust, and it was two feet long. It was also slender as a thread. It looked like an inked line someone was nervously drawing over and over. Later I learned that it was a horse-hair worm. The larvae of horsehair worms live as parasites in land insects; the aquatic adults can get to be a yard long. I don't know how it gets from the insect to the pond, or from the pond to the insect, for that matter, or why on earth it needs such an extreme shape. If the one I saw had been so much as an inch longer or a shave thinner, I doubt if I would ever have come back.

The plankton bloom is what interests me. The plankton animals are all those microscopic drifting animals that so staggeringly outnumber us. In the spring they are said to "bloom," like so many poppies. There may be five times as many of these teeming creatures in spring as in summer. Among them are the protozoans—amoebae and other rhizopods, and millions of various flagellates and ciliates; gelatinous moss animalcules or byrozoans; rotifers—which wheel around either free or in colonies; and all the diverse crustacean minutiae—copepods, ostracods, and cladocerans like the abundant daphnias. All these drifting animals multiply in sundry bizarre fashions, eat tiny plants or each other, die, and drop to the pond's bottom. Many of them have quite refined means of locomotion—they whirl, paddle, swim, slog, whip, and sinuate—but since they are so small, they are no match against even the least current in the water. Even such a sober limnologist as Robert E. Coker characterizes the movement of plankton as "milling around."

A cup of duck-pond water looks like a seething broth. If I carry the cup home and let the sludge settle, the animalcules sort themselves out, and I can concentrate them further by dividing them into two clear glass bowls. One bowl I paint all black except for a single circle where the light shines through; I leave the other bowl clear except for a single black circle against the light. Given a few hours, the light-loving creatures make their feeble way to the clear circle, and the shade-loving creatures to the black. Then, if I want to, I can harvest them with a pipette and examine them under a microscope.

There they loom and disappear as I fiddle with the focus. I run the eyepiece around until I am seeing the drop magnified three hundred times, and I squint at the little rotifer called monostyla. It zooms around excitedly, crashing into strands of spirogyra alga or zipping around the frayed edge of a clump of debris. The creature is a flattened oval; at its "head" is a circular fringe of whirling cilia, and at its "tail" a single long spike, so that it is shaped roughly like a horseshoe crab. But it is so incredibly small, as multicelled animals go, that it is translucent, even transparent, and I have a hard time telling if it is above or beneath a similarly transparent alga. Two monostyla drive into view from opposite directions; they meet, bump, reverse, part. I keep thinking that if I listen closely I will hear the high whine of tiny engines. As their drop heats from the light on the mirror, the rotifers skitter more and more frantically; as it dries, they pale and begin to stagger, and at last can muster only a halting twitch. Then I either wash the whole batch down the sink's drain, or in a rush of sentiment walk out to the road by starlight and dump them in a puddle. Tinker Creek where I live is too fast and rough for most of them.

I don't really look forward to these microscopic forays: I have been almost knocked off my kitchen chair on several occasions when, as I was following with strained eyes the tiny career of a monostyla rotifer, an enormous red round-worm whipped into the scene, blocking everything, and writhing in huge, flapping convulsions that seemed to sweep my face and fill the kitchen. I do it as a moral exercise; the microscope at my forehead is a kind of phylactery, a constant reminder of the facts of creation that I would just as soon forget. You can buy your child a microscope and say grandly, "Look, child, at the Jungle in a Little Drop." The boy looks, plays around with pond water and bread mold and onion sprouts for a month or two, and then starts shooting baskets or racing cars, leaving the microscope on the basement table staring fixedly at its own mirror forever— and you say he's growing up. But in the puddle or pond, in the city reservoir, ditch, or Atlantic Ocean, the rotifers still spin and munch, the daphnia still filter and are filtered, and the copepods still swarm hanging with clusters of eggs. These are real creatures with real organs leading real lives, one by one. I can't pretend they're not there. If I have life, sense, energy, will, so does a rotifer. The monostyla goes to the dark spot on the bowl: To which circle am I heading? I can move around right smartly in a calm; but in a real wind, in a change of weather, in a riptide, am I really moving, or am I "milling around"?

I was created from a clot and set in proud, free motion: so were they. So was this rotifer created, this monostyla with its body like a light bulb in which pale organs hang in loops; so was this paramecium created, with a thousand propulsive hairs jerking in unison, whipping it from here to there across a drop and back. *Ad majorem Dei gloriam*?

Somewhere, and I can't find where, I read about an Eskimo hunter who asked the local missionary priest, "If I did not know about God and sin, would I go to hell?" "No," said the priest, "not if you did not know." "Then why," asked the Eskimo earnestly, "did you tell me?" If I did not know about the rotifers and paramecia, and all the bloom of plankton clogging the dying pond, fine; but since I've seen it I must somehow deal with it, take it into account. "Never lose a holy curiosity," Einstein said; and so I lift my microscope down from the shelf, spread a drop of duck pond on a glass slide, and try to look spring in the eye.

CHAPTER 8

Intricacy

I

A ROSY, COMPLEX LIGHT fills my kitchen at the end of these lengthening June days. From an explosion on a nearby star eight minutes ago, the light zips through space, particle-wave, strikes the planet, angles on the continent, and filters through a mesh of land dust: clay bits, sod bits, tiny windborne insects, bacteria, shreds of wing and leg, gravel dust, grits of carbon, and dried cells of grass, bark, and leaves. Reddened, the light inclines into this valley over the green western mountains; it sifts between pine needles on northern slopes, and through all the mountain blackjack oak and haw, whose leaves are unclenching, one by one, and making an intricate, toothed and lobed haze. The light crosses the valley, threads through the screen on my open kitchen window, and gilds the painted wall. A plank of brightness bends from the wall and extends over the goldfish bowl on the table where I sit. The goldfish's side catches the light and bats it my way; I've an eyeful of fishscale and star.

This Ellery cost me twenty-five cents. He is a deep redorange, darker than most goldfish. He steers short distances mainly with his slender red lateral fins; they seem to provide impetus for going backward, up, or down. It took me a few days to discover his ventral fins; they are completely transparent and all but invisible—dream fins. He also has a short anal fin, and a tail that is deeply notched and perfectly transparent at the two tapered tips. He can extend his mouth, so that it looks like a length of pipe; he can shift the angle of his eyes in his head so he can look before and behind himself, instead of simply out to his side. His belly, what there is of it, is white ventrally, and a patch of this white extends up his sides—the variegated Ellery. When he opens his gill slits he shows a thin crescent of silver where the flap overlapped—as though all his brightness were sunburn.

For this creature, as I said, I paid twenty-five cents. I had never bought an animal before. It was very simple; I went to a store in Roanoke called "Wet Pets"; I handed the man a quarter, and he handed me a knotted plastic bag bouncing with water in which a green plant floated and the goldfish swam. This fish, two bits' worth, has a coiled gut, a spine radiating fine bones, and a brain. Just before I sprinkle his food flakes into his bowl, I rap three times on the bowl's edge; now he is conditioned, and swims to the surface when I rap. And, he has a heart.

Once, years ago, I saw red blood cells whip, one by one, through the capillaries in a goldfish's transparent tail. The goldfish was etherized. Its head lay in a wad of wet cotton wool; its tail lay on a tray under a dissecting microscope, one of those wonderful light-gathering microscopes with two eyepieces like a stereoscope in which the world's fragments—even the skin on my finger—look brilliant with myriads of colored lights, and as deep as any alpine landscape. The red blood cells in the goldfish's tail streamed and coursed through narrow channels invisible save for glistening threads of thickness in the general translucency. They never wavered or slowed or ceased flowing, like the creek itself; they streamed redly around, up, and on, one by one, more, and more, without end. (The energy of that pulse reminds me of something about the human body: if you sit absolutely perfectly balanced on the end of your spine, with your legs either crossed tailor-fashion or drawn up together, and your arms forward on your legs, then even if you hold your breath, your body will rock with the energy of your heartbeat, forward and back, effortlessly, for as long as you want to remain balanced.) Those red blood cells are coursing in Ellery's tail now, too, in just that way, and through his mouth and eyes as well, and through mine. I've never forgotten the sight of those cells; I think of it when I see the fish in his bowl; I think of it lying in bed at night, imagining that if I concentrate enough I might be able to feel in my fingers' capillaries the small knockings and flow of those circular dots, like a string of beads drawn through my hand.

Something else is happening in the goldfish bowl. There on the kitchen table, nourished by the simple plank of complex light, the plankton is blooming. The water yellows and clouds; a transparent slime coats the leaves of the water plant, elodea; a blue-green film of single-celled algae clings to the glass. And I have to clean the doggone bowl.

I'll spare you the details: it's the plant I'm interested in. While Ellery swims in the stoppered sink, I rinse the algae down the drain of another sink, wash the gravel, and rub the elodea's many ferny leaves under running water until they feel clean.

The elodea is not considered much of a plant. Aquarists use it because it's available and it gives off oxygen completely submersed; laboratories use it because its leaves are only two cells thick. It's plentiful, easy to grow, and cheap —like the goldfish. And, like the goldfish, its cells have unwittingly performed for me on a microscope's stage.

I was in a laboratory, using a very expensive microscope. I peered through the deep twin eyepieces and saw again that color-charged, glistening world. A thin, oblong leaf of elodea, a quarter of an inch long, lay on a glass slide sopping wet and floodlighted brilliantly from below. In the circle of light formed by the two eyepieces trained at the translucent leaf, I saw a clean mosaic of almost colorless cells. The cells were large—eight or nine of them, magnified four hundred and fifty times, packed the circle—so that I could easily see what I had come to see: the streaming of chloroplasts.

Chloroplasts bear chlorophyll; they give the green world its color, and they carry out the business of photosynthesis. Around the inside perimeter of each gigantic cell trailed a continuous loop of these bright green dots. They spun like paramecia; they pulsed, pressed, and thronged. A change of focus suddenly revealed the eddying currents of the river of transparent cytoplasm, a sort of "ether" to the chloroplasts, or "space-time," in which they have their tiny being. Back to the green dots: they shone, they swarmed in ever-shifting files around and around the edge of the cell; they wandered, they charged, they milled, raced, and ran at the edge of apparent nothingness, the empty-looking inner cell;

they flowed and trooped greenly, up against the vegetative wall.

All the green in the planted world consists of these whole, rounded chloroplasts wending their ways in water. If you analyze a molecule of chlorophyll itself, what you get is one hundred thirty-six atoms of hydrogen, carbon, oxygen, and nitrogen arranged in an exact and complex relationship around a central ring. At the ring's center is a single atom of magnesium. Now: If you remove the atom of magnesium and in its exact place put an atom of iron, you get a molecule of hemoglobin. The iron atom combines with all the other atoms to make red blood, the streaming red dots in the goldfish's tail.

It is, then, a small world there in the goldfish bowl, and a very large one. Say the nucleus of any atom in the bowl were the size of a cherry pit: its nearest electron would revolve around it one hundred seventy-five yards away. A whirling air in his swim bladder balances the goldfish's weight in the water; his scales overlap, his feathery gills pump and filter; his eyes work, his heart beats, his liver absorbs, his muscles contract in a wave of extending ripples. The daphnias he eats have eyes and jointed legs. The algae the daphnias eat have green cells stacked like checkers or winding in narrow ribbons like spiral staircases up long columns of emptiness. And so on diminishingly down. We have not yet found the dot so small it is uncreated, as it were, like a metal blank, or merely roughed in—and we never shall. We go down landscape after mobile, sculpture after collage, down to molecular structures like a mob dance in Breughel, down to atoms airy and balanced as a canvas by Klee, down to atomic particles, the heart of the matter, as spirited and wild as any El Greco saints. And it all works. "Nature," said Thoreau in his journal, "is mythical and mystical always, and spends her whole genius on the least work." The creator, I would add, churns out the intricate texture of least works that is the world with a spendthrift genius and an extravagance of care. This is the point.

I am sitting here looking at a goldfish bowl and busting my brain. *Ich kann nicht anders.* I am sitting here, you are sitting there. Say even that you are sitting across this kitchen table from me right now. Our eyes meet; a consciousness snaps back and forth. What we know, at least for starters, is: here we—so incontrovertibly—are. This is our life, these are our lighted seasons, and then we die. (You die, you die; first you go wet, and then you go dry.) In the meantime, in between time, we can see. The scales are fallen from our eyes, the cataracts are cut away, and we can work at making sense of the color-patches we see in an effort to discover *where* we so incontrovertibly are. It's common sense: when you move in, you try to learn the neighborhood.

I am as passionately interested in where I am as is a lone sailor sans sextant in a ketch on the open ocean. What else is he supposed to be thinking about? Fortunately, like the sailor, I have at the moment a situation which allows me to devote considerable hunks of time to seeing what I can see, and trying to piece it together. I've learned the names of some color-patches, but not the meanings. I've read books. I've gathered statistics feverishly: The average temperature of our planet is 57° Fahrenheit. Of the 29% of all land that is above water, over a third is given to grazing. The average size of all living animals, including man, is almost that of a housefly. The earth is mostly granite, which in turn is mostly oxygen. The most numerous of animals big enough to see are the copepods, the mites, and the springtails; of plants, the algae, the sedge. In these Appalachians we have found a coal bed with 120 seams, meaning

120 forests that just happened to fall into water, heaped like corpses in drawers. And so on. These statistics, and all the various facts about subatomic particles, quanta, neutrinos, and so forth, constitute in effect the infrared and ultraviolet light at either end of the spectrum. They are too big and too small to see, to understand; they are more or less invisible to me though present, and peripheral to me in a real sense because I do not understand even what I can easily see. I would like to see it all, to understand it, but I must start somewhere, so I try to deal with the giant water bug in Tinker Creek and the flight of three hundred redwings from an Osage orange, with the goldfish bowl and the snakeskin, and let those who dare worry about the birthrate and population explosion among solar systems.

So I think about the valley. And it occurs to me more and more that everything I have seen is wholly gratuitous. The giant water bug's predations, the frog's croak, the tree with the lights in it are not in any real sense necessary per se to the world or to its creator. Nor am I. The creation in the first place, being itself, is the only necessity, for which I would die, and I shall. The point about that being, as I know it here and see it, is that, as I think about it, it accumulates in my mind as an extravagance of minutiae. The sheer fringe and network of detail assumes primary importance. That there are so many details seems to be the most important and visible fact about the creation. If you can't see the forest for the trees, then look at the trees; when you've looked at enough trees, you've seen a forest, you've got it. If the world is gratuitous, then the fringe of a goldfish's fin is a million times more so. The first question—the one crucial one—of the creation of the universe and the existence of something as a sign and an affront to nothing, is a blank one. I can't think about it. So it is to the fringe of that question that I affix my attention, the fringe of the fish's fin, the intricacy of the world's spotted and speckled detail.

The old Kabbalistic phrase is "the Mystery of the Splintering of the Vessels." The words refer to the shrinking or imprisonment of essences within the various husk-covered forms of emanation or time. The Vessels splintered and solar systems spun; ciliated rotifers whirled in still water, and newts with gills laid tracks in the silt-bottomed creek. Not only did the Vessels splinter: they splintered exceeding fine. Intricacy, then, is the subject, the intricacy of the created world.

You are God. You want to make a forest, something to hold the soil, lock up solar energy, and give off oxygen. Wouldn't it be simpler just to rough in a slab of chemicals, a green acre of goo?

You are a man, a retired railroad worker who makes replicas as a hobby. You decide to make a replica of one tree, the longleaf pine your great-grandfather planted—just a replica—it doesn't have to work. How are you going to do it? How long do you think you might live, how good is your glue? For one thing, you are going to have to dig a hole and stick your replica trunk in the ground halfway to China if you want the thing to stand up. Because you will have to work fairly big; if your replica is too small, you'll be unable to handle the slender, three-sided needles, affix them in clusters of three in fascicles, and attach those laden fascicles to flexible twigs. The twigs themselves must be covered by "many silvery-white, fringed, long-spreading scales." Are your pine cones' scales "thin, flat, rounded at the apex, the exposed portions (closed cone) reddish brown, often wrinkled, armed on the back with a small, reflexed prickle, which curves toward the base of the scale"?

When you loose the lashed copper wire trussing the replica limbs to the trunk, the whole tree collapses like an umbrella.

You are a starling. I've seen you fly through a longleaf pine without missing a beat.

You are a sculptor. You climb a great ladder; you pour grease all over a growing longleaf pine. Next, you build a hollow cylinder like a cofferdam around the entire pine, and grease its inside walls. You climb your ladder and spend the next week pouring wet plaster into the cofferdam, over and inside the pine. You wait; the plaster hardens. Now open the walls of the dam, split the plaster, saw down the tree, remove it, discard, and your intricate sculpture is ready: this is the shape of part of the air.

You are a chloroplast moving in water heaved one hundred feet above ground. Hydrogen, carbon, oxygen, nitrogen in a ring around magnesium. . . . You are evolution; you have only begun to make trees. You are God—are you tired? finished?

Intricacy means that there is a fluted fringe to the something that exists over against nothing, a fringe that rises and spreads, burgeoning in detail. Mentally reverse positive and negative space, as in the plaster cast of the pine, and imagine emptiness as a sort of person, a boundless person consisting of an elastic, unformed clay. (For the moment forget that the air in our atmosphere is "something," and count it as "nothing," the sculptor's negative space.) The clay man completely surrounds the holes in him, which are galaxies and solar systems. The holes in him part, expand, shrink, veer, circle, spin. He gives like water, he spreads and fills unseeing. Here is a ragged hole, our earth, a hole that makes torn and frayed edges in his side, mountains and pines. And here is the shape of one swift, raveling edge, a feather-hole on a flying goose's hollow wing extended over the planet. Five hundred barbs of emptiness prick into clay from either side of a central, flexible shaft. On each barb are two fringes of five hundred barbules apiece, making a million barbules on each feather, fluted and hooked in a matrix of clasped hollowness. Through the fabric of this form the clay man shuttles unerringly, and through the other feather-holes, and the goose, the pine forest, the planet, and so on.

In other words, even on the perfectly ordinary and clearly visible level, creation carries on with an intricacy unfathomable and apparently uncalled for. The lone ping into being of the first hydrogen atom *ex nihilo* was so unthinkably, violently radical, that surely it ought to have been enough, more than enough. But look what happens. You open the door and all heaven and hell break loose.

Evolution, of course, is the vehicle of intricacy. The stability of simple forms is the sturdy base from which more complex stable forms might arise, forming in turn more complex forms, and so on. The stratified nature of this stability, like a house built on rock on rock on rock, performs, in Jacob Branowski's terms, as the "ratchet" that prevents the whole shebang from "slipping back." Bring a feather into the house, and a piano; put a sculpture on the roof, sure, and fly banners from the lintels—the house will hold.

There are, for instance, two hundred twenty-eight separate and distinct muscles in the head of an ordinary caterpillar. Again, of an ostracod, a common fresh-water crustacean of the sort I crunch on by the thousands every time I set foot in Tinker Creek, I read, "There is one eye situated at the fore-end of the animal. The food canal lies just below the hinge, and around the mouth are the feathery feeding appendages which collect the food. . . . Behind them is a foot which is clawed and this is partly used for removing unwanted particles from the feeding appendages." Or again, there are, as I have said, six million leaves on a big elm. All right . . . but they are toothed, and the teeth themselves are toothed. How many notches and barbs is that to a world? In and out go the intricate leaf edges, and "don't nobody know why." All the theories botanists have devised to explain the functions of various leaf-shapes tumble under an avalanche of inconsistencies. They simply don't know, can't imagine.

I have often noticed that these things, which obsess me, neither bother nor impress other people even slightly. I am horribly apt to approach some innocent at a gathering and, like the ancient mariner, fix him with a wild glitt'ring eye and say, "Do you know that in the head of the caterpillar of the ordinary goat moth there are two hundred twenty-eight separate muscles?" The poor wretch flees. I am not making chatter; I mean to change his life. I seem to possess an organ that others lack, a sort of trivia machine.

When I was young I thought that all human beings had an organ inside each lower eyelid which caught things that got in the eye. I don't know where I imagined I'd learned this piece of anatomy. Things got in my eye, and then they went away, so I supposed that they had fallen into my eye-pouch. This eye-pouch was a slender, thin-walled purse, equipped with frail digestive powers that enabled it eventually to absorb eyelashes, strands of fabric, bits of grit, and anything else that might stray into the eye. Well, the existence of this eye-pouch, it turned out, was all in my mind, and, it turns out, it is apparently there still, a brain-pouch, catching and absorbing small bits that fall deeply into my open eye.

All I can remember from a required zoology course years ago, for instance, is a lasting impression that there is an item in the universe called a Henle's loop. Its terrestrial abode is in the human kidney. I just refreshed my memory on the subject. The Henle's loop is an attenuated oxbow or U-turn made by an incredibly tiny tube in the nephron of the kidney. The nephron in turn is a filtering structure which produces urine and reabsorbs nutrients. This business is so important that one fifth of all the heart's pumped blood goes to the kidneys.

There is no way to describe a nephron; you might hazard into a fairly good approximation of its structure if you threw about fifteen yards of string on the floor. If half the string fell into a very narrow loop, that would be the Henle's loop. Two other bits of string that rumpled up and tangled would be the "proximal convoluted tubule" and the "distal convoluted tubule," shaped just so. But the heart of the matter would be a very snarled clump of string, "an almost spherical tuft of parallel capillaries," which is the glomerulus, or Malpighian body. This is the filter to end all filters, supplied with afferent and efferent arterioles and protected by a double-walled capsule. Compared to the glomerulus, the Henle's loop is rather unimportant. By going from here to there in such a roundabout way, the Henle's loop packs a great deal of filtering tubule into a very narrow space. But the delicate oxbow of tissue, looping down so far, and then up, is really a peripheral extravagance, which is why I remembered it, and a beautiful one, like a meander in a creek.

Now the point of all this is that there are a million nephrons in each human kidney. I've got two million glomeruli, two million Henle's loops, and I made them all myself, without the least effort. They're undoubtedly my finest work. What an elaboration, what an extravagance! The proximal segment of the tubule, for instance, "is composed of irregular cuboidal cells with characteristic brush-like striations (brush border) at the internal, or luminal, border." Here are my own fringed necessities, a veritable forest of pines.

Van Gogh, you remember, called the world a study that didn't come off. Whether it "came off" is a difficult question. The chloroplasts do stream in the leaf as if propelled by a mighty, invisible breath; but on the other hand, a certain sorrow arises, welling up in Shadow Creek, and from those lonely banks it appears that all our intricate fringes, however beautiful, are really the striations of a universal and undeserved flaying. But, Van Gogh: a *study* it is not. This is the truth of the pervading intricacy of the world's detail: the creation is not a study, a roughed-in sketch; it is supremely, meticulously created, created abundantly, extravagantly, and in fine.

Along with intricacy, there is another aspect of the creation that has impressed me in the course of my wanderings. Look again at the horsehair worm, a yard long and thin as a thread, whipping through the duck pond, or tangled with others of its kind in a slithering Gordian knot. Look at an overwintering ball of buzzing bees, or a turtle under ice breathing through its pumping cloaca. Look at the fruit of the Osage orange tree, big as a grapefruit, green, convoluted as any human brain. Or look at a rotifer's translucent gut: something orange and powerful is surging up and down like a piston, and something small and round is spinning in place like a flywheel. Look, in short, at practically anything

—the coot's feet, the mantis's face, a banana, the human ear —and see that not only did the creator create everything, but that he is apt to create *anything*. He'll stop at nothing.

There is no one standing over evolution with a blue pencil to say, "Now that one, there, is absolutely ridiculous, and I won't have it." If the creature makes it, it gets a "stet." Is our taste so much better than the creator's? Utility to the creature is evolution's only aesthetic consideration. Form follows function in the created world, so far as I know, and the creature that functions, however bizarre, survives to perpetuate its form. Of the intricacy of form, I know some answers and not others: I know why the barbules on a feather hook together, and why the Henle's loop loops, but not why the elm tree's leaves zigzag, or why butterfly scales and pollen are shaped just so. But of the *variety* of form itself, of the multiplicity of forms, I know nothing. Except that, apparently, anything goes. This holds for forms of behavior as well as design—the mantis munching her mate, the frog wintering in mud, the spider wrapping a hummingbird, the pine processionary straddling a thread. Welcome aboard. A generous spirit signs on this motley crew.

Take, for instance, the African Hercules beetle, which is so big, according to Edwin Way Teale, "it drones over the countryside at evening with a sound like an approaching airplane." Or, better, take to heart Teale's description of South American honey ants. These ants have abdomens that can stretch to enormous proportions. "Certain members of the colony act as storage vessels for the honeydew gathered by the workers. They never leave the nest. With abdomens so swollen they cannot walk, they cling to the roof of their underground chamber, regurgitating food to the workers when it is needed." I read these things, and those ants are as present to me as if they hung from my kitchen ceiling, or down the vaults of my skull, pulsing live jars, engorged vats, teats, with an eyed animal at the head thinking—what?

Blake said, "He who does not prefer Form to Colour is a Coward!" I often wish the creator had been more of a coward, giving us many fewer forms and many more colors. Here is an interesting form, one closer to home. This is the larva, or nymph, of an ordinary dragonfly. The wingless nymphs are an inch long and fat as earthworms. They stalk everywhere on the floors of valley ponds and creeks, sucking water into their gilled rectums. But it is their faces I'm interested in. According to Howard Ensign Evans, a dragonfly larva's "lower lip is enormously lengthened, and has a double hinge joint so that it can be pulled back beneath the body when not in use; the outer part is expanded and provided with stout hooks, and in resting position forms a 'mask' that covers much of the face of the larva. The lip is capable of being thrust forward suddenly, and the terminal hooks are capable of grasping prey well in front of the larva and pulling it back to the sharp, jagged mandibles. Dragonfly larvae prey on many kinds of small insects occuring in the water, and the large ones are well able to handle small fish."

The world is full of creatures that for some reason seem stranger to us than others, and libraries are full of books describing them—hagfish, platypuses, lizardlike pangolins four feet long with bright green, lapped scales like umbrella-tree leaves on a bush hut roof, butterflies emerging from anthills, spiderlings wafting through the air clutching tiny silken balloons, horseshoe crabs . . . the creator creates. Does he stoop, does he speak, does he save, succor, prevail? Maybe. But he creates; he creates everything and anything.

Of all known forms of life, only about ten percent are still living today. All other forms—fantastic plants, ordinary plants, living animals with unimaginably various wings, tails, teeth, brains—are utterly and forever gone. That is a great many forms that have been created. Multiplying ten times the number of living forms today yields a profusion that is quite beyond what I consider thinkable. Why so many forms? Why not just that one hydrogen atom? The creator goes off on one wild, specific tangent after another, or millions simultaneously, with an exuberance that would seem to be unwarranted, and with an abandoned energy sprung from an unfathomable font. What is going on here? The point of the dragonfly's terrible lip, the giant water bug, birdsong, or the beautiful dazzle and flash of sunlighted minnows, is not that it all fits together like clockwork—for it doesn't, particularly, not even inside the goldfish bowl—but that it all flows so freely wild, like the creek, that it all surges in such a free, fringed tangle. Freedom is the world's water and weather, the world's nourishment freely given, its soil and sap: and the creator loves pizzazz.

II

What I aim to do is not so much learn the names of the shreds of creation that flourish in this valley, but to keep myself open to their meanings, which is to try to impress myself at all times with the fullest possible force of their very reality. I want to have things as multiply and intricately as possible present and visible in my mind. Then I might be able to sit on the hill by the burnt books where the starlings fly over, and see not only the starlings, the grass field, the quarried rock, the viney woods, Hollins Pond, and the mountains beyond, but also, and simultaneously, feathers' barbs, springtails in the soil, crystal in rock, chloroplasts streaming, rotifers pulsing, and the shape of the air in the pines. And, if I try to keep my eye on quantum physics, if I try to keep up with astronomy and cosmology, and really believe it all, I might ultimately be able to make out the landscape of the universe. Why not?

Landscape consists in the multiple, overlapping intricacies and forms that exist in a given space at a moment in time. Landscape is the texture of intricacy, and texture is my present subject. Intricacies of detail and varieties of form build up into textures. A bird's feather is an intricacy; the bird is a form; the bird in space in relation to air, forest, continent, and so on, is a thread in a texture. The moon has its texture, too, its pitted and carved landscapes in even its flattest seas. The planets are more than smooth spheres; the galaxy itself is a fleck of texture, binding and bound. But here on earth texture interests us supremely. Wherever there is life, there is twist and mess: the frizz of an arctic lichen, the tangle of brush along a bank, the dogleg of a dog's leg, the way a line has got to curve, split, or knob. The planet is characterized by its very jaggedness, its random heaps of mountains, its frayed fringes of shore.

Think of a globe, a revolving globe on a stand. Think of a contour globe, whose mountain ranges cast shadows, whose continents rise in bas-relief above the oceans. But then: think of how it *really* is. These heights aren't just suggested; they're there. Pliny, who knew the world was round, figured that when it was all surveyed the earth would be seen to resemble in shape, not a sphere, but a pineapple, pricked by irregularities. When I think of walking across a continent I think of all the neighborhood hills, the tiny grades up which children drag their sleds. It is all so sculptured, three-dimensional, casting a shadow. What if you had an enormous globe in relief that was so huge it showed roads and houses—a geological survey globe, a quarter of a mile to an inch—of the whole world, and the ocean floor! Looking at it, you would know what had to be left out: the free-standing sculptural arrangement of furniture in rooms, the jumble of broken rocks in a creek bed, tools in a box, labyrinthine ocean liners, the shape of snapdragons, walrus. Where is the one thing you care about on earth, the molding of one face? The relief globe couldn't begin to show trees, between whose overlapping boughs birds raise broods, or the furrows in bark, where whole creatures, creatures easily visible, live out their lives and call it world enough.

What do I make of all this texture? What does it mean about the kind of world in which I have been set down? The texture of the world, its filigree and scrollwork, means that there is the possibility for beauty here, a beauty inexhaustible in its complexity, which opens to my knock, which answers in me a call I do not remember calling, and which trains me to the wild and extravagant nature of the spirit I seek.

In the eighteenth century, when educated European tourists visited the Alps, they deliberately blindfolded their eyes to shield themselves from the evidence of the earth's horrid irregularity. It is hard to say if this was not merely affectation, for today, newborn infants, who have not yet been taught our ideas of beauty, repeatedly show in tests that they prefer complex to simple designs. At any rate, after the Romantic Revolution, and after Darwin, I might add, our conscious notions of beauty changed. Were the earth as smooth as a ball bearing, it might be beautiful seen from another planet, as the rings of Saturn are. But here we live and move; we wander up and down the banks of the creek, we ride a railway through the Alps, and the landscape shifts and changes. Were the earth smooth, our brains would be smooth as well; we would wake, blink, walk two steps to get the whole picture, and lapse into a dreamless sleep. Because we are living people, and because we are on the receiving end of beauty, another element necessarily enters the question. The texture of space is a condition of time. Time is the warp and matter the weft of the woven texture of beauty in space, and death is the hurtling shuttle. Did those eighteenth-century people think they were immortal? Or were their carriages stalled to rigidity, so that they knew they would never move again, and, panicked, they reached for their blindfolds?

What I want to do, then, is add time to the texture, paint the landscape on an unrolling scroll, and set the giant relief globe spinning on its stand.

Last year I had a very unusual experience. I was awake, with my eyes closed, when I had a dream. It was a small dream about time.

I was dead, I guess, in deep black space high up among many white stars. My own consciousness had been disclosed to me, and I was happy. Then I saw far below me a long, curved band of color. As I came closer, I saw that it stretched endlessly in either direction, and I understood that I was seeing all the time of the planet where I had lived. It looked like a woman's tweed scarf; the longer I studied any one spot, the more dots of color I saw. There was no end to the deepness and variety of the dots. At length I started to look for my time, but, although more and more specks of color and deeper and more intricate textures appeared in the fabric, I couldn't find my time, or any time at all that I recognized as being near my time. I couldn't make out so much as a pyramid. Yet as I looked at the band of time, all the individual people, I understood with special clarity, were living at that very moment with great emotion, in intricate detail, in their individual times and places, and they were dying and being replaced by ever more people, one by one, like stitches in which whole worlds of feeling and energy were wrapped, in a never-ending cloth. I re-membered suddenly the color and texture of our life as we knew it—these things had been utterly forgotten—and I thought as I searched for it on the limitless band, "That was a good time then, a good time to be living." And I be-gan to remember our time.

I recalled green fields with carrots growing, one by one, in slender rows. Men and women in bright vests and scarves came and pulled the carrots out of the soil and carried them in baskets to shaded kitchens, where they scrubbed them with yellow brushes under running water. I saw white-faced cattle lowing and wading in creeks, with dust on the whorled and curly white hair between their ears. I saw May apples in forests, erupting through leaf-strewn paths. Cells on the root hairs of sycamores split and divided, and apples grew spotted and striped in the fall. Mountains kept their cool caves, and squirrels raced home to their nests through sunlight and shade.

I remembered the ocean, and I seemed to be in the ocean myself, swimming over orange crabs that looked like coral, or off the deep Atlantic banks where whitefish school. Or again I saw the tops of poplars, and the whole sky brushed with clouds in pallid streaks, under which wild ducks flew with outstretched necks, and called, one by one, and flew on.

All these things I saw. Scenes grew in depth and sunlit detail before my eyes, and were replaced by ever more scenes, as I remembered the life of my time with increasing feeling.

At last I saw the earth as a globe in space, and I recalled the ocean's shape and the form of continents, saying to my-self with surprise as I looked at the planet, "Yes, that's how it was then; that part there we called . . . 'France.' " I was filled with the deep affection of nostalgia—and then I opened my eyes.

We all ought to be able to conjure up sights like these at will, so that we can keep in mind the scope of texture's motion in time. It is a pity we can't watch it on a screen. John Dee, the Elizabethan geographer and mathematician, dreamed up a great idea, which is just what we need. You shoot a mirror up into space so that it is traveling faster than the speed of light (there's the rub). Then you can look in the mirror and watch all the earth's previous history unfolding as on a movie screen. Those people who shoot endless time-lapse films of unfurling roses and tulips have the wrong idea. They should train their cameras instead on the melting of pack ice, the green filling of ponds, the tidal swing of the Severn Bore. They should film the glaciers of Greenland, some of which creak along at such a fast clip that even the dogs bark at them. They should film the invasion of the southernmost Canadian tundra by the northernmost spruce-fir-forest, which is happening right now at the rate of a mile every ten years. When the last ice sheet receded from the North American continent, the earth rebounded ten feet. Wouldn't that have been a sight to see?

People say that a good seat in the backyard affords as accurate and inspiring a vantage point on the plant earth as any observation tower on Alpha Centauri. They are wrong. We see through a glass darkly. We find ourselves in the middle of a movie, or, God help us, a take for a movie, and we don't know what's on the rest of the film.

Say you could look through John Dee's mirror whizzing through space; say you could heave our relief globe into motion like a giant top and breathe life on its surface; say you could view a time-lapse film of our planet: What would you see? Transparent images moving through light, "an infinite storm of beauty."

The beginning is swaddled in mists, blasted by random blinding flashes. Lava pours and cools; seas boil and flood. Clouds materialize and shift; now you can see the earth's face through only random patches of clarity. The land shudders and splits, like pack ice rent by a widening lead. Mountains burst up, jutting, and dull and soften before your eyes, clothed in forests like felt. The ice rolls up, grinding green land under water forever; the ice rolls back. Forests erupt and disappear like fairy rings. The ice rolls up—mountains are mowed into lakes, land rises wet from the sea like a surfacing whale—the ice rolls back.

A blue-green streaks the highest ridges, a yellow-green spreads from the south like a wave up a strand. A red dye seems to leak from the north down the ridges and into the valleys, seeping south; a white follows the red, then yellow-green washes north, then red spreads again, then white, over and over, making patterns of color too swift and intricate to follow. Slow the film. You see dust storms, locusts, floods, in dizzying flash-frames.

Zero in on a well-watered shore and see smoke from fires drifting. Stone cities rise, spread, and crumble, like patches of alpine blossoms that flourish for a day an inch above the permafrost, that iced earth no root can suck, and wither in an hour. New cities appear, and rivers sift silt onto their rooftops; more cities emerge and spread in lobes like lichen on rock. The great human figures of history, those intricate, spirited tissues that roamed the earth's surface, are a wavering blur whose split second in the light was too brief an exposure to yield any image but the hunched, shadowless figures of ghosts. The great herds of caribou pour into the valleys like slag, and trickle back, and pour, a brown fluid.

Slow it down more, come closer still. A dot appears, a flesh-flake. It swells like a balloon; it moves, circles, slows, and vanishes. This is your life.

Our life is a faint tracing on the surface of mystery. The surface of mystery is not smooth, any more than the planet is smooth; not even a single hydrogen atom is smooth, let alone a pine. Nor does it fit together; not even the chlorophyll and hemoglobin molecules are a perfect match, for, even after the atom of iron replaces the magnesium, long streamers of disparate atoms trail disjointedly from the rims of the molecules' loops. Freedom cuts both ways. Mystery itself is as fringed and intricate as the shape of the air in time. Forays into mystery cut bays and fine fiords, but the forested mainland itself is implacable both in its bulk and in its most filigreed fringe of detail. "Every religion that does not affirm that God is hidden," said Pascal flatly, "is not true."

What is man, that thou art mindful of him? This is where the great modern religions are so unthinkably radical: the love of God! For we can see that we are as many as the leaves of trees. But it could be that our faithlessness is a cowering cowardice born of our very smallness, a massive failure of imagination. Certainly nature seems to exult in abounding radicality, extremism, anarchy. If we were to judge nature by its common sense or likelihood, we wouldn't believe the world existed. In nature, improbabilities are the one stock in trade. The whole creation is one lunatic fringe. If creation had been left up to me, I'm sure I wouldn't have had the imagination or courage to do more than shape a single, reasonably sized atom, smooth as a snowball, and let it go at that. No claims of any and all revelations could be so far-fetched as a single giraffe.

The question from agnosticism is, Who turned on the

lights? The question from faith is, Whatever for? Thoreau climbs Mount Katahdin and gives vent to an almost outraged sense of the reality of the things of this world: "I fear bodies, I tremble to meet them. What is this Titan that has possession of me? Talk of mysteries!—Think of our life in nature,—daily to be shown matter, to come in contact with it,—rocks, trees, wind on our cheeks! the *solid* earth! the *actual* world! the *common* sense! *Contact! Contact!* Who are we? *where* are we?" The Lord God of gods, the Lord God of gods, he knoweth. . . .

Sir James Jeans, British astronomer and physicist, suggested that the universe was beginning to look more like a great thought than a great machine. Humanists seized on the expression, but it was hardly news. We knew, looking around, that a thought branches and leafs, a tree comes to a conclusion. But the question of who is thinking the thought is more fruitful than the question of who made the machine, for a machinist can of course wipe his hands and leave, and his simple machine still hums; but if the thinker's attention strays for a minute, his simplest thought ceases altogether. And, as I have stressed, the place where we so incontrovertibly find ourselves, whether thought or machine, is at least not in any way simple.

Instead, the landscape of the world is "ring-streaked, speckled, and spotted," like Jacob's cattle culled from Laban's herd. Laban had been hard, making Jacob serve seven years in his fields for Rachel, and then giving him instead Rachel's sister, Leah, withholding Rachel until he had served another seven years. When Laban finally sent Jacob on his way, he agreed that Jacob could have all those cattle, sheep, and goats from the herd that were ring-streaked, speckled, and spotted. Jacob pulled some tricks of his own, and soon the strongest and hardiest of Laban's fecund flocks were born ringstreaked, speckled, and spotted.

Jacob set out for Canaan with his wives and twelve sons, the fathers of the twelve tribes of Israel, and with these cattle that are Israel's heritage, into Egypt and out of Egypt, just as the intricate speckled and spotted world is ours.

Intricacy is that which is given from the beginning, the birthright, and in intricacy is the hardiness of complexity that ensures against the failure of all life. This is our heritage, the piebald landscape of time. We walk around; we see a shred of the infinite possible combinations of an infinite variety of forms.

Anything can happen; any pattern of speckles may appear in a world ceaselessly bawling with newness. I see red blood stream in shimmering dots inside a goldfish's tail; I see the stout, extensible lip of a dragonfly nymph that can pierce and clasp a goldfish; and I see the clotted snarls of bright algae that snare and starve the nymph. I see engorged, motionless ants regurgitate pap to a colony of pawing workers, and I see sharks limned in light twist in a raised and emerald wave.

The wonder is—given the errant nature of freedom and the burgeoning of texture in time—the wonder is that all the forms are not monsters, that there is beauty at all, grace gratuitous, pennies found, like mockingbird's free fall. Beauty itself is the fruit of the creator's exuberance that grew such a tangle, and the grotesques and horrors bloom from that same free growth, that intricate scramble and twine up and down the conditions of time.

This, then, is the extravagant landscape of the world, given, given with pizzazz, given in good measure, pressed down, shaken together, and running over.

CHAPTER 9

Flood

IT'S SUMMER. We had some deep spring sunshine about a month ago, in a drought; the nights were cold. It's been gray sporadically, but not oppressively, and rainy for a week, and I would think: When is the real hot stuff coming, the mind-melting weeding weather? It was rainy again this morning, the same spring rain, and then this afternoon a different rain came: a pounding, three-minute shower. And when it was over, the cloud dissolved to haze. I can't see Tinker Mountain. It's summer now: the heat is on. It's summer now all summer long.

The season changed two hours ago. Will my life change as well? This is a time for resolutions, revolutions. The animals are going wild. I must have seen ten rabbits in as many minutes. Baltimore orioles are here; brown thrashers seem to be nesting down by Tinker Creek across the road.

The coot is still around, big as a Thanksgiving turkey, and as careless; it doesn't even glance at a barking dog.

The creek's up. When the rain stopped today I walked across the road to the downed log by the steer crossing. The steers were across the creek, a black clot on a distant hill. High water had touched my log, the log I sit on, and dumped a smooth slope of muck in its lee. The water itself was an opaque pale green, like pulverized jade, still high and very fast, lightless, like no earthly water. A dog I've never seen before, thin as death, was flushing rabbits.

A knot of yellow, fleshy somethings had grown up by the log. They didn't seem to have either proper stems or proper flowers, but instead only blind, featureless growth, like etiolated potato sprouts in a root cellar. I tried to dig one up from the crumbly soil, but they all apparently grew from a single, well-rooted corm, so I let them go.

Still, the day had an air of menace. A broken whiskey bottle by the log, the brown tip of a snake's tail disappearing between two rocks on the hill at my back, the rabbit the dog nearly caught, the rabies I knew was in the county, the bees who kept unaccountably fumbling at my forehead with their furred feet . . .

I headed over to the new woods by the creek, the motorbike woods. They were strangely empty. The air was so steamy I could barely see. The ravine separating the woods from the field had filled during high water, and a dead tan mud clogged it now. The horny orange roots of one tree on the ravine's jagged bank had been stripped of soil; now the roots hung, an empty net in the air, clutching an incongruous light bulb stranded by receding waters. For the entire time that I walked in the woods, four jays flew around me very slowly, acting generally odd, and screaming on two held notes. There wasn't a breath of wind.

Coming out of the woods, I heard loud shots; they reverberated ominously in the damp air. But when I walked up the road, I saw what it was, and the dread quality of the whole afternoon vanished at once. It was a couple of garbage trucks, huge trash compacters humped like armadillos, and they were making their engines backfire to impress my neighbors' pretty daughters, high school girls who had just been let off the school bus. The long-haired girls strayed into giggling clumps at the corner of the road; the garbage trucks sped away gloriously, as if they had been the Tarleton twins on thoroughbreds cantering away from the gates of Tara. In the distance a white vapor was rising from the waters of Carvin's Cove and catching in trailing tufts in the mountains' sides. I stood on my own porch, exhilarated, unwilling to go indoors.

It was just this time last year that we had the flood. It was Hurricane Agnes, really, but by the time it got here, the weather bureau had demoted it to a tropical storm. I see by a clipping I saved that the date was June twenty-first, the solstice, midsummer's night, the longest daylight of the year; but I didn't notice it at the time. Everything was so exciting, and so very dark.

All it did was rain. It rained, and the creek started to rise. The creek, naturally, rises every time it rains; this didn't seem any different. But it kept raining, and, that morning of the twenty-first, the creek kept rising.

That morning I'm standing at my kitchen window. Tinker Creek is out of its four-foot banks, way out, and it's still coming. The high creek doesn't look like our creek. Our creek splashes transparently over a jumble of rocks; the high creek obliterates everything in flat opacity. It looks like somebody else's creek that has usurped or eaten our creek and is roving frantically to escape, big and ugly, like a blacksnake caught in a kitchen drawer. The color is foul,

a rusty cream. Water that has picked up clay soils looks
worse than other muddy waters, because the particles of clay
are so fine; they spread out and cloud the water so that you
can't see light through even an inch of it in a drinking
glass.

Everything looks different. Where my eye is used to
depth, I see the flat water, near, too near. I see trees I never
noticed before, the black verticals of their rain-soaked
trunks standing out of the pale water like pilings for a
rotted dock. The stillness of grassy banks and stony ledges
is gone; I see rushing, a wild sweep and hurry in one direction, as swift and compelling as a waterfall. The Atkins
kids are out in their tiny rain gear, staring at the monster
creek. It's risen up to their gates; the neighbors are gathering; I go out.

I hear a roar, a high windy sound more like air than
like water, like the run-together whaps of a helicopter's
propeller after the engine is off, a high million rushings.
The air smells damp and acrid, like fuel oil, or insecticide.
It's raining.

I'm in no danger; my house is high. I hurry down the
road to the bridge. Neighbors who have barely seen each
other all winter are there, shaking their heads. Few have
ever seen it before: the water is *over* the bridge. Even when
I see the bridge now, which I do every day, I still can't
believe it: the water was *over* the bridge, a foot or two over
the bridge, which at normal times is eleven feet above the
surface of the creek.

Now the water is receding slightly; someone has produced empty metal drums, which we roll to the bridge and
set up in a square to keep cars from trying to cross. It takes
a bit of nerve even to stand on the bridge; the flood has
ripped away a wedge of concrete that buttressed the bridge
on the bank. Now one corner of the bridge hangs appar-

ently unsupported while water hurls in an arch just inches
below.

It's hard to take it all in, it's all so new. I look at the
creek at my feet. It smashes under the bridge like a fist, but
there is no end to its force; it hurtles down as far as I can
see till it lurches round the bend, filling the valley, flatten-
ing, mashing, pushed, wider and faster, till it fills my brain.

It's like a dragon. Maybe it's because the bridge we are
on is chancy, but I notice that no one can help imagining
himself washed overboard, and gauging his chances for
survival. You couldn't live. Mark Spitz couldn't live. The
water arches where the bridge's supports at the banks prevent its enormous volume from going wide, forcing it to go
high; that arch drives down like a diving whale, and would
butt you on the bottom. "You'd never know what hit you,"
one of the men says. But if you survived that part and managed to surface . . . ? How fast can you live? You'd need
a windshield. You couldn't keep your head up; the water
under the surface is fastest. You'd spin around like a sock
in a clothes dryer. You couldn't grab onto a tree trunk
without leaving that arm behind. No, you couldn't live.
And if they ever found you, your gut would be solid red
clay.

It's all I can do to stand. I feel dizzy, drawn, mauled.
Below me the floodwater roils to a violent froth that looks
like dirty lace, a lace that continuously explodes before my
eyes. If I look away, the earth moves backwards, rises and
swells, from the fixing of my eyes at one spot against the
motion of the flood. All the familiar land looks as though
it were not solid and real at all, but painted on a scroll like
a backdrop, and that unrolled scroll has been shaken, so the
earth sways and the air roars.

Everything imaginable is zipping by, almost too fast to
see. If I stand on the bridge and look downstream, I get

dizzy; but if I look upstream, I feel as though I am looking up the business end of an avalanche. There are dolls, split wood and kindling, dead fledgling songbirds, bottles, whole bushes and trees, rakes and garden gloves. Wooden, rough-hewn railroad ties charge by faster than any express. Lattice fencing bobs along, and a wooden picket gate. There are so many white plastic gallon milk jugs that when the flood ultimately recedes, they are left on the grassy banks looking from a distance like a flock of white geese.

I expect to see anything at all. In this way, the creek is more like itself when it floods than at any other time: mediating, bringing things down. I wouldn't be at all surprised to see John Paul Jones coming round the bend, standing on the deck of the *Bon Homme Richard,* or Amelia Earhart waving gaily from the cockpit of her floating Lockheed. Why not a cello, a basket of breadfruit, a casket of antique coins? Here comes the Franklin expedition on snowshoes, and the three magi, plus camels, afloat on a canopied barge!

The whole world is in flood, the land as well as the water. Water streams down the trunks of trees, drips from hat-brims, courses across roads. The whole earth seems to slide like sand down a chute; water pouring over the least slope leaves the grass flattened, silver side up, pointing downstream. Everywhere windfall and flotsam twigs and leafy boughs, wood from woodpiles, bottles, and saturated straw spatter the ground or streak it in curving windrows. Tomatoes in flat gardens are literally floating in mud; they look as though they have been dropped whole into a boiling, brown-gravy stew. The level of the water table is at the top of the toe of my shoes. Pale muddy water lies on the flat so that it all but drowns the grass; it looks like a hideous parody of a light snow on the field, with only the dark tips of the grass blades visible.

When I look across the street, I can't believe my eyes. Right behind the road's shoulder are waves, waves whipped in rhythmically peaking scallops, racing downstream. The hill where I watched the praying mantis lay her eggs is a waterfall that splashes into a brown ocean. I can't even remember where the creek usually runs—it is everywhere now. My log is gone for sure, I think—but in fact, I discover later, it holds, rammed between growing trees. Only the cable suspending the steers' fence is visible, and not the fence itself; the steers' pasture is entirely in flood, a brown river. The river leaps its banks and smashes into the woods where the motorbikes go, devastating all but the sturdiest trees. The water is so deep and wide it seems as though you could navigate the *Queen Mary* in it, clear to Tinker Mountain.

What do animals do in these floods? I see a drowned muskrat go by like he's flying, but they all couldn't die; the water rises after every hard rain, and the creek is still full of muskrats. This flood is higher than their raised sleeping platforms in the banks; they must just race for high ground and hold on. Where do the fish go, and what do they do? Presumably their gills can filter oxygen out of this muck, but I don't know how. They must hide from the current behind any barriers they can find, and fast for a few days. They must: otherwise we'd have no fish; they'd all be in the Atlantic Ocean. What about herons and kingfishers, say? They can't see to eat. It usually seems to me that when I see any animal, its business is urgent enough that it couldn't easily be suspended for forty-eight hours. Crayfish, frogs, snails, rotifers? Most things must simply die. They couldn't live. Then I suppose that when the water goes down and clears, the survivors have a field day with no competition. But you'd think the bottom would be knocked out of the food chain—the whole pyramid would have no base plankton, and it would crumble, or crash with a thud. Maybe enough spores and larvae and eggs are constantly being borne down from slower upstream waters to repopulate. . . I don't know.

Some little children have discovered a snapping turtle as big as a tray. It's hard to believe that this creek could support a predator that size: its shell is a foot and a half across, and its head extends a good seven inches beyond the shell. When the children—in the company of a shrunken terrier —approach it on the bank, the snapper rears up on its thick front legs and hisses very impressively. I had read earlier that since turtles' shells are rigid, they don't have bellows lungs; they have to gulp for air. And, also since their shells are rigid, there's only room for so much inside, so when they are frightened and planning a retreat, they have to expel air from their lungs to make room for head and feet —hence the malevolent hiss.

The next time I look, I see that the children have somehow maneuvered the snapper into a washtub. They're waving a broom handle at it in hopes that it will snap the wood like a matchstick, but the creature will not deign to oblige. The kids are crushed; all their lives they've heard that this is the one thing you do with a snapping turtle—you shove a broom handle near it, and it "snaps it like a matchstick." It's nature's way; it's sure-fire. But the turtle is having none of it. It avoids the broom handle with an air of patiently repressed rage. They let it go, and it beelines down the bank, dives unhesitatingly into the swirling floodwater, and that's the last we see of it.

A cheer comes up from the crowd on the bridge. The truck is here with a pump for the Bowerys' basement, hooray! We roll away the metal drums, the truck makes it over the bridge, to my amazement—the crowd cheers again. State police cruise by; everything's fine here; downstream people are in trouble. The bridge over by the Bings' on Tinker Creek looks like it's about to go. There's a tree trunk wedged against its railing, and a section of concrete is out. The Bings are away, and a young couple is living there, "taking care of the house." What can they do? The husband drove to work that morning as usual; a few hours later, his wife was evacuated from the front door in a *motorboat*.

I walk to the Bings'. Most of the people who are on our bridge eventually end up over there; it's just down the road. We straggle along in the rain, gathering a crowd. The men who work away from home are here, too; their wives have telephoned them at work this morning to say that the creek is rising fast, and they'd better get home while the gettin's good.

There's a big crowd already there; everybody knows that the Bings' is low. The creek is coming in the recreation-room windows; it's halfway up the garage door. Later that day people will haul out everything salvageable and try to dry it: books, rugs, furniture—the lower level was filled from floor to ceiling. Now on this bridge a road crew is trying to chop away the wedged tree trunk with a long-handled ax. The handle isn't so long that they don't have to stand on the bridge, in Tinker Creek. I walk along a low brick wall that was built to retain the creek away from the house at high water. The wall holds just fine, but now that the creek's receding, it's retaining water around the house. On the wall I can walk right out into the flood and stand in the middle of it. Now on the return trip I meet a young man who's going in the opposite direction. The wall is one brick wide; we can't pass. So we clasp hands and lean out backwards over the turbulent water; our feet interlace like teeth on a zipper, we pull together, stand, and continue on our ways. The kids have spotted a rattlesnake draping it-self out of harm's way in a bush; now they all want to walk over the brick wall to the bush, to get bitten by the snake.

The little Atkins kids are here, and they are hopping up and down. I wonder if I hopped up and down, would the bridge go? I could stand at the railing as at the railing of a steamboat, shouting deliriously, "Mark three! Quarter-less-three! Half twain! Quarter twain! . . ." as the current bore the broken bridge out of sight around the bend before she sank. . . .

Everyone else is standing around. Some of the women are carrying curious plastic umbrellas that look like diving bells—umbrellas they don't put up, but on; they don't get under, but in. They can see out dimly, like goldfish in bowls. Their voices from within sound distant, but with an underlying cheerfulness that plainly acknowledges, "Isn't this ridiculous?" Some of the men are wearing their fishing hats. Others duck their heads under folded newspapers held not very high in an effort to compromise between keeping their heads dry and letting rain run up their sleeves. Following some form of courtesy, I guess, they lower these newspapers when they speak with you, and squint politely into the rain.

Women are bringing coffee in mugs to the road crew. They've barely made a dent in the tree trunk, and they're giving up. It's a job for power tools; the water's going down anyway, and the danger is past. Some kid starts doing tricks on a skateboard; I head home.

On the same day that I was standing on bridges here over Tinker Creek, a friend, Lee Zacharias, was standing on a bridge in Richmond over the James River. It was a calm day there, with not a cloud in the skies. The James River was up a mere nine feet, which didn't look too unusual. But floating in the river was everything under the bright sun. As Lee watched, chicken coops raced by, chunks of houses, porches, stairs, whole uprooted trees—and finally a bloated dead horse. Lee knew, all of Richmond knew: it was coming.

There the James ultimately rose thirty-two feet. The whole town was under water, and all the electrical power was out. When Governor Holton signed the emergency relief bill—which listed our county among the federal disaster areas—he had to do it by candlelight.

That night a curious thing happened in the blacked-out Governor's mansion. Governor Holton walked down an upstairs hall and saw, to his disbelief, a lightbulb glowing in a ceiling fixture. It was one of three bulbs, all dead—the whole city was dead—but that one bulb was giving off a faint electrical light. He stared at the thing, scratched his head, and summoned an electrician. The electrician stared at the thing, scratched his head, and announced, "Impossible." The governor went back to bed, and the electrician went home. No explanation has ever been found.

Later Agnes would move on up into Maryland, Pennsylvania, and New York, killing people and doing hundreds of millions of dollars worth of damage. Here in Virginia alone it killed twelve people and ruined 166 million dollars worth of property. But it hit Pennsylvania twice, coming and going. I talked to one of the helicopter pilots who had helped airlift ancient corpses from a flooded cemetery in Wilkes-Barre, Pennsylvania. The flood left the bodies stranded on housetops, in trees; the pilots, sickened, had to be relieved every few hours. The one I talked to, in a little sandwich shop at the Peaks of Otter on the Blue Ridge Parkway, preferred Vietnam. We were lucky here.

This winter I heard a final flood story, about an extra dividend that the flood left the Bings, a surprise as unexpected as a baby in a basket on a stoop.

The Bings came home and their house was ruined, but somehow they managed to salvage almost everything, and live as before. One afternoon in the fall a friend went to visit them; as he was coming in, he met a man coming out, a professor with a large volume under his arm. The Bings led my friend inside and into the kitchen, where they proudly opened the oven door and showed him a giant mushroom—which they were baking to serve to guests the following day. The professor with the book had just been verifying its edibility. I imagined the mushroom, wrinkled, black, and big as a dinner plate, erupting overnight mysteriously in the Bings' living room—from the back of an upholstered couch, say, or from a still-damp rug under an armchair.

Alas, the story as I had fixed it in my mind proved to be only partly true. The Bings often cook wild mushrooms, and they know what they're doing. This particular mushroom had grown outside, under a sycamore, on high ground that the flood hadn't touched. So the flood had nothing to do with it. But it's still a good story, and I like to think that the flood left them a gift, a consolation prize, so that for years to come they will be finding edible mushrooms here and there about the house, dinner on the bookshelf, hors d'oeuvres in the piano. It would have been nice.

CHAPTER 10

Fecundity

I

I WAKENED MYSELF last night with my own shouting. It must have been that terrible yellow plant I saw pushing through the flood-damp soil near the log by Tinker Creek, the plant as fleshy and featureless as a slug, that erupted through the floor of my brain as I slept, and burgeoned into the dream of fecundity that woke me up.

I was watching two huge luna moths mate. Luna moths are those fragile ghost moths, fairy moths, whose five-inch wings are swallow-tailed, a pastel green bordered in silken lavender. From the hairy head of the male sprouted two enormous, furry antennae that trailed down past his ethereal wings. He was on top of the female, hunching repeatedly with a horrible animal vigor.

It was the perfect picture of utter spirituality and utter degradation. I was fascinated and could not turn away my eyes. By watching them I in effect permitted their mating to take place and so committed myself to accepting the consequences—all because I wanted to see what would happen. I wanted in on a secret.

And then the eggs hatched and the bed was full of fish. I was standing across the room in the doorway, staring at the bed. The eggs hatched before my eyes, on my bed, and a thousand chunky fish swarmed there in a viscid slime. The fish were firm and fat, black and white, with triangular bodies and bulging eyes. I watched in horror as they squirmed three feet deep, swimming and oozing about in the glistening, transparent slime. Fish in the bed! —and I awoke. My ears still rang with the foreign cry that had been my own voice.

For nightmare you eat wild carrot, which is Queen Anne's lace, or you chew the black seeds of the male peony. But it was too late for prevention, and there is no cure. What root or seed will erase that scene from my mind? Fool, I thought: child, you child, you ignorant, innocent fool. What did you expect to see—angels? For it was understood in the dream that the bed full of fish was my own fault, that if I had turned away from the mating moths the hatching of their eggs wouldn't have happened, or at least would have happened in secret, elsewhere. I brought it upon myself, this slither, this swarm.

I don't know what it is about fecundity that so appalls. I suppose it is the teeming evidence that birth and growth, which we value, are ubiquitous and blind, that life itself is so astonishingly cheap, that nature is as careless as it is bountiful, and that with extravagance goes a crushing waste that will one day include our own cheap lives, Henle's loops and all. Every glistening egg is a memento mori.

After a natural disaster such as a flood, nature "stages a comeback." People use the optimistic expression without any real idea of the pressures and waste the comeback involves. Now, in late June, things are popping outside. Creatures extrude or vent eggs; larvae fatten, split their shells, and eat them; spores dissolve or explode; root hairs multiply, corn puffs on the stalk, grass yields seed, shoots erupt from the earth turgid and sheathed; wet muskrats, rabbits, and squirrels slide into the sunlight, mewling and blind; and everywhere watery cells divide and swell, swell and divide. I can like it and call it birth and regeneration, or I can play the devil's advocate and call it rank fecundity —and say that it's hell that's a-poppin'.

This is what I plan to do. Partly as a result of my terrible dream, I have been thinking that the landscape of the intricate world that I have painted is inaccurate and lopsided. It is too optimistic. For the notion of the infinite variety of detail and the multiplicity of forms is a pleasing one; in complexity are the fringes of beauty, and in variety are generosity and exuberance. But all this leaves something vital out of the picture. It is not one pine I see, but a thousand. I myself am not one, but legion. And we are all going to die.

In this repetition of individuals is a mindless stutter, an imbecilic fixedness that must be taken into account. The driving force behind all this fecundity is a terrible pressure I also must consider, the pressure of birth and growth, the pressure that splits the bark of trees and shoots out seeds, that squeezes out the egg and bursts the pupa, that hungers and lusts and drives the creature relentlessly toward its own death. Fecundity, then, is what I have been thinking about, fecundity and the pressure of growth. Fecundity is an ugly word for an ugly subject. It is ugly, at least, in the eggy animal world. I don't think it is for plants.

I never met a man who was shaken by a field of identical blades of grass. An acre of poppies and a forest of spruce boggle no one's mind. Even ten square miles of wheat gladdens the hearts of most people, although it is really as unnatural and freakish as the Frankenstein monster; if man were to die, I read, wheat wouldn't survive him more than three years. No, in the plant world, and especially among the flowering plants, fecundity is not an assault on human values. Plants are not our competitors; they are our prey and our nesting materials. We are no more distressed at their proliferation than an owl is at a population explosion among field mice.

After the flood last year I found a big tulip-tree limb that had been wind-thrown into Tinker Creek. The current dragged it up on some rocks on the bank, where receding waters stranded it. A month after the flood I discovered that it was growing new leaves. Both ends of the branch were completely exposed and dried. I was amazed. It was like the old fable about the corpse's growing a beard; it was as if the woodpile in my garage were suddenly to burst greenly into leaf. The way plants persevere in the bitterest of circumstances is utterly heartening. I can barely keep from unconsciously ascribing a will to these plants, a do-or-die courage, and I have to remind myself that coded cells and mute water pressure have no idea how grandly they are flying in the teeth of it all.

In the lower Bronx, for example, enthusiasts found an ailanthus tree that was fifteen feet long growing from the corner of a garage roof. It was rooted in and living on "dust and roofing cinders." Even more spectacular is a desert plant, *Ibervillea sonorae*—a member of the gourd family—that Joseph Wood Krutch describes. If you see this plant in the desert, you see only a dried chunk of loose wood. It has neither roots nor stems; it's like an old gray knothole. But it is alive. Each year before the rainy season comes, it sends out a few roots and shoots. If the rain arrives, it grows flowers and fruits; these soon wither away, and it reverts to a state as quiet as driftwood.

Well, the New York Botanical Garden put a dried *Ibervillea sonorae* on display in a glass case. "For seven years," says Joseph Wood Krutch, "without soil or water, simply lying in the case, it put forth a few anticipatory shoots and then, when no rainy season arrived, dried up again, hoping for better luck next year." That's what I call flying in the teeth of it all.

(It's hard to understand why no one at the New York Botanical Garden had the grace to splash a glass of water on the thing. Then they could say on their display case label, "This is a live plant." But by the eighth year what they had was a dead plant, which is precisely what it had looked like all along. The sight of it, reinforced by the label "Dead *Ibervillea sonorae*," would have been most melancholy to visitors to the botanical garden. I suppose they just threw it away.)

The growth pressure of plants can do an impressive variety of tricks. Bamboo can grow three feet in twenty-four hours, an accomplishment that is capitalized upon, *legendarily*, in that exquisite Asian torture in which a victim is strapped to a mesh bunk a mere foot above a bed of healthy bamboo plants whose wood-like tips have been sharpened. For the first eight hours he is fine, if jittery; then he starts turning into a collander, by degrees.

Down at the root end of things, blind growth reaches astonishing proportions. So far as I know, only one real experiment has even been performed to determine the extent and rate of root growth, and when you read the figures, you see why. I have run into various accounts of this experiment, and the only thing they don't tell you is how many lab assistants were blinded for life.

The experimenters studied a single grass plant, winter rye. They let it grow in a greenhouse for four months; then they gingerly spirited away the soil—under microscopes, I imagine—and counted and measured all the roots and root hairs. In four months the plant had set forth 378 miles of roots—that's about three miles a day—in 14 million distinct roots. This is mighty impressive, but when they get down to the root hairs, I boggle completely. In those same four months the rye plant created 14 *billion* root hairs, and those little strands placed end-to-end just about wouldn't quit. In a single *cubic inch* of soil, the length of the root hairs totaled 6000 miles.

Other plants use the same water power to heave the rock earth around as though they were merely shrugging off a silken cape. Rutherford Platt tells about a larch tree whose root had cleft a one-and-one-half ton boulder and hoisted it a foot into the air. Everyone knows how a sycamore root will buckle a sidewalk, a mushroom will shatter a cement basement floor. But when the first real measurements of this awesome pressure were taken, nobody could believe the figures.

Rutherford Platt tells the story in *The Great American Forest,* one of the most interesting books ever written: "In 1875, a Massachusetts farmer, curious about the growing power of expanding apples, melons and squashes, harnessed a squash to a weight-lifting device which had a dial like a grocer's scale to indicate the pressure exerted by the expanding fruit. As the days passed, he kept piling on counterbalancing weight; he could hardly believe his eyes when he saw his vegetables quietly exerting a lifting force of 5 thousand pounds per square inch. When nobody believed him, he set up exhibits of harnessed squashes and invited the public to come and see. The *Annual Report of the Massachusetts Board of Agriculture,* 1875, reported: 'Many thousands of men, women, and children of all classes of society visited it. *Mr. Penlow* watched it day and night, making hourly observations; *Professor Parker* was moved to write a poem about it; *Professor Seelye* declared that he positively stood in awe of it.' "

All this is very jolly. Unless perhaps I were strapped down above a stand of growing, sharpened bamboo, I am unlikely to feel the faintest queasiness either about the growth pressure of plants, or their fecundity. Even when the plants get in the way of human "culture," I don't mind. When I read how many thousands of dollars a city like New York has to spend to keep underground water pipes free of ailanthus, ginko, and sycamore roots, I cannot help but give a little cheer. After all, water pipes are almost always an excellent source of water. In a town where resourcefulness and beating the system are highly prized, these primitive trees can fight city hall and win.

But in the animal world things are different, and human feelings are different. While we're in New York, consider the cockroaches under the bed and the rats in the early morning clustered on the porch stoop. Apartment houses are hives of swarming roaches. Or again: in one sense you could think of Manhattan's land as high-rent, high-rise real estate; in another sense you could see it as an enormous breeding ground for rats, acres and acres of rats. I suppose that the rats and the cockroaches don't do so much actual damage as the roots do; nevertheless, the prospect does not please. Fecundity is anathema only in the animal. "Acres and acres of rats" has a suitably chilling ring to it that is decidedly lacking if I say, instead, "acres and acres of tulips."

The landscape of earth is dotted and smeared with masses of apparently identical individual animals, from the great Pleistocene herds that blanketed grasslands to the gluey gobs of bacteria that clog the lobes of lungs. The oceanic breeding grounds of pelagic birds are as teeming and cluttered as any human Calcutta. Lemmings blacken the earth and locusts the air. Grunion run thick in the ocean, corals pile on pile, and protozoans explode in a red tide stain. Ants take to the skies in swarms, mayflies hatch by the millions, and molting cicadas coat the trunks of trees. Have you seen the rivers run red and lumpy with salmon?

Consider the ordinary barnacle, the rock barnacle. Inside every one of those millions of hard white cones on the rocks —the kind that bruises your heel as you bruise its head—is of course a creature as alive as you or I. Its business in life is this: when a wave washes over it, it sticks out twelve feathery feeding appendages and filters the plankton for food. As it grows, it sheds its skin like a lobster, enlarges its shell, and reproduces itself without end. The larvae "hatch into the sea in milky clouds." The barnacles encrusting a single half mile of shore can leak into the water a million million larvae. How many is that to a human mouthful? In sea water they grow, molt, change shape wildly, and eventually, after several months, settle on the rocks, turn into adults, and build shells. Inside the shells they have to shed their skins. Rachel Carson was always finding the old skins; she reported: "Almost every container of sea water that I bring up from the shore is flecked with white, semitransparent objects. . . . Seen under the microscope, every detail of structure is perfectly represented. . . . In the little cellophane-like replicas I can count the joints of the appendages; even the bristles, growing at the bases of the joints, seem to have been slipped intact out of their casings." All in all, rock barnacles may live four years.

My point about rock barnacles is those million million larvae "in milky clouds" and those shed flecks of skin. Sea water seems suddenly to be but a broth of barnacle bits. Can I fancy that a million million human infants are more real?

What if God has the same affectionate disregard for us that we have for barnacles? I don't know if each barnacle larva is of itself unique and special, or if we the people are essentially as interchangeable as bricks. My brain is full of numbers; they swell and would split my skull like a shell. I examine the trapezoids of skin covering the back of my hands like blown dust motes moistened to clay. I have hatched, too, with millions of my kind, into a milky way that spreads from an unknown shore.

I have seen the mantis's abdomen dribbling out eggs in wet bubbles like tapioca pudding glued to a thorn. I have seen a film of a termite queen as big as my face, dead white and featureless, glistening with slime, throbbing and pulsing out rivers of globular eggs. Termite workers, who looked like tiny longshoremen unloading the *Queen Mary*, licked each egg as fast as it was extruded to prevent mold. The whole world is an incubator for incalculable numbers of eggs, each one coded minutely and ready to burst.

The egg of a parasite chalcid wasp, a common small wasp, multiplies unassisted, making ever more identical eggs. The female lays a single fertilized egg in the flaccid tissues of its live prey, and that one egg divides and divides. As many as two thousand new parasitic wasps will hatch to feed on the host's body with identical hunger. Similarly— only more so—Edwin Way Teale reports that a lone aphid, without a partner, breeding "unmolested" for one year, would produce so many living aphids that, although they are only a tenth of an inch long, together they would extend into space twenty-five hundred *light-years*. Even the average goldfish lays five thousand eggs, which she will eat as fast as she lays, if permitted. The sales manager of Ozark Fisheries in Missouri, which raises commercial goldfish for the likes of me, said, "We produce, measure, and sell our product by the ton." The intricacy of Ellery and aphids multiplied mindlessly into tons and light-years is more than extravagance; it is holocaust, parody, glut.

The pressure of growth among animals is a kind of terrible hunger. These billions must eat in order to fuel their surge to sexual maturity so that they may pump out more billions of eggs. And what are the fish on the bed going to eat, or the hatched mantises in the Mason jar going to eat, but each other? There is a terrible innocence in the benumbed world of the lower animals, reducing life there to a universal chomp. Edwin Way Teale, in *The Strange Lives of Familiar Insects*—a book I couldn't live without—describes several occasions of meals mouthed under the pressure of a hunger that knew no bounds.

You remember the dragonfly nymph, for instance, which stalks the bottom of the creek and the pond in search of live prey to snare with its hooked, unfolding lip. Dragonfly nymphs are insatiable and mighty. They clasp and devour whole minnows and fat tadpoles. Well, a dragonfly nymph, says Teale, "has even been seen climbing up out of the water on a plant to attack a helpless dragonfly emerging, soft and rumpled, from its nymphal skin." Is this where I draw the line?

It is between mothers and their offspring that these feedings have truly macabre overtones. Look at lacewings. Lacewings are those fragile green insects with large, rounded transparent wings. The larvae eat enormous numbers of aphids, the adults mate in a fluttering rush of instinct, lay eggs, and die by the millions in the first cold snap of fall. Sometimes, when a female lays her fertile eggs on a green leaf atop a slender stalked thread, she is hungry. She pauses in her laying, turns around, and eats her eggs one by one, then lays some more, and eats them, too.

Anything can happen, and anything does; what's it all about? Valerie Eliot, T. S. Eliot's widow, wrote in a letter to the London *Times*: "My husband, T. S. Eliot, loved to recount how late one evening he stopped a taxi. As he got in the driver said: 'You're T. S. Eliot.' When asked how he knew, he replied: 'Ah, I've got an eye for a celebrity. Only the other evening I picked up Bertrand Russell, and I said to him, "Well, Lord Russell, what's it all about," and, do you know, he couldn't tell me.'" Well, Lord God, asks the delicate, dying lacewing whose mandibles are wet with the juice secreted by her own ovipositor, what's it all about? ("And do you know . . .")

Planarians, which live in the duck pond, behave similarly. They are those dark laboratory flatworms that can regenerate themselves from almost any severed part. Arthur Koestler writes, "during the mating season the worms become cannibals, devouring everything alive that comes their way, including their own previously discarded tails which were in the process of growing a new head." Even such sophisticated mammals as the great predator cats occasionally eat their cubs. A mother cat will be observed licking the area around the umbilical cord of the helpless newborn. She licks, she licks, she licks until something snaps in her brain, and she begins eating, starting there, at the vulnerable belly.

Although mothers devouring their own offspring is patently the more senseless, somehow the reverse behavior is the more appalling. In the death of the parent in the jaws of its offspring I recognize a universal drama that chance occurrence has merely telescoped, so that I can see all the players at once. Gall gnats, for instance, are common small flies. Sometimes, according to Teale, a gall gnat larva, which does not resemble the adult in the least, and which has certainly not mated, nevertheless produces within its body eggs, live eggs, which then hatch within its soft tissues. Sometimes the eggs hatch alive even within the quiescent body of the pupa. The same incredible thing occasionally occurs within the fly genus *Miastor*, again to both larvae and pupae. "These eggs hatch within their bodies and the ravenous larvae which emerge immediately begin devouring their parents." In this case, I know what it's all about, and I wish I didn't. The parents die, the next generation lives, *ad majorem gloriam*, and so it goes. If the new generation hastens the death of the old, it scarcely matters; the old has served its one purpose, and the direct processing of proteins is tidily all in the family. But think of the invisible swelling of ripe eggs inside the pupa as wrapped and rigid as a mummified Egyptian queen! The eggs burst, shatter her belly, and emerge alive, awake, and hungry from a mummy case which they crawl over like worms and feed on till it's gone. And then they turn to the world.

"To prevent a like fate," Teale continues, "some of the ichneumon flies, those wasplike parasites which deposit their eggs in the body tissues of caterpillars, have to scatter their eggs while in flight at times when they are unable to find their prey and the eggs are ready to hatch within their bodies."

You are an ichneumon. You mated and your eggs are fertile. If you can't find a caterpillar on which to lay your eggs, your young will starve. When the eggs hatch, the young will eat any body in which they find themselves, so if you don't kill them by emitting them broadcast over the landscape, they'll eat you alive. But if you let them drop over the fields you will probably be dead yourself, of old age, before they even hatch to starve, and the whole show will be over and done, and a wretched one it was. You feel them coming, and coming, and you struggle to rise. . . .

Not that the ichneumon is making any conscious choice. If she were, her dilemma would be truly the stuff of tragedy; Aeschylus need have looked no further than the ichneumon. That is, it would be the stuff of real tragedy if only Aeschylus and I could convince you that the ichneumon is really and truly as alive as we are, and that what happens to it matters. Will you take it on faith?

Here is one last story. It shows that the pressures of growth gang aft a-gley. The clothes moth, whose caterpillar eats wool, sometimes goes into a molting frenzy which Teale blandly describes as "curious": "A curious paradox in molting is the action of a clothes-moth larva with insufficient food. It sometimes goes into a 'molting frenzy,' changing its skin repeatedly and getting smaller and smaller with each change." Smaller and smaller . . . can you imagine the frenzy? Where shall we send our sweaters? The diminution process could, in imagination, extend to infinity, as the creature frantically shrinks and shrinks and shrinks to the size of a molecule, then an electron, but never can shrink to absolute nothing and end its terrible hunger. I feel like Ezra: "And when I heard this thing, I rent my garment and my mantle, and plucked off the hair of my head and of my beard, and sat down astonied."

II

I am not kidding anyone if I pretend that these awesome pressures to eat and breed are wholly mystifying. The million million barnacle larvae in a half mile of shore water, the rivers of termite eggs, and the light-years of aphids ensure the living presence, in a scarcely concerned world, of ever more rock barnacles, termites, and aphids.

It's chancy out there. Dog whelks eat rock barnacles, worms invade their shells, shore ice razes them from the rocks and grinds them to a powder. Can you lay aphid eggs faster than chickadees can eat them? Can you find a caterpillar, can you beat the killing frost?

As far as lower animals go, if you lead a simple life you probably face a boring death. Some animals, however, lead such complicated lives that not only do the chances for any one animal's death at any minute multiply greatly, but so also do the *varieties* of the deaths it might die. The ordained paths of some animals are so rocky they are preposterous. The horsehair worm in the duck pond, for instance, wriggling so serenely near the surface, is the survivor of an impossible series of squeaky escapes. I did a bit of research into the life cycles of these worms, which are shaped exactly like hairs from a horse's tail, and learned that although scientists are not exactly sure what happens to any one species of them, they think it might go something like this:

You start with long strands of eggs wrapped around vegetation in the duck pond. The eggs hatch, the larvae emerge, and each seeks an aquatic host, say a dragonfly nymph. The larva bores into the nymph's body, where it feeds and grows and somehow escapes. Then if it doesn't get eaten it swims over to the shore where it encysts on submersed plants. This is all fairly improbable, but not impossibly so.

Now the coincidences begin. First, presumably, the water level of the duck pond has to drop. This exposes the vegetation so that the land host organism can get at it without drowning. Horsehair worms have various land hosts, such as crickets, beetles, and grasshoppers. Let's say ours can only make it if a grasshopper comes along. Fine. But the grasshopper had best hurry, for there is only so much fat stored in the encysted worm, and it might starve. Well, here comes just the right species of grasshopper, and it is obligingly feeding on shore vegetation. Now I have not observed any extensive grazing of grasshoppers on any grassy shores, but obviously it must occur. Bingo, then, the grasshopper just happens to eat the encysted worm.

The cyst bursts. The worm emerges in all its hideous length, up to thirty-six inches, inside the body of the grasshopper, on which it feeds. I presume that the worm must eat enough of its host to stay alive, but not so much that the grasshopper will keel over dead far from water. Entomologists have found tiger beetles dead and dying on the water whose insides were almost perfectly empty except for the white coiled bodies of horsehair worms. At any rate, now the worm is almost an adult, ready to reproduce. But first it's got to get out of this grasshopper.

Biologists don't know what happens next. If at the critical stage the grasshopper is hopping in a sunny meadow away from a duck pond or ditch, which is entirely likely, then the story is over. But say it happens to be feeding near the duck pond. The worm perhaps bores its way out of the grasshopper's body, or perhaps is excreted. At any rate, there it is on the grass, drying out. Now the biologists have to go so far as to invoke a "heavy rain," falling from heaven at this fortuitous moment, in order to get the horsehair worm back into the water where it can mate and lay more seemingly doomed eggs. You'd be thin, too.

Other creatures have it just about as easy. A blood fluke starts out as an egg in human feces. If it happens to fall into fresh water it will live only if it happens to encounter a certain species of snail. It changes in the snail, swims out, and now needs to find a human being in the water in order to bore through his skin. It travels around in the man's blood, settles down in the blood vessels of his intestine, and turns into a sexually mature blood fluke, either male or female. Now it has to find another fluke, of the opposite sex, who also just happens to have traveled the same circuitous route and landed in the same unfortunate man's intestinal blood vessels. Other flukes lead similarly improbable lives, some passing through as many as four hosts.

But it is for gooseneck barnacles that I reserve the largest measure of awe. Recently I saw photographs taken by members of the *Ra* expedition. One showed a glob of tar as big as a softball, jetsam from a larger craft, which Heyerdahl and his crew spotted in the middle of the Atlantic Ocean. The tar had been in the sea for a long time; it was overgrown with gooseneck barnacles. The gooseneck barnacles were entirely incidental, but for me they were the most interesting thing about the whole expedition. How many gooseneck barnacle larvae must be dying out there in the middle of vast oceans for every one that finds a glob of tar to fasten to? You've seen gooseneck barnacles washed up on the beach; they grow on old ship's timber, driftwood, strips of rubber—anything that's been afloat in the sea long enough. They do not resemble rock barnacles in the least, although the two are closely related. They have pinkish shells extending in a flattened oval from a flexible bit of "gooseneck" tissue that secures them to the substratum.

I have always had a fancy for these creatures, but I'd always assumed that they lived near shores, where chance floating holdfasts are more likely to occur. What are they doing—what are the larvae doing—out there in the middle of the ocean? They drift and perish, or, by some freak accident in a world where anything can happen, they latch and flourish. If I dangled my hand from the deck of the

Ra into the sea, could a gooseneck barnacle fasten there? If I gathered a cup of ocean water, would I be holding a score of dying and dead barnacle larvae? Should I throw them a chip? What kind of a world is this, anyway? Why not make fewer barnacle larvae and give them a decent chance? Are we dealing in life, or in death?

I have to look at the landscape of the blue-green world again. Just think: in all the clean beautiful reaches of the solar system, our planet alone is a blot; our planet alone has death. I have to acknowledge that the sea is a cup of death and the land is a stained altar stone. We the living are survivors huddled on flotsam, living on jetsam. We are escapees. We wake in terror, eat in hunger, sleep with a mouthful of blood.

Death: W. C. Fields called death "the Fellow in the Bright Nightgown." He shuffles around the house in all the corners I've forgotten, all the halls I dare not call to mind or visit for fear I'll glimpse the hem of his shabby, dazzling gown disappearing around a turn. This is the monster evolution loves. How could it be?

The faster death goes, the faster evolution goes. If an aphid lays a million eggs, several might survive. Now, my right hand, in all its human cunning, could not make one aphid in a thousand years. But these aphid eggs—which run less than a dime a dozen, which run absolutely free—can make aphids as effortlessly as the sea makes waves. Wonderful things, wasted. It's a wretched system. Arthur Stanley Eddington, the British physicist and astronomer who died in 1944, suggested that all of "Nature" could conceivably run on the same deranged scheme. "If indeed she has no greater aim than to provide a home for her greatest experiment, Man, it would be just like her methods to scatter a million stars whereof one might haply achieve her purpose." I doubt very much that this is the aim, but it seems clear on all fronts that this is the method.

Say you are the manager of the Southern Railroad. You figure that you need three engines for a stretch of track between Lynchburg and Danville. It's a mighty steep grade. So at fantastic effort and expense you have your shops make nine thousand engines. Each engine must be fashioned just so, every rivet and bolt secure, every wire twisted and wrapped, every needle on every indicator sensitive and accurate.

You send all nine thousand of them out on the runs. Although there are engineers at the throttles, no one is manning the switches. The engines crash, collide, derail, jump, jam, burn. . . . At the end of the massacre you have three engines, which is what the run could support in the first place. There are few enough of them that they can stay out of each others' paths.

You go to your board of directors and show them what you've done. And what are they going to say? You know what they're going to say. They're going to say: It's a hell of a way to run a railroad.

Is it a better way to run a universe?

Evolution loves death more than it loves you or me. This is easy to write, easy to read, and hard to believe. The words are simple, the concept clear—but you don't believe it, do you? Nor do I. How could I, when we're both so lovable? Are my values then so diametrically opposed to those that nature preserves? This is the key point.

Must I then part ways with the only world I know? I had thought to live by the side of the creek in order to shape my life to its free flow. But I seem to have reached a point where I must draw the line. It looks as though the creek is not buoying me up but dragging me down. Look: Cock Robin may die the most gruesome of slow deaths, and nature is no less pleased; the sun comes up, the creek rolls on, the survivors still sing. I cannot feel that way about your death, nor you about mine, nor either of us about the robin's—or even the barnacles'. We value the individual supremely, and nature values him not a whit. It looks for the moment as though I might have to reject this creek life unless I want to be utterly brutalized. Is human culture with its values my only real home after all? Can it possibly be that I should move my anchor-hold to the side of a library? This direction of thought brings me abruptly to a fork in the road where I stand paralyzed, unwilling to go on, for both ways lead to madness.

Either this world, my mother, is a monster, or I myself am a freak.

Consider the former: the world is a monster. Any three-year-old can see how unsatisfactory and clumsy is this whole business of reproducing and dying by the billions. We have not yet encountered any god who is as merciful as a man who flicks a beetle over on its feet. There is not a people in the world who behaves as badly as praying mantises. But wait, you say, there is no right and wrong in nature; right and wrong is a human concept. Precisely: we are moral creatures, then, in an amoral world. The universe that suckled us is a monster that does not care if we live or die —does not care if it itself grinds to a halt. It is fixed and blind, a robot programmed to kill. We are free and seeing; we can only try to outwit it at every turn to save our skins.

This view requires that a monstrous world running on chance and death, careening blindly from nowhere to nowhere, somehow produced wonderful us. I came from the world, I crawled out of a sea of amino acids, and now I must whirl around and shake my fist at that sea and cry Shame! If I value anything at all, then I must blindfold my eyes when I near the Swiss Alps. We must as a culture disassemble our telescopes and settle down to backslapping. We little blobs of soft tissue crawling around on this one planet's skin are right, and the whole universe is wrong.

Or consider the alternative.

Julian of Norwich, the great English anchorite and theologian, cited, in the manner of the prophets, these words from God: "See, I am God: see, I am in all things: see, I never lift my hands off my works, nor ever shall, without end. . . . How should anything be amiss?" But now not even the simplest and best of us sees things the way Julian did. It seems to us that plenty is amiss. So much is amiss that I must consider the second fork in the road, that creation itself is blamelessly, benevolently askew by its very free nature, and that it is only human feeling that is freakishly amiss. The frog that the giant water bug sucked had, presumably, a rush of pure feeling for about a second, before its brain turned to broth. I, however, have been sapped by various strong feelings about the incident almost daily for several years.

Do the barnacle larvae care? Does the lacewing who eats her eggs care? If they do not care, then why am I making all this fuss? If I am a freak, then why don't I hush?

Our excessive emotions are so patently painful and harmful to us as a species that I can hardly believe that they evolved. Other creatures manage to have effective matings and even stable societies without great emotions, and they have a bonus in that they need not ever mourn. (But some higher animals have emotions that we think are similar to ours: dogs, elephants, otters, and the sea mammals mourn their dead. Why do that to an otter? What creator could be so cruel, not to kill otters, but to let them care?) It would seem that emotions are the curse, not death—emotions that appear to have devolved upon a few freaks as a special curse from Malevolence.

All right then. It is our emotions that are amiss. We are freaks, the world is fine, and let us all go have lobotomies to restore us to a natural state. We can leave the library then, go back to the creek lobotomized, and live on its banks as untroubled as any muskrat or reed. You first.

Of the two ridiculous alternatives, I rather favor the second. Although it is true that we are moral creatures in an amoral world, the world's amorality does not make it a monster. Rather, I am the freak. Perhaps I don't need a lobotomy, but I could use some calming down, and the creek is just the place for it. I must go down to the creek again. It is where I belong, although as I become closer to it, my fellows appear more and more freakish, and my home in the library more and more limited. Imperceptibly at first, and now consciously, I shy away from the arts, from the human emotional stew. I read what the men with telescopes and microscopes have to say about the landscape. I read about the polar ice, and I drive myself deeper and deeper into exile from my own kind. But, since I cannot avoid the library altogether—the human culture that taught me to speak in its tongue—I bring human values to the creek, and so save myself from being brutalized.

What I have been after all along is not an explanation but a picture. This is the way the world is, altar and cup, lit by the fire from a star that has only begun to die. My rage and shock at the pain and death of individuals of my kind is the old, old mystery, as old as man, but forever fresh, and completely unanswerable. My reservations about the fecundity and waste of life among other creatures is, however, mere squeamishness. After all, I'm the one having the nightmares. It is true that many of the creatures live and die abominably, but I am not called upon to pass judgment.

Nor am I called upon to live in that same way, and those creatures who are, are mercifully unconscious.

I don't want to cut this too short. Let me pull the camera back and look at that fork in the road from a distance, in the larger context of the speckled and twining world. It could be that the fork will disappear, or that I will see it to be but one of many interstices in a network, so that it is impossible to say which line is the main part and which is the fork.

The picture of fecundity and its excesses and of the pressures of growth and its accidents is of course no different from the picture I painted before of the world as an intricate texture of a bizarre variety of forms. Only now the shadows are deeper. Extravagance takes on a sinister, wastrel air, and exuberance blithers. When I added the dimension of time to the landscape of the world, I saw how freedom grew the beauties and horrors from the same live branch. This landscape is the same as that one, with a few more details added, and a different emphasis. I see squashes expanding with pressure and a hunk of wood rapt on the desert floor. The rye plant and the Bronx ailanthus are literally killing themselves to make seeds, and the animals to lay eggs. Instead of one goldfish swimming in its intricate bowl, I see tons and tons of goldfish laying and eating billions and billions of eggs. The point of all the eggs is of course to make goldfish one by one—nature loves the *idea* of the individual, if not the individual himself—and the point of a goldfish is pizzazz. This is familiar ground. I merely failed to mention that it is death that is spinning the globe.

It is harder to take, but surely it's been thought about. I cannot really get very exercised over the hideous appearance and habits of some deep-sea jellies and fishes, and I exercise easy. But about the topic of my own death I am decidedly touchy. Nevertheless, the two phenomena are two branches of the same creek, the creek that waters the world. Its source is freedom, and its network of branches is infinite. The graceful mockingbird that falls drinks there and sips in the same drop a beauty that waters its eyes and a death that fledges and flies. The petals of tulips are flaps of the same doomed water that swells and hatches in the ichneumon's gut.

That something is everywhere and always amiss is part of the very stuff of creation. It is as though each clay form had baked into it, fired into it, a blue streak of nonbeing, a shaded emptiness like a bubble that not only shapes its very structure but that also causes it to list and ultimately explode. We could have planned things more mercifully, perhaps, but our plan would never get off the drawing board until we agreed to the very compromising terms that are the only ones that being offers.

The world has signed a pact with the devil; it had to. It is a covenant to which every thing, even every hydrogen atom, is bound. The terms are clear: if you want to live, you have to die; you cannot have mountains and creeks without space, and space is a beauty married to a blind man. The blind man is Freedom, or Time, and he does not go anywhere without his great dog Death. The world came into being with the signing of the contract. A scientist calls it the Second Law of Thermodynamics. A poet says, "The force that through the green fuse drives the flower/Drives my green age." This is what we know. The rest is gravy.

CHAPTER 11

Stalking

I

SUMMER: I GO DOWN to the creek again, and lead a creek life. I watch and stalk.

The Eskimos' life changes in summer, too. The caribou flee from the inland tundra's mosquitos to the windy shores of the Arctic Ocean, and coastal Eskimos hunt them there. In the old days before they had long-range rifles, the men had to approach the wary animals very closely for a kill. Sometimes, waiting for a favorable change of weather so they could rush in unseen and unscented, the Eskimos would have to follow the fleet herds on foot for days, sleepless.

Also in summer they dredge for herring with nets from shoreline camps. In the open water off the Mackenzie River delta, they hunt the white whale (the beluga) and bearded seal. They paddle their slender kayaks inland to fresh water and hunt muskrats, too, which they used to snare or beat with sticks.

To travel from camp to camp in summer, coastal Eskimos ply the open seas in big umiaks paddled by women. They eat fish, goose or duck eggs, fresh meat, and anything else they can get, including fresh "salad" of greens still raw in a killed caribou's stomach and dressed with the delicate acids of digestion.

On St. Lawrence Island, women and children are in charge of netting little birds. They have devised a cruel and ingenious method: after they net a few birds with great effort and after much stalking, they thread them alive and squawking through their beaks' nostrils, and fly them like living kites at the end of long lines. The birds fly frantically, trying to escape, but they cannot, and their flapping efforts attract others of their kind, curious—and the Eskimos easily net the others.

They used to make a kind of undershirt out of bird skins, which they wore under fur parkas in cold weather, and left on inside the igloos after they'd taken the parkas off. It was an elaborate undertaking, this making of a bird-skin shirt, requiring thousands of tiny stitches. For thread they had the stringy sinew found along a caribou's backbone. The sinew had to be dried, frayed, and twisted into a clumsy thread. Its only advantages were that it swelled in water, making seams more or less waterproof, and it generally contained a minute smear of fat, so if they were starving they could suck their sewing thread and add maybe five minutes to their lives. For needles they had shards of bone, which got thinner and shorter every time they pushed through tough skins, so that an old needle might be little more than a barely enclosed slit. When the Eskimos first met the advanced culture of the south, men and women alike admired it first and foremost for its sturdy sewing needles. For it is understood that without good clothing, you perish. A crewman from a whaler with a paper of needles in his pocket could save many lives, and was welcome everywhere as the rich and powerful always are.

I doubt that they make bird-skin shirts anymore, steel needles or no. They do not do many of the old things at all any more, except in my mind, where they hunt and stitch well, with an animal skill, in silhouette always against white oceans of ice.

Down here, the heat is on. Even a bird-skin shirt would be too much. In the cool of the evening I take to the bridges over the creek. I am prying into secrets again, and taking my chances. I might see anything happen; I might see nothing but light on the water. I walk home exhilarated or becalmed, but always changed, alive. "It scatters and gathers," Heraclitus said, "it comes and goes." And I want to be in the way of its passage, and cooled by its invisible breath.

In summer, I stalk. Summer leaves obscure, heat dazzles, and creatures hide from the red-eyed sun, and me. I have to seek things out. The creatures I seek have several senses and free will; it becomes apparent that they do not wish to be seen. I can stalk them in either of two ways. The first is not what you think of as true stalking, but it is the *Via negativa,* and as fruitful as actual pursuit. When I stalk this way I take my stand on a bridge and wait, emptied. I put myself in the way of the creature's passage, like spring Eskimos at a seal's breathing hole. Something might come; something might go. I am Newton under the apple tree, Buddha under the bo. Stalking the other way, I forge my own passage seeking the creature. I wander the banks; what I find, I follow, doggedly, like Eskimos haunting the caribou herds. I am Wilson squinting after the traces of electrons in a cloud chamber; I am Jacob at Peniel wrestling with the angel.

Fish are hard to see either way. Although I spend most of the summer stalking muskrats, I think it is fish even more than muskrats that by their very mystery and hiddenness crystalize the quality of my summer life at the creek. A thick spawning of fish, a bedful of fish, is too much, horror; but I walk out of my way in hopes of glimpsing three bluegills bewitched in a pool's depth or rising to floating petals or bubbles.

The very act of trying to see fish makes them almost impossible to see. My eyes are awkward instruments whose casing is clumsily outsized. If I face the sun along a bank I cannot see into the water; instead of fish I see water striders, the reflected undersides of leaves, birds' bellies, clouds and blue sky. So I cross to the opposite bank and put the sun at my back. Then I can see into the water perfectly within the blue shadow made by my body; but as soon as that shadow looms across them, the fish vanish in a flurry of flashing tails.

Occasionally by waiting still on a bridge or by sneaking smoothly into the shade of a bankside tree, I see fish slowly materialize in the shallows, one by one, swimming around and around in a silent circle, each one washed in a blue like the sky's and all as tapered as tears. Or I see them suspended in a line in deep pools, parallel to the life-giving current, literally "streamlined." Because fish have swim bladders filled with gas that balances their weight in the water, they are actually hanging from their own bodies, as it were, as gondolas hang from balloons. They wait suspended and seemingly motionless in clear water; they look dead, under a spell, or captured in amber. They look like the expressionless parts hung in a mobile, which has apparently suggested itself to mobile designers. Fish! They manage to be so water-colored. Theirs is not the color of the bottom but the color of the light itself, the light dissolved like a powder in the water. They disappear and reappear as if by spontaneous generation: sleight of fish.

I am coming around to fish as spirit. The Greek acronym for some of the names of Christ yields *ichthys*, Christ as fish, and fish as Christ. The more I glimpse the fish in Tinker Creek, the more satisfying the coincidence becomes, the richer the symbol, not only for Christ but for the spirit as well. The people must live. Imagine for a Mediterranean people how much easier it is to haul up free, fed fish in nets than to pasture hungry herds on those bony hills and feed them through a winter. To say that holiness is a fish is a statement of the abundance of grace; it is the equivalent of affirming in a purely materialistic culture that money does indeed grow on trees. "Not as the world gives do I give to you"; these fish are spirit food. And revelation is a study in stalking: "Cast the net on the right side of the ship, and ye shall find."

Still—of course—there is a risk. More men in all of time have died at fishing than at any other human activity except perhaps the making of war. You go out so far . . . and you are blown, or stove, or swamped, and never seen again. Where are the fish? Out in the underwater gaps, out where the winds are, wary, adept, invisible. You can lure them, net them, troll for them, club them, clutch them, chase them up an inlet, stun them with plant juice, catch them in a wooden wheel that runs all night—and you still might starve. They are there, they are certainly there, free, food, and wholly fleeting. You can see them if you want to; catch them if you can.

It scatters and gathers; it comes and goes. I might see a

monstrous carp heave out of the water and disappear in a smack of foam, I might see a trout emerge in a riffle under my dangling hand, or I might see only a flash of back parts fleeing. It is the same all summer long, all year long, no matter what I seek. Lately I have given myself over almost entirely to stalking muskrats—eye food. I found out the hard way that waiting is better than pursuing; now I usually sit on a narrow pedestrian bridge at a spot where the creek is shallow and wide. I sit alone and alert, but stilled in a special way, waiting and watching for a change in the water, for the tremulous ripples rising in intensity that signal the appearance of a living muskrat from the underwater entrance to its den. Muskrats are cautious. Many, many evenings I wait without seeing one. But sometimes it turns out that the focus of my waiting is misdirected, as if Buddha had been expecting the fall of an apple. For when the muskrats don't show, something else does.

I positively ruined the dinner of a green heron on the creek last week. It was fairly young and fairly determined not to fly away, but not to be too foolhardy, either. So it had to keep an eye on me. I watched it for half an hour, during which time it stalked about in the creek moodily, expanding and contracting its incredible, brown-streaked neck. It made only three lightning-quick stabs at strands of slime for food, and all three times occurred when my head was turned slightly away.

The heron was in calm shallows; the deepest water it walked in went two inches up its orange legs. It would go and get something from the cattails on the side, and, when it had eaten it—tossing up its beak and contracting its throat in great gulps—it would plod back to a dry sandbar in the center of the creek which seemed to serve as its observation tower. It wagged its stubby tail up and down;

its tail was so short it did not extend beyond its folded
wings.

Mostly it just watched me warily, as if I might shoot it,
or steal its minnows for my own supper, if it did not stare
me down. But my only weapon was stillness, and my only
wish its continued presence before my eyes. I knew it would
fly away if I made the least false move. In half an hour it
got used to me—as though I were a bicycle somebody had
abandoned on the bridge, or a branch left by high water. It
even suffered me to turn my head slowly, and to stretch my
aching legs very slowly. But finally, at the end, some least
motion or thought set it off, and it rose, glancing at me
with a cry, and winged slowly away upstream, around a
bend, and out of sight.

I find it hard to see anything about a bird that it does not
want seen. It demands my full attention. Several times waiting for muskrats, however, I have watched insects doing
various special things who were, like the mantis laying her
eggs, happily oblivious to my presence. Twice I was not certain what I had seen.

Once it was a dragonfly flying low over the creek in an
unusual rhythm. I looked closely; it was dipping the tip of
its abdomen in the water very quickly, over and over. It was
flying in a series of tight circles, just touching the water at
the very bottom arc of each circle. The only thing I could
imagine it was doing was laying eggs, and this later proved
to be the case. I actually saw this, I thought—I actually saw
a dragonfly laying her eggs not five feet away.

It is this peculiar stitching motion of the dragonfly's
abdomen that earned it the name "darning needle"—parents used to threaten their children by saying that, if the
children told lies, dragonflies would hover over their faces
as they slept and sew their lips together. Interestingly, I

read that only the great speed at which the egg-laying female dragonfly flies over the water prevents her from being "caught by the surface tension and pulled down." And at that same great speed the dragonfly I saw that day whirred away, downstream: a drone, a dot, and then gone.

Another time I saw a water strider behaving oddly. When there is nothing whatsoever to see, I watch the water striders skate over the top of the water, and I watch the six dots of shade—made by their feet dimpling the water's surface—slide dreamily over the bottom silt. Their motion raises tiny ripples or wavelets ahead of them over the water's surface, and I had noticed that when they feel or see these ripples coming towards them, they tend to turn away from the ripples' source. In other words, they avoid each other. I figure this behavior has the effect of distributing them evenly over an area, giving them each a better chance at whatever it is they eat.

But one day I was staring idly at the water when something out of the ordinary triggered my attention. A strider was skating across the creek purposefully instead of randomly. Instead of heading away from ripples made by another insect, it was racing towards them. At the center of the ripples I saw that some sort of small fly had fallen into the water and was struggling to right itself. The strider acted extremely "interested"; it jerked after the fly's frantic efforts, following it across the creek and back again, inching closer and closer like Eskimos stalking caribou. The fly could not escape the surface tension. Its efforts were diminishing to an occasional buzz; it floated against the bank, and the strider pursued it there—but I could not see what happened, because overhanging grasses concealed the spot.

Again, only later did I learn what I had seen. I read that striders are attracted to any light. According to William H. Amos, "Often the attracting light turns out to be the reflections off the ripples set up by an insect trapped on the surface, and it is on such creatures that the striders feed." They suck them dry. Talk about living on jetsam! At any rate, it will be easy enough to watch for this again this summer. I especially want to see if the slow ripples set up by striders themselves reflect less light than the ripples set up by trapped insects—but it might be years before I happen to see another insect fall on the water among striders. I was lucky to have seen it once. Next time I will know what is happening, and if they want to play the last bloody act offstage, I will just part the curtain of grasses and hope I sleep through the night.

II

Learning to stalk muskrats took me several years.

I've always known there were muskrats in the creek. Sometimes when I drove late at night my headlights' beam on the water would catch the broad lines of ripples made by a swimming muskrat, a bow wave, converging across the water at the raised dark vee of its head. I would stop the car and get out: nothing. They eat corn and tomatoes from my neighbors' gardens, too, by night, so that my neighbors were always telling me that the creek was full of them. Around here, people call them "mushrats"; Thoreau called them "Musquashes." They are not of course rats at all (let alone squashes). They are more like diminutive beavers, and, like beavers, they exude a scented oil from musk glands under the base of the tail—hence the name. I had read in several respectable sources that muskrats are so wary they are almost impossible to observe. One expert who made a full-time study of large populations, mainly by examining "sign" and performing autopsies on corpses, said he often went for weeks at a time without seeing a single living muskrat.

One hot evening three years ago, I was standing more or less *in* a bush. I was stock-still, looking deep into Tinker Creek from a spot on the bank opposite the house, watching a group of bluegills stare and hang motionless near the bottom of a deep, sunlit pool. I was focused for depth. I had long since lost myself, lost the creek, the day, lost everything but still amber depth. All at once I couldn't see. And then I could: a young muskrat had appeared on top of the water, floating on its back. Its forelegs were folded langorously across its chest; the sun shone on its upturned belly. Its youthfulness and rodent grin, coupled with its ridiculous method of locomotion, which consisted of a lazy wag of the tail assisted by an occasional dabble of a webbed hind foot, made it an enchanting picture of decadence, dissipation, and summer sloth. I forgot all about the fish.

But in my surprise at having the light come on so suddenly, and at having my consciousness returned to me all at once and bearing an inverted muskrat, I must have moved and betrayed myself. The kit—for I know now it was just a young kit—righted itself so that only its head was visible above water, and swam downstream, away from me. I extricated myself from the bush and foolishly pursued it. It dove sleekly, reemerged, and glided for the opposite bank. I ran along the bankside brush, trying to keep it in sight. It kept casting an alarmed look over its shoulder at me. Once again it dove, under a floating mat of brush lodged in the bank, and disappeared. I never saw it again. (Nor have I ever, despite all the muskrats I have seen, again seen a muskrat floating on its back.) But I did not know muskrats then; I waited panting, and watched the shadowed bank. Now I know that I cannot outwait a muskrat who knows I am there. The most I can do is get "there" quietly, while it is still in its hole, so that it never knows, and wait there until it emerges. But then all I knew was that I wanted to see more muskrats.

I began to look for them day and night. Sometimes I would see ripples suddenly start beating from the creek's side, but as I crouched to watch, the ripples would die. Now I know what this means, and have learned to stand perfectly still to make out the muskrat's small, pointed face hidden under overhanging bank vegetation, watching me. That summer I haunted the bridges, I walked up creeks and down, but no muskrats ever appeared. You must just have to be there, I thought. You must have to spend the rest of your life standing in bushes. It was a once-in-a-lifetime thing, and you've had your once.

Then one night I saw another, and my life changed. After that I knew where they were in numbers, and I knew when to look. It was late dusk; I was driving home from a visit with friends. Just on the off chance I parked quietly by the creek, walked out on the narrow bridge over the shallows, and looked upstream. Someday, I had been telling myself for weeks, someday a muskrat is going to swim right through that channel in the cattails, and I am going to see it. That is precisely what happened. I looked up into the channel for a muskrat, and there it came, swimming right toward me. Knock; seek; ask. It seemed to swim with a side-to-side, sculling motion of its vertically flattened tail. It looked bigger than the upside-down muskrat, and its face more reddish. In its mouth it clasped a twig of tulip tree. One thing amazed me: it swam right down the middle of the creek. I thought it would hide in the brush along the edge; instead, it plied the waters as obviously as an aquaplane. I could just look and look.

But I was standing on the bridge, not sitting, and it saw me. It changed its course, veered towards the bank, and disappeared behind an indentation in the rushy shoreline. I felt a rush of such pure energy I thought I would not need to breathe for days.

That innocence of mine is mostly gone now, although I felt almost the same pure rush last night. I have seen many muskrats since I learned to look for them in that part of the creek. But still I seek them out in the cool of the evening, and still I hold my breath when rising ripples surge from under the creek's bank. The great hurrah about wild animals is that they exist at all, and the greater hurrah is the actual moment of seeing them. Because they have a nice dignity, and prefer to have nothing to do with me, not even as the simple objects of my vision. They show me by their very wariness what a prize it is simply to open my eyes and behold.

Muskrats are the bread and butter of the carnivorous food chain. They are like rabbits and mice: if you are big enough to eat mammals, you eat them. Hawks and owls prey on them, and foxes; so do otters. Minks are their special enemies; minks live near large muskrat populations, slinking in and out of their dens and generally hanging around like mantises outside a beehive. Muskrats are also subject to a contagious blood disease that wipes out whole colonies. Sometimes, however, their whole populations explode, just like lemmings', which are their near kin; and they either die by the hundreds or fan out across the land migrating to new creeks and ponds.

Men kill them, too. One Eskimo who hunted muskrats for a few weeks each year strictly as a sideline says that in fourteen years he killed 30,739 muskrats. The pelts sell, and the price is rising. Muskrats are the most important fur animal on the North American continent. I don't know what they bring on the Mackenzie River delta these days, but around here, fur dealers, who paid $2.90 in 1971, now pay $5.00 a pelt. They make the pelts into coats, calling the fur anything but muskrat: "Hudson seal" is typical. In the old days, after they had sold the skins, trappers would sell the meat, too, calling it "marsh rabbit." Many people still stew muskrat.

Keeping ahead of all this slaughter, a female might have as many as five litters a year, and each litter contains six or seven or more muskrats. The nest is high and dry under the bank; only the entrance is under water, usually by several feet, to foil enemies. Here the nests are marked by simple holes in a creek's clay bank; in other parts of the country muskrats build floating, conical winter lodges which are not only watertight, but edible to muskrats.

The very young have a risky life. For one thing, even snakes and raccoons eat them. For another, their mother is easily confused, and may abandon one or two of a big litter here or there, forgetting as it were to count noses. The newborn hanging on their mother's teats may drop off if the mother has to make a sudden dive into the water, and sometimes these drown. The just-weaned young have a rough time, too, because new litters are coming along so hard and fast that they have to be weaned before they really know how to survive. And if the just-weaned young are near starving, they might eat the newborn—if they can get to them. Adult muskrats, including their own mothers, often kill them if they approach too closely. But if they live through all these hazards, they can begin a life of swimming at twilight and munching cattail roots, clover, and an occasional crayfish. Paul Errington, a usually solemn authority, writes, "The muskrat nearing the end of its first month may be thought of as an independent enterprise in a very modest way."

The wonderful thing about muskrats in my book is that they cannot see very well, and are rather dim, to boot. They are extremely wary if they know I am there, and will out-wait me every time. But with a modicum of skill and mini-mum loss of human dignity, such as it is, I can be right "there," and the breathing fact of my presence will never penetrate their narrow skulls.

What happened last night was not only the ultimate in muskrat dimness, it was also the ultimate in human intru-sion, the limit beyond which I am certain I cannot go. I would never have imagined I could go that far, actually to sit beside a feeding muskrat as beside a dinner partner at a crowded table.

What happened was this. Just in the past week I have been frequenting a different place, one of the creek's name-less feeder streams. It is mostly a shallow trickle joining several pools up to three feet deep. Over one of these pools is a tiny pedestrian bridge known locally, if at all, as the troll bridge. I was sitting on the troll bridge about an hour before sunset, looking upstream about eight feet to my right where I know the muskrats have a den. I had just lighted a cigarette when a pulse of ripples appeared at the mouth of the den, and a muskrat emerged. He swam straight toward me and headed under the bridge.

Now the moment a muskrat's eyes disappear from view under a bridge, I go into action. I have about five seconds to switch myself around so that I will be able to see him very well when he emerges on the other side of the bridge. I can easily hang my head over the other side of the bridge, so that when he appears from under me, I will be able to count his eyelashes if I want. The trouble with this maneu-ver is that, once his beady eyes appear again on the other side, I am stuck. If I move again, the show is over for the evening. I have to remain in whatever insane position I happen to be caught, for as long as I am in his sight, so that I stiffen all my muscles, bruise my ankles on the concrete, and burn my fingers on the cigarette. And if the muskrat goes out on a bank to feed, there I am with my face hanging a foot over the water, unable to see anything but crayfish. So I have learned to take it easy on these five-second flings.

When the muskrat went under the bridge, I moved so I could face downstream comfortably. He reappeared, and I had a good look at him. He was eight inches long in the body, and another six in the tail. Muskrat tails are black and scaled, flattened not horizontally, like beavers' tails, but vertically, like a belt stood on edge. In the winter, muskrats' tails sometimes freeze solid, and the animals chew off the frozen parts up to about an inch of the body. They must swim entirely with their hind feet, and have a terrible time steering. This one used his tail as a rudder and only occasionally as a propeller; mostly he swam with a pedaling motion of his hind feet, held very straight and moving down and around, "toeing down" like a bicycle racer. The soles of his hind feet were strangely pale; his toenails were pointed in long cones. He kept his forelegs still, tucked up to his chest.

The muskrat clambered out on the bank across the stream from me, and began feeding. He chomped down on a ten-inch weed, pushing it into his mouth steadily with both forepaws as a carpenter feeds a saw. I could hear his chewing; it sounded like somebody eating celery sticks. Then he slid back into the water with the weed still in his mouth, crossed under the bridge, and, instead of returning to his den, rose erect on a submerged rock and calmly polished off the rest of the weed. He was about four feet away from me. Immediately he swam under the bridge again, hauled himself out on the bank, and unerringly found the same spot on the grass, where he devoured the weed's stump.

All this time I was not only doing an elaborate about-face every time his eyes disappeared under the bridge, but I was also smoking a cigarette. He never noticed that the configuration of the bridge metamorphosed utterly every time he went under it. Many animals are the same way: they can't see a thing unless it's moving. Similarly, every time he turned his head away, I was free to smoke the cigarette, although of course I never knew when he would suddenly turn again and leave me caught in some wretched position. The galling thing was, he was downwind of me and my cigarette: was I really going through all this for a creature without any sense whatsoever?

After the weed stump was gone, the muskrat began ranging over the grass with a nervous motion, chewing off mouthfuls of grass and clover near the base. Soon he had gathered a huge, bushy mouthful; he pushed into the water, crossed under the bridge, swam towards his den, and dove.

When he launched himself again shortly, having apparently cached the grass, he repeated the same routine in a businesslike fashion, and returned with another shock of grass.

Out he came again. I lost him for a minute when he went under the bridge; he did not come out where I expected him. Suddenly to my utter disbelief he appeared on the bank next to me. The troll bridge itself is on a level with the low bank; there I was, and there he was, at my side. I could have touched him with the palm of my hand without straightening my elbow. He was ready to hand.

Foraging beside me he walked very humped up, maybe to save heat loss through evaporation. Generally, whenever he was out of water he assumed the shape of a shmoo; his shoulders were as slender as a kitten's. He used his fore-paws to part clumps of grass extremely tidily; I could see the flex in his narrow wrists. He gathered mouthfuls of grass and clover less by actually gnawing than by biting hard near the ground, locking his neck muscles, and pushing up jerkily with his forelegs.

His jaw was underslung, his black eyes close set and glistening, his small ears pointed and furred. I will have to try and see if he can cock them. I could see the water-slicked long hairs of his coat, which gathered in rich brown strands that emphasized the smooth contours of his body, and which parted to reveal the paler, softer hair like rabbit fur underneath. Despite his closeness, I never saw his teeth or belly.

After several minutes of rummaging about in the grass at my side, he eased into the water under the bridge and paddled to his den with the jawful of grass held high, and that was the last I saw of him.

In the forty minutes I watched him, he never saw me, smelled me, or heard me at all. When he was in full view of course I never moved except to breathe. My eyes would move, too, following his, but he never noticed. I even swallowed a couple of times: nothing. The swallowing thing interested me because I had read that, when you are trying to hand-tame wild birds, if you inadvertently swallow, you ruin everything. The bird, according to this theory, thinks you are swallowing in anticipation, and off it goes. The muskrat never twitched. Only once, when he was feeding from the opposite bank about eight feet away from me, did he suddenly rise upright, all alert—and then he immediately resumed foraging. But he never knew I was there.

I never knew I was there, either. For that forty minutes last night I was as purely sensitive and mute as a photographic plate; I received impressions, but I did not print out captions. My own self-awareness had disappeared; it seems now almost as though, had I been wired with electrodes, my EEG would have been flat. I have done this sort of thing so often that I have lost self-consciousness about moving slowly and halting suddenly; it is second nature to me now. And I have often noticed that even a few minutes of this self-forgetfulness is tremendously invigorating. I wonder if we do not waste most of our energy just by spending every waking minute saying hello to ourselves. Martin Buber quotes an old Hasid master who said, "When you walk across the fields with your mind pure and holy, then from all the stones, and all growing things, and all animals, the sparks of their soul come out and cling to you, and then they are purified and become a holy fire in you." This is one way of describing the energy that comes, using the specialized Kabbalistic vocabulary of Hasidism.

I have tried to show muskrats to other people, but it rarely works. No matter how quiet we are, the muskrats stay hidden. Maybe they sense the tense hum of consciousness, the buzz from two human beings who in the silence cannot help but be aware of each other, and so of themselves. Then too, the other people invariably suffer from a self-consciousness that prevents their stalking well. It used to bother me, too: I just could not bear to lose so much dignity that I would completely alter my whole way of being for a muskrat. So I would move or look around or scratch my nose, and no muskrats would show, leaving me alone with my dignity for days on end, until I decided that it was worth my while to learn—from the muskrats themselves—how to stalk.

The old, classic rule for stalking is, "Stop often 'n' set frequent." The rule cannot be improved upon, but muskrats will permit a little more. If a muskrat's eyes are out of sight, I can practically do a buck-and-wing on his tail, and he'll never notice. A few days ago I approached a muskrat feeding on a bank by the troll bridge simply by taking as many gliding steps towards him as possible while his head was turned. I spread my weight as evenly as I could, so that he wouldn't feel my coming through the ground, and so that no matter when I became visible to him, I could pause motionless until he turned away again without having to balance too awkwardly on one leg.

When I got within ten feet of him, I was sure he would flee, but he continued to browse nearsightedly among the mown clovers and grass. Since I had seen just about everything I was ever going to see, I continued approaching just to see when he would break. To my utter bafflement, he never broke. I broke first. When one of my feet was six inches from his back, I refused to press on. He could see me perfectly well, of course, but I was stock-still except when he lowered his head. There was nothing left to do but kick him. Finally he returned to the water, dove, and vanished. I do not know to this day if he would have permitted me to keep on walking right up his back.

It is not always so easy. Other times I have learned that the only way to approach a feeding muskrat for a good look is to commit myself to a procedure so ridiculous that only a total unself-consciousness will permit me to live with myself. I have to ditch my hat, line up behind a low boulder, and lay on my belly to inch snake-fashion across twenty feet of bare field until I am behind the boulder itself and able to hazard a slow peek around it. If my head moves from around the boulder when the muskrat's head happens to be turned, then all is well. I can be fixed into position and still by the time he looks around. But if he sees me move my head, then he dives into the water, and the whole belly-crawl routine was in vain. There is no way to tell ahead of time; I just have to chance it and see.

I have read that in the unlikely event that you are caught in a stare-down with a grizzly bear, the best thing to do is talk to him softly and pleasantly. Your voice is supposed to have a soothing effect. I have not yet had occasion to test this out on grizzly bears, but I can attest that it does not work on muskrats. It scares them witless. I have tried time and again. Once I watched a muskrat feeding on a bank ten feet away from me; after I had looked my fill I had nothing to lose, so I offered a convivial greeting. Boom. The terrified muskrat flipped a hundred and eighty degrees in the air, nose-dived into the grass at his feet, and disappeared. The earth swallowed him; his tail shot straight up in the air and then vanished into the ground without a sound. Muskrats make several emergency escape holes along a bank for just this very purpose, and they don't like to feed too far away from them. The entire event was most impressive, and illustrates the relative power in nature of the word and the sneak.

Stalking is a pure form of skill, like pitching or playing chess. Rarely is luck involved. I do it right or I do it wrong; the muskrat will tell me, and that right early. Even more than baseball, stalking is a game played in the actual present. At every second, the muskrat comes, or stays, or goes, depending on my skill.

Can I stay still? How still? It is astonishing how many people cannot, or will not, hold still. I could not, or would not, hold still for thirty minutes inside, but at the creek I slow down, center down, empty. I am not excited; my breathing is slow and regular. In my brain I am not saying, Muskrat! Muskrat! There! I am saying nothing. If I must hold a position, I do not "freeze." If I freeze, locking my muscles, I will tire and break. Instead of going rigid, I go calm. I center down wherever I am; I find a balance and repose. I retreat—not inside myself, but outside myself, so that I am a tissue of senses. Whatever I see is plenty, abundance. I am the skin of water the wind plays over; I am petal, feather, stone.

III

Living this way by the creek, where the light appears and vanishes on the water, where muskrats surface and dive, and redwings scatter, I have come to know a special side of nature. I look to the mountains, and the mountains still slumber, blue and mute and rapt. I say, it gathers; the world abides. But I look to the creek, and I say: it scatters, it comes and goes. When I leave the house the sparrows flee and hush; on the banks of the creek jays scream in alarm, squirrels race for cover, tadpoles dive, frogs leap, snakes freeze, warblers vanish. Why do they hide? I will not hurt them. They simply do not want to be seen. "Nature," said Heraclitus, "is wont to hide herself." A fleeing mockingbird unfurls for a second a dazzling array of white fans . . . and disappears in the leaves. Shane! . . . Shane! Nature flashes the old mighty glance—the come-hither look—drops the handkerchief, turns tail, and is gone. The nature I know is old touch-and-go.

I wonder whether what I see and seem to understand about nature is merely one of the accidents of freedom, repeated by chance before my eyes, or whether it has any counterpart in the worlds beyond Tinker Creek. I find in quantum mechanics a world symbolically similar to my world at the creek.

Many of us are still living in the universe of Newtonian physics, and fondly imagine that real, hard scientists have no use for these misty ramblings, dealing as scientists do with the measurable and known. We think that at least the physical causes of physical events are perfectly knowable, and that, as the results of various experiments keep coming in, we gradually roll back the cloud of unknowing. We remove the veils one by one, painstakingly, adding knowledge to knowledge and whisking away veil after veil, until at last we reveal the nub of things, the sparkling equation from whom all blessings flow. Even wildman Emerson accepted the truly pathetic fallacy of the old science when he wrote grudgingly towards the end of his life, "When the microscope is improved, we shall have the cells analysed, and all will be electricity, or somewhat else." All we need to do is perfect our instruments and our methods, and we can collect enough data like birds on a string to predict physical events from physical causes.

But in 1927 Werner Heisenberg pulled out the rug, and our whole understanding of the universe toppled and collapsed. For some reason it has not yet trickled down to the man on the street that some physicists now are a bunch of wild-eyed, raving mystics. For they have perfected their instruments and methods just enough to whisk away the crucial vein, and what stands revealed is the Cheshire cat's grin.

The Principle of Indeterminacy, which saw the light in the summer of 1927, says in effect that you cannot know both a particle's velocity and position. You can guess statistically what any batch of electrons might do, but you cannot predict the career of any one particle. They seem to be as free as dragonflies. You can perfect your instruments and your methods till the cows come home, and you will never ever be able to measure this one basic thing. It cannot be done.

The electron is a muskrat; it cannot be perfectly stalked. And nature is a fan dancer born with a fan; you can wrestle her down, throw her on the stage and grapple with her for the fan with all your might, but it will never quit her grip. She comes that way; the fan is attached.

It is not that we lack sufficient information to know both a particle's velocity and its position; that would have been a perfectly ordinary situation well within the understanding of classical physics. Rather, we know now for sure that there is no knowing. You can determine the position, and your figure for the velocity blurs into vagueness; or, you can determine the velocity, but whoops, there goes the position. The use of instruments and the very fact of an observer seem to bollix the observations; as a consequence, physicists are saying that they cannot study nature per se, but only their own investigation of nature. And I can only see blue-gills within my own blue shadow, from which they immediately flee.

The Principle of Indeterminacy turned science inside-out. Suddenly determinism goes, causality goes, and we are left with a universe composed of what Eddington calls, "mind-stuff." Listen to these physicists: Sir James Jeans, Eddington's successor, invokes "fate," saying that the future "may rest on the knees of whatever gods there be." Eddington says that "the physical world is entirely abstract and without 'actuality' apart from its linkage to consciousness." Heisenberg himself says, "method and object can no longer be separated. *The scientific world-view has ceased to be a scientific view in the true sense of the word.*" Jeans says that science can no longer remain opposed to the notion of free will. Heisenberg says, "there is a higher power, not influenced by our wishes, which finally decides and judges." Eddington says that our dropping causality as a result of the Principle of Indeterminacy "leaves us with no clear distinction between the Natural and the Supernatural." And so forth.

These physicists are once again mystics, as Kepler was, standing on a rarefied mountain pass, gazing transfixed into an abyss of freedom. And they got there by experimental method and a few wild leaps such as Einstein made. What a pretty pass!

All this means is that the physical world as we understand it now is more like the touch-and-go creek world I see than it is like the abiding world of which the mountains seem to speak. The physicists' particles whiz and shift like rotifers in and out of my microscope's field, and that this valley's ring of granite mountains is an airy haze of those same particles I must believe. The whole universe is a swarm of those wild, wary energies, the sun that glistens from the wet hairs on a muskrat's back and the stars which the mountains obscure on the horizon but which catch from on high in Tinker Creek. It is all touch and go. The heron flaps away; the dragonfly departs at thirty miles an hour; the water strider vanishes under a screen of grass; the muskrat dives, and the ripples roll from the bank, and flatten, and cease altogether.

Moses said to God, "I beseech thee, shew me thy glory." And God said, "Thou canst not see my face: for there shall no man see me, and live." But he added, "There is a place by me, and thou shalt stand upon a rock: and it shall come to pass, while my glory passeth by, that I will put thee in a clift of the rock, and will cover thee with my hand while I pass by: And I will take away mine hand, and thou shalt see my back parts: but my face shall not be seen." So Moses went up on Mount Sinai, waited still in a clift of the rock, and saw the back parts of God. Forty years later he went up on Mount Pisgah, and saw the promised land across the Jordan, which he was to die without ever being permitted to enter.

Just a glimpse, Moses: a clift in the rock here, a mountaintop there, and the rest is denial and longing. You have to stalk everything. Everything scatters and gathers; everything comes and goes like fish under a bridge. You have to stalk the spirit, too. You can wait forgetful anywhere, for anywhere is the way of his fleet passage, and hope to catch him by the tail and shout something in his ear before he wrests away. Or you can pursue him wherever you dare, risking the shrunken sinew in the hollow of the thigh; you can bang at the door all night till the innkeeper relents, if he ever relents; and you can wail till you're hoarse or worse the cry for incarnation always in John Knoepfle's poem: "and christ is red rover . . . and the children are calling/ come over come over." I sit on a bridge as on Pisgah or Sinai, and I am both waiting becalmed in a clift of the rock and banging with all my will, calling like a child beating on a door: Come on out! . . . I know you're there.

And then occasionally the mountains part. The tree with the lights in it appears, the mockingbird falls, and time unfurls across space like an oriflamme. Now we rejoice. The news, after all, is not that muskrats are wary, but that they can be seen. The hem of the robe was a Nobel Prize to Heisenberg; he did not go home in disgust. I wait on the bridges and stalk along banks for those moments I cannot predict, when a wave begins to surge under the water, and ripples strengthen and pulse high across the creek and back again in a texture that throbs. It is like the surfacing of an impulse, like the materialization of fish, this rising, this coming to a head, like the ripening of nutmeats still in their husks, ready to split open like buckeyes in a field, shining with newness. "Surely the Lord is in this place; and I knew it not." The fleeing shreds I see, the back parts, are a gift, an abundance. When Moses came down from the clift in Mount Sinai, the people were afraid of him: the very skin on his face shone.

Do the Eskimos' faces shine, too? I lie in bed alert: I am with the Eskimos on the tundra who are running after the click-footed caribou, running sleepless and dazed for days, running spread out in scraggling lines across the glacier-ground hummocks and reindeer moss, in sight of the ocean, under the long-shadowed pale sun, running silent all night long.

CHAPTER 12

Nightwatch

I STOOD IN THE LUCAS MEADOW in the middle of a barrage of grasshoppers. There must have been something about the rising heat, the falling night, the ripeness of grasses— something that mustered this army in the meadow where they have never been in such legions before. I must have seen a thousand grasshoppers, alarums and excursions clicking over the clover, knee-high to me.

I had stepped into the meadow to feel the heat and catch a glimpse of the sky, but these grasshoppers demanded my attention, and became an event in themselves. Every step I took detonated the grass. A blast of bodies like shrapnel exploded around me; the air burst and whirred. There were grasshoppers of all sizes, grasshoppers yellow, green and black, short-horned, long-horned, slant-faced, band-winged, spur-throated, cone-headed, pygmy, spotted, striped and barred. They sprang in salvos, dropped in the air, and clung unevenly to stems and blades with their legs spread for balance, as redwings ride cattail reeds. They clattered around my ears; they ricocheted off my calves with an instant clutch and release of tiny legs.

I was in shelter, but open to the sky. The meadow was clean, the world new, and I washed by my walk over the waters of the dam. A new, wild feeling descended upon me and caught me up. What if these grasshoppers were locusts, I thought; what if I were the first man in the world, and stood in a swarm?

I had been reading about locusts. Hordes of migrating locusts have always appeared in arid countries, and then disappeared as suddenly as they had come. You could actually watch them lay eggs all over a plain, and the next year there would be no locusts on the plain. Entomologists would label their specimens, study their structure, and never find a single one that was alive—until years later they would be overrun again. No one knew in what caves or clouds the locusts hid between plagues.

In 1921 a Russian naturalist named Uvarov solved the mystery. Locusts are grasshoppers: they are the same animal. Swarms of locusts are ordinary grasshoppers gone berserk.

If you take ordinary grasshoppers of any of several species from any of a number of the world's dry regions—including the Rocky Mountains—and rear them in glass jars under crowded conditions, they go into the migratory phase. That is, they turn into locusts. They literally and physically change from Jekyll to Hyde before your eyes. They will even change, all alone in their jars, if you stimulate them by a rapid succession of artificial touches. Imperceptibly at first, their wings and wing-covers elongate. Their drab color heightens, then saturates more and more, until it locks at the hysterical locust yellows and pinks. Stripes and dots appear on the wing-covers; these deepen to a glittering black. They lay more egg-pods than grasshoppers. They are restless, excitable, voracious. You now have jars full of plague.

Under ordinary conditions, inside the laboratory and out in the deserts, the eggs laid by these locusts produce ordinary solitary grasshoppers. Only under special conditions—such as droughts that herd them together in crowds near available food—do the grasshoppers change. They shun food and shelter and seek only the jostle and clack of their kind. Their ranks swell; the valleys teem. One fine day they take to the air.

In full flight their millions can blacken the sky for nine hours, and when they land, it's every man to your tents, O Israel. "A fire devoureth before them; and behind them a flame burneth: the land is as the garden of Eden before them, and behind them a desolate wilderness; yea, and nothing shall escape them." One writer says that if you feed one a blade of grass, "the eighteen components of its jaws go immediately into action, lubricated by a brown saliva which looks like motor oil." Multiply this action by millions, and you hear a new sound: "The noise their myriad jaws make when engaged in their work of destruction can be realized by any one who has fought a prairie fire or heard the flames passing along before a brisk wind, the low crackling and rasping." Every contour of the land, every twig, is inches deep in bodies, so the valleys seethe and the hills tremble. Locusts: it is an old story.

A man lay down to sleep in a horde of locusts, Will Barker says. Instantly the suffocating swarm fell on him and knit him in a clicking coat of mail. The metallic mouth parts meshed and pinched. His friends rushed in and woke him at once. But when he stood up, he was bleeding from the throat and wrists.

The world has locusts, and the world has grasshoppers. I was up to my knees in the world.

Not one of these insects in this meadow could change into a locust under any circumstance. I am King of the Meadow, I thought, and raised my arms. Instantly grasshoppers burst all around me, describing in the air a blur of angular trajectories which ended in front of my path in a wag of grasses. As *if* I were king, dilly-dilly.

A large gray-green grasshopper hit with a clack on my shirt, and stood on my shoulder, panting. "Boo," I said, and it clattered off. It landed on a grass head several yards away. The grass bucked and sprang from the impact like a bronc, and the grasshopper rode it down. When the movement ceased, I couldn't see the grasshopper.

I walked on, one step at a time, both instigating and receiving this spray of small-arms fire. I had to laugh. I'd been had. I wanted to see the creatures, and they were gone. The only way I could see them in their cunning was to frighten them in their innocence. No charm or cleverness of mine could conjure or draw them; I could only flush them, triggering the grossest of their instincts, with the physical bluntness of my passage. To them I was just so much trouble, a horde of commotion, like any rolling stone. Wait! Where did you go? Does not any one of you, with your eighteen mouth-parts, wish to have a word with me here in the Lucas meadow? Again I raised my arms: there you are. And then gone. The grasses slammed. I was exhilarated, flushed. I was the serf of the meadow, exalted; I was the bride who waits with her lamp filled. A new wind was stirring; I had received the grasshoppers the way

I received this wind. All around the meadow's rim the highest trees heaved soundlessly.

I walked back toward the cottage, maneuvering the whole squadron from one end of the meadow to the other. I'd been had all along by grasshoppers, muskrats, mountains—and like any sucker, I come back for more. They always get you in the end, and when you know it from the beginning, you have to laugh. You come for the assault, you come for the flight—but really you know you come for the laugh.

This is the fullness of late summer now; the green of what is growing and grown conceals. I can watch a muskrat feed on a bank for ten minutes, harvesting shocks of grass that bristle and droop from his jaws, and when he is gone I cannot see any difference in the grass. If I spread the patch with my hands and peer closely, I am hard put to locate any damage from even the most intense grazing. Nothing even looks trampled. Does everything else but me pass so lightly? When the praying mantis egg cases hatched in June, over a period of several days, I watched the tiny translucent mantises leap about leggily on the egg case, scraggle down the hedge's twigs, and disappear in the grass. In some places I could see them descend in a line like a moving bridge from stem to ground. The instant they crossed the horizon and entered the grass, they vanished as if they had jumped off the edge of the world.

Now it is early September, and the paths are clogged. I look to water to see sky. It is the time of year when a honeybee beats feebly at the inside back window of every parked car. A frog flies up for every foot of bank, bubbles tangle in a snare of blue-green algae, and Japanese beetles hunch doubled on the willow leaves. The sun thickens the air to jelly; it bleaches, flattens, dissolves. The skies are a milky haze—nowhere, do-nothing summer skies. Every kid I see has a circular grid on his forehead, a regular cross-hatching of straight lines, from spending his days leaning into screen doors.

I had come to the Lucas place to spend a night there, to let come what may. The Lucas place is paradise enow. It has everything: old woods, young woods, cliffs, meadows, slow water, fast water, caves. All it needs is a glacier extending a creaking foot behind the cottage. This magic garden is just on the other side of the oxbow in Tinker Creek; it is secluded because it is hard to approach. I could have followed the rock cliff path through the old woods, but in summer that path is wrapped past finding in saplings, bushes, kudzu, and poison oak. I could have tacked down the shorn grass terraces next to the cliff, but to get there I would have had to pass a vicious dog, who is waiting for the day I forget to carry a stick. So I planned on going the third way, over the dam.

I made a sandwich, filled a canteen, and slipped a palm-sized flashlight into my pocket. Then all I had to do was grab a thin foam pad and my sleeping bag, walk down the road, over the eroded clay hill where the mantis laid her eggs, along the creek downstream to the motorbike woods, and through the woods' bike trail to the dam.

I like crossing the dam. If I fell, I might not get up again. The dam is three or four feet high; a thick green algae, combed by the drag and sudden plunge of the creek's current, clings to its submersed, concrete brim. Below is a jumble of fast water and rocks. But I face this threat every time I cross the dam, and it is always exhilarating. The tightest part is at the very beginning. That day as always I faced the current, planted my feet firmly, stepped sideways instead of striding, and I soon emerged dripping in a new world.

Now, returning from my foray into the grasshopper meadow, I was back where I started, on the bank that separates the cottage from the top of the dam, where my sleeping bag, foam pad, and sandwich lay. The sun was setting invisibly behind the cliffs' rim. I unwrapped the sandwich and looked back over the way I had come, as if I could have seen the grasshoppers spread themselves again over the wide meadow and hide enfolded in its thickets and plush.

This is what I had come for, just this, and nothing more. A fling of leafy motion on the cliffs, the assault of real things, living and still, with shapes and powers under the sky—this is my city, my culture, and all the world I need. I looked around.

What I call the Lucas place is only a part of the vast Lucas property. It is one of the earliest clearings around here, a garden in the wilderness; every time I cross the dam and dry my feet on the bank, I feel like I've just been born. Now to my right the creek's dammed waters were silent and deep, overhung by and reflecting bankside tulip and pawpaw and ash. The creek angled away out of sight upstream; this was the oxbow, and the dam spanned its sharpest arc. Downstream the creek slid over the dam and slapped along sandstone ledges and bankside boulders, exhaling a cooling breath of mist before disappearing around the bend under the steep wooded cliff.

I stood ringed and rimmed in heights, locked and limned, in a valley within a valley. Next to the cliff fell a grassy series of high terraces, suitable for planting the hanging gardens of Babylon. Beyond the terraces, forest erupted again wherever it could eke a roothold on the sheer vertical rock. In one place, three caves cut into the stone vaults, their entrances hidden by honeysuckle. One of the caves was so small only a child could enter it crawling; one was big enough to explore long after you have taken the initiatory turns that shut out the light; the third was huge and shallow, filled with cut wood and chicken wire, and into its nether wall extended another tiny cave in which a groundhog reared her litter this spring.

Ahead of me in the distance I could see where the forested cliffs mined with caves gave way to overgrown terraces that once must have been cleared. Now they were tangled in saplings swathed in honeysuckle and wild rose brambles. I always remember trying to fight my way up that steepness one winter when I first understood that even January is not muscle enough to subdue the deciduous South. There were clear trails through the undergrowth— I saw once I was in the thick of it—but they were rabbit paths, unfit for anyone over seven inches tall. I had emerged scratched, pricked, and panting in the Lucas peach orchard, which is considerably more conveniently approached by the steep gravel drive that parallels the creek.

In the flat at the center of all this rimrock was the sunlit grasshopper meadow, and facing the meadow, tucked up between the grass terrace and the creek's dam, was the heart of the city, the Lucas cottage.

I stepped to the porch. My footfall resounded; the cliffs rang back the sound, and the clover and grasses absorbed it. The Lucas cottage was in fact mostly porch, airy and winged. Gray-painted two-by-fours wobbled around three sides of the cottage, split, smashed, and warped long past plumb. Beams at the porch's four corners supported a low, peaked roof that vaulted over both the porch and the cottage impartially, lending so much importance to the already huge porch that it made the cottage proper seem an afterthought, as Adam seems sometimes an afterthought in Eden. For years an old inlaid chess table with a broken carved pedestal leaned against the cottage on one wing of the porch; the contrasting brown patches of weathered inlay curled up in curves like leaves.

The cottage was scarcely longer than the porch was deep. It was a one-room cottage; you could manage (I've thought this through again and again—building more spartan mansions, o my soul) a cot, a plank window-desk, a chair (two for company, as the man says), and some narrow shelves. The cottage is mostly windows—there are five—and the windows are entirely broken, so that my life inside the cottage is mostly Tinker Creek and mud dauber wasps.

It's a great life—luxurious, really. The cottage is wired for electricity; a bare-bulb socket hangs from the unfinished wood ceiling. There is a stovepipe connection in the roof. Beyond the porch on the side away from the creek is a big brick fireplace suitable for grilling whole steers. The steers themselves are fattening just five minutes away, up the hill and down into the pasture. The trees that shade the cottage are walnuts and pecans. In the spring the edge of the up-stream creek just outside the cottage porch comes up in yellow daffodils, all the way up to the peach orchard.

That day it was dark inside the cottage, as usual; the five windows framed five films of the light and living world. I crunched to the creekside window, walking on the layer of glass shards on the floor, and stood to watch the creek lurch over the dam and round the shaded bend under the cliff, while bumblebees the size of ponies fumbled in the fragrant flowers that flecked the bank. A young cotton-tail rabbit bounded into view and froze. It crouched under my window with its ears flattened to its skull and its body motionless, the picture of adaptive invisibility. With one ridiculous exception. It was so very young, and its shoulder itched so maddeningly, that it whapped away at the spot noisily with a violent burst of a hind leg—and then resumed its frozen alert. Over the dam's drop of waters, two dog-faced sulphur butterflies were fighting. They touched and parted, ascending in a vertical climb, as though they were racing up an invisible spiraling vine.

All at once something wonderful happened, although at first it seemed perfectly ordinary. A female goldfinch suddenly hove into view. She lighted weightlessly on the head of a bankside purple thistle and began emptying the seedcase, sowing the air with down.

The lighted frame of my window filled. The down rose and spread in all directions, wafting over the dam's waterfall and wavering between the tulip trunks and into the meadow. It vaulted towards the orchard in a puff; it hovered over the ripening pawpaw fruit and staggered up the steep-faced terrace. It jerked, floated, rolled, veered, swayed. The thistledown faltered toward the cottage and gusted clear to the motorbike woods; it rose and entered the shaggy arms of pecans. At last it strayed like snow, blind and sweet, into the pool of the creek upstream, and into the race of the creek over rocks down. It shuddered onto the tips of growing grasses, where it poised, light, still wracked by errant quivers. I was holding my breath. Is this where we live, I thought, in this place at this moment, with the air so light and wild?

The same fixity that collapses stars and drives the mantis to devour her mate eased these creatures together before my eyes: the thick adept bill of the goldfinch, and the feathery, coded down. How could anything be amiss? If I myself were lighter and frayed, I could ride these small winds, too, taking my chances, for the pleasure of being so purely played.

The thistle is part of Adam's curse. "Cursed is the ground for thy sake; in sorrow shalt thou eat of it all the days of thy life; Thorns also and thistles shall it bring forth to thee." A terrible curse: But does the goldfinch eat thorny sorrow with the thistle, or do I? If this furling air is fallen, then the fall was happy indeed. If this creekside garden is sorrow, then I seek martyrdom. This crown of thorns sits light on my skull, like wings. The Venetian Baroque painter Tiepolo painted Christ as a red-lipped infant clutching a goldfinch; the goldfinch seems to be looking around in search of thorns. Creation itself was the fall, a burst into the thorny beauty of the real.

The goldfinch here on the fringed thistletop was burying her head with each light thrust deeper into the seedcase. Her fragile legs braced to her task on the vertical, thorny stem; the last of the thistledown sprayed and poured. Is there anything I could eat so lightly, or could I die so fair? With a ruffle of feathered wings the goldfinch fluttered away, out of range of the broken window's frame and toward the deep blue shade of the cliffs where late fireflies already were rising alight under trees. I was weightless; my bones were taut skins blown with buoyant gas; it seemed that if I inhaled too deeply, my shoulders and head would waft off. Alleluia.

Later I lay half out of my sleeping bag on a narrow shelf of flat ground between the cottage porch and the bank to the dam. I lay where a flash flood would reach me, but we have had a flood; the time is late. The night was clear; when the fretwork of overhead foliage rustled and parted, I could see the pagan stars.

Sounds fell all about me; I vibrated like still water ruffed by wind. Cicadas—which Donald E. Carr calls "the guns of August"—were out in full force. Their stridulations mounted over the meadow and echoed from the rim of cliffs, filling the air with a plaintive, mysterious urgency.

I had heard them begin at twilight, and was struck with the way they actually do "start up," like an out-of-practice orchestra, creaking and grinding and all out of synch. It had sounded like someone playing a cello with a wide-toothed comb. The frogs added their unlocatable notes, which always seem to me to be so arbitrary and anarchistic, and crickets piped in, calling their own tune which they have been calling since the time of Pliny, who noted bluntly of the cricket, it "never ceaseth all night long to creak very shrill."

Earlier a bobwhite had cried from the orchardside cliff, now here, now there, and his round notes swelled sorrowfully over the meadow. A bobwhite who is still calling in summer is lorn; he has never found a mate. When I first read this piece of information, every bobwhite call I heard sounded tinged with desperation, suicidally miserable. But now I am somehow cheered on my way by that solitary signal. The bobwhite's very helplessness, his obstinate Johnny-two-notedness, takes on an aura of dogged pluck. God knows what he is thinking in those pendant silences between calls. God knows what I am. But: bob*white*. (Somebody showed me once how to answer a bobwhite in the warbling, descending notes of the female. It works like a charm. But what can I do with a charmed circle of male bobwhites but weep? Still, I am brutalized enough that I give the answering call occasionally, just to get a rise out of the cliffs, and a bitter laugh.) Yes, it's tough, it's tough, that goes without saying. But isn't waiting itself and longing a wonder, being played on by wind, sun, and shade?

In his famous *Camping and Woodcraft,* Horace Kephart sounds a single ominous note. He writes in parentheses: "Some cannot sleep well in a white tent under a full moon." Every time I think of it, I laugh. I like the way that handy woodsy tip threatens us with the thrashings of the spirit.

I was in no tent under leaves, sleepless and glad. There was no moon at all; along the world's coasts the sea tides would be springing strong. The air itself also has lunar tides: I lay still. Could I feel in the air an invisible sweep and surge, and an answering knock in my lungs? Or could I feel the starlight? Every minute on a square mile of this land—on the steers and the orchard, on the quarry, the meadow, and creek—one ten thousandth of an ounce of starlight spatters to earth. What percentage of an ounce did that make on my eyes and cheeks and arms, tapping and nudging as particles, pulsing and stroking as waves? Straining after these tiny sensations, I nearly rolled off the world when I heard, and at the same time felt through my hips' and legs' bones on the ground, the bang and shudder of distant freight trains coupling.

Night risings and fallings filled my mind, free excursions carried out invisibly while the air swung up and back and the starlight rained. By day I had watched water striders dimple and jerk over the deep bankside water slowed by the dam. But I knew that sometimes a breath or call stirs the colony, and new forms emerge with wings. They cluster at night on the surface of their home waters and then take to the air in a rush. Migrating, they sail over meadows, under trees, cruising, veering towards a steady gleam in a flurry of glistening wings: "phantom ships in the air."

Now also in the valley night a skunk emerged from his underground burrow to hunt pale beetle grubs in the dark. A great horned owl folded his wings and dropped from the sky, and the two met on the bloodied surface of earth. Spreading over a distance, the air from that spot thinned to a frail sweetness, a tinctured wind that bespoke real creatures and real encounters at the edge . . . events, events. Over my head black hunting beetles crawled up into the high limbs of trees, killing more caterpillars and pupae than they would eat.

I had read once about a mysterious event of the night that is never far from my mind. Edwin Way Teale described an occurrence so absurd that it vaults out of the world of strange facts and into that startling realm where power and beauty hold sovereign sway.

The sentence in Teale is simple: "On cool autumn nights, eels hurrying to the sea sometimes crawl for a mile or more across dewy meadows to reach streams that will carry them to salt water." These are adult eels, silver eels, and this descent that slid down my mind is the fall from a long spring ascent the eels made years ago. As one-inch elvers they wriggled and heaved their way from the salt sea up the coastal rivers of America and Europe, upstream always into "the quiet upper reaches of rivers and brooks, in lakes and ponds—sometimes as high as 8,000 feet above sea level." There they had lived without breeding "for at least eight years." In the late summer of the year they reached maturity, they stopped eating, and their dark color vanished. They turned silver; now they are heading to the sea. Down streams to rivers, down rivers to the sea, south in the North Atlantic where they meet and pass billions of north-bound elvers, they are returning to the Sargasso Sea, where, in floating sargassum weed in the deepest waters of the Atlantic, they will mate, release their eggs, and die. This, the whole story of eels at which I have only just hinted, is extravagant in the extreme, and food for another kind of thought, a thought about the meaning of such wild, incomprehensible gestures. But it was feeling with which I was concerned under the walnut tree by the side of the Lucas cottage and dam. My mind was on that meadow.

Imagine a chilly night and a meadow; balls of dew droop from the curved blades of grass. All right: the grass at the edge of the meadow begins to tremble and sway. Here come the eels. The largest are five feet long. All are silver. They stream into the meadow, sift between grasses and clover, veer from your path. There are too many to count. All you see is a silver slither, like twisted ropes of water falling roughly, a one-way milling and mingling over the meadow and slide to the creek. Silver eels in the night: a barely-made-out seething as far as you can squint, a squirming, jostling torrent of silver eels in the grass. If I saw that sight, would I live? If I stumbled across it, would I ever set foot from my door again? Or would I be seized to join that compelling rush, would I cease eating, and pale, and abandon all to start walking?

Had this place always been so, and had I not known it? There were blowings and flights, tossings and heaves up the air and down to grass. Why didn't God let the animals in Eden name the man; why didn't I wrestle the grasshopper on my shoulder and pin him down till he called my name? I was thistledown, and now I seemed to be grass, the receiver of grasshoppers and eels and mantises, grass the windblown and final receiver.

For the grasshoppers and thistledown and eels went up and came down. If you watch carefully the hands of a juggler, you see they are almost motionless, held at precise angles, so that the balls seem to be of their own volition describing a perfect circle in the air. The ascending arc is the hard part, but our eyes are on the smooth and curving fall. Each falling ball seems to trail beauty as its afterimage, receding faintly down the air, almost disappearing, when lo, another real ball falls, shedding its transparent beauty, and another. . . .

And it all happens so dizzyingly fast. The goldfinch I had seen was asleep in a thicket; when she settled to sleep, the weight of her breast locked her toes around her perch. Wasps were asleep with their legs hanging loose, their jaws jammed into the soft stems of plants. Everybody grab a handle: we're spinning headlong down.

I am puffed clay, blown up and set down. That I fall like Adam is not surprising: I plunge, waft, arc, pour, and dive. The surprise is how good the wind feels on my face as I fall. And the other surprise is that I ever rise at all. I rise when I receive, like grass.

I didn't know, I never have known, what spirit it is that descends into my lungs and flaps near my heart like an eagle rising. I named it full-of-wonder, highest good, voices. I shut my eyes and saw a tree stump hurled by wind, an enormous tree stump sailing sideways across my vision, with a wide circular brim of roots and soil like a tossed top hat.

And what if those grasshoppers had been locusts descending, I thought, and what if I stood awake in a swarm? I cannot ask for more than to be so wholly acted upon, flown at, and lighted on in throngs, probed, knocked, even bitten. A little blood from the wrists and throat is the price I would willingly pay for that pressure of clacking weights on my shoulders, for the scent of deserts, ground-fire in my ears—for being so in the clustering thick of things, rapt and enwrapped in the rising and falling real world.

CHAPTER 13

The Horns of
the Altar

I

THERE WAS A SNAKE at the quarry with me tonight. It lay shaded by cliffs on a flat sandstone ledge above the quarry's dark waters. I was thirty feet away, sitting on the forest path overlook, when my eye caught the dark scrawl on the rocks, the lazy sinuosity that can only mean snake. I approached for a better look, edging my way down the steep rock cutting, and saw that the snake was only twelve or thirteen inches long. Its body was thick for its length. I came closer still, and saw the unmistakable undulating bands of brown, the hourglasses: copperhead.

I never step a foot out of the house, even in winter, without a snakebite kit in my pocket. Mine is a small kit in rubber casing about the size of a shotgun shell; I slapped my pants instinctively to fix in my mind its location. Then I stomped hard on the ground a few times and set down beside the snake.

The young copperhead was motionless on its rock. Although it lay in a loose sprawl, all I saw at first was a camouflage pattern of particolored splotches confused by the rushing speckles of light in the weeds between us, and by the deep twilight dark of the quarry pond beyond the rock. Then suddenly the form of its head emerged from the confusion: burnished brown, triangular, blunt as a stone ax. Its head and the first four inches of its body rested on airy nothing an inch above the rock. I admired the snake. Its scales shone with newness, bright and buffed. Its body was perfect, whole and unblemished. I found it hard to believe it had not just been created on the spot, or hatched fresh from its mother, so unscathed and clean was its body, so unmarked by any passage.

Did it see me? I was only four feet away, seated on the weedy cliff behind the sandstone ledge; the snake was between me and the quarry pond. I waved an arm in its direction: nothing moved. Its low-forehead glare and lipless reptile smirk revealed nothing. How could I tell where it was looking, what it was seeing? I squinted at its head, staring at those eyes like the glass eyes of a stuffed warbler, at those scales like shields canted and lapped just so, to frame an improbable, unfathomable face.

Yes, it knew I was there. There was something about its eyes, some alien alertness . . . what on earth must it be like to have scales on your face? All right then, copperhead. I know you're here, you know I'm here. This is a big night. I dug my elbows into rough rock and dry soil and settled back on the hillside to begin the long business of waiting out a snake.

The only other poisonous snake around here is the timber rattler, *Crotalus horridus horridus*. These grow up to six feet long in the mountains, and as big as your thigh. I've never seen one in the wild; I don't know how many have seen me. I see copperheads, though, sunning in the dust, disappearing into rock cliff chinks, crossing dirt roads at twilight. Copperheads have no rattle, of course, and, at least in my experience, they do not give way. You walk around a copperhead—if you see it. Copperheads are not big enough or venomous enough to kill adult humans readily, but they do account for far and away the greatest number of poisonous snakebites in North America: there are so many of them, and people, in the Eastern woodlands. It always interests me when I read about new studies being done on pit vipers; the team of herpetologists always seems to pick my neck of the woods for its fieldwork. I infer that we have got poisonous snakes as East Africa has zebras or the tropics have orchids—they are our specialty, our stock-in-trade. So I try to keep my eyes open. But I don't worry: you have to live pretty far out to be more than a day from a hospital. And worrying about getting it in the face from a timber rattler is like worrying about being struck by a meteorite: life's too short. Anyway perhaps the actual bite is painless.

One day I was talking about snakes to Mrs. Mildred Sink, who operates a switchboard. A large pane separated us, and we were talking through a circular hole in the glass. She was seated in a dark room little bigger than a booth. As we talked, red lights on her desk would flash. She would glance at them, then back at me, and, finishing her point with careful calmness, she would fix on me a long, significant look to hold my attention while her hand expertly sought the button and pushed it. In this way she handled incoming calls and told me her snake story.

When she was a girl, she lived in the country just north of here. She had a brother four years old. One bright summer day her brother and her mother were sitting quietly in the big room of the log cabin. Her mother had her sewing in her lap and was bent over it in concentration. The little boy was playing with wooden blocks on the floor. "Ma," he said, "I saw a snake." "Where?" "Down by the spring." The woman stitched the hem of a cotton dress, gathering the material with her needle and drawing it smooth with her hand. The little boy piled his blocks carefully, this way and that. After a while he said, "Ma, it's too dark in here, I can't see." She looked up and the boy's leg was swollen up as big around as his body.

Mrs. Sink nodded at me emphatically and then heeded the flashing light on the panel before her. She turned away; this caller was taking time. I waved and caught her eye; she waved, and I left.

The copperhead in front of me was motionless; its head still hung in the air above the sandstone rock. I thought of poking at it with a weed, but rejected the notion. Still, I wished it would do something. Marston Bates tells about an English ecologist, Charles Elton, who said, with his Britishness fully unfurled, "All cold-blooded animals . . . spend an unexpectedly large proportion of their time doing nothing at all, or at any rate nothing in particular." That is precisely what this one was doing.

I noticed its tail. It tapered to nothingness. I started back at the head and slid my eye down its body slowly: taper, taper, taper, scales, tiny scales, air. Suddenly the copperhead's tail seemed to be the most remarkable thing I had ever seen. I wished I tapered like that somewhere. What if

I were a shaped balloon blown up through the tip of a finger?

Here was this blood-filled, alert creature, this nerved rope of matter, really here instead of not here, splayed soft and solid on a rock by the slimmest of chances. It was a thickening of the air spread from a tip, a rush into being, eyeball and blood, through a pin-hole rent. Every other time I had ever seen this rock it had been a flat sandstone rock over the quarry pond; now it hosted and bore this chunk of fullness that parted the air around it like a driven wedge. I looked at it from the other direction. From tail to head it spread like the lines of a crescendo, widening from stillness to a turgid blast; then at the bulging jaws it began contracting again, diminuendo, till at the tip of its snout the lines met back at the infinite point that corners every angle, and that space once more ceased being a snake.

While this wonder engaged me, something happened that was so unusual and unexpected that I can scarcely believe I saw it. It was ridiculous.

Night had been rising like a ground vapor from the blackened quarry pool. I heard a mosquito sing in my ear; I waved it away. I was looking at the copperhead. The mosquito landed on my ankle; again, I idly brushed it off. To my utter disbelief, it lighted on the copperhead. It squatted on the copperhead's back near its "neck," and bent its head to its task. I was riveted. I couldn't see the mosquito in great detail, but I could make out its lowered head that seemed to bore like a well drill through surface rock to fluid. Quickly I looked around to see if I could find anyone—any hunter going to practice shooting beer cans, any boy on a motorbike—to whom I could show this remarkable sight while it lasted.

To the best of my knowledge, it lasted two or three full

minutes; it seemed like an hour. I could imagine the snake, like the frog sucked dry by the giant water bug, collapsing to an empty bag of skin. But the snake never moved, never indicated any awareness. At last the mosquito straightened itself, fumbled with its forelegs about its head like a fly, and sluggishly took to the air, where I lost it at once. I looked at the snake; I looked beyond the snake to the ragged chomp in the hillside where years before men had quarried stone; I rose, brushed myself off, and walked home.

Is this what it's like, I thought then, and think now: a little blood here, a chomp there, and still we live, trampling the grass? Must everything whole be nibbled? Here was a new light on the intricate texture of things in the world, the actual plot of the present moment in time after the fall: the way we the living are nibbled and nibbling—not held aloft on a cloud in the air but bumbling pitted and scarred and broken through a frayed and beautiful land.

II

When I reached home, I turned first to the bookshelf, to see if I could possibly have seen what I thought I had. All I could find was this sentence in Will Barker's book, *Familiar Insects of North America*: "The bite of the female [Mosquito, *Culex pipiens*] is effected with a little drill that can puncture many types of body covering—even the leathery skin of a frog or the overlapping scales on a snake." All right then; maybe I *had* seen it. Anything can happen in any direction; the world is more chomped than I'd dreamed.

It is mid-September now; I can see in the fading light the jagged holes in the leaves of the mock-orange hedge outside my study window. The more closely I look, the more I doubt that there is a single whole, unblemished leaf left on the bush. I go out again and examine the leaves one by one, first of the mock orange outside my study, then of the cherry tree in the yard. In the blue light I see scratched and peeled stems, leaves that are half-eaten, rusted, blighted, blistered, mined, snipped, smutted, pitted, puffed, sawed, bored, and rucked. Where have I been all summer while the world has been eaten?

I remember something else I saw this week. I passed on the road by the creek a small boy bearing aloft an enormous foot-long snapping turtle. The boy was carrying the turtle —which was stretching and snapping wildly in the air—at arm's length, and his arms must have been tired, for he asked me plaintively, "Do you have a box?" when I was on foot myself and quite clearly did not have a box. I admired the turtle, but the boy was worried. "He's got bleachers," he said. "Bleachers?" "You know, they suck your blood." Oh. I had noticed the black leech drooping like a tar tear down the turtle's thick shell. The boy showed me another one, almost two inches long, fixed to the granular skin under the turtle's foreleg. "Will they kill him?" the boy asked. "Will he live?" Many, if not most, of the wild turtles I see harbor leeches. I assured him that the turtle would live. For most creatures, being parasitized is a way of life—if you call that living.

I think of the fox that Park Service Ranger Gene Parker told me about. The fox sprawled naked and pink-skinned in a mountain field, unable to rise, dying of mange. I think of the swimming bluegill I saw at the Lawsons', upstream in Tinker Creek on the other side of Tinker Mountain. One of its eyes was blinded by an overgrowth of white water mold, a white that spread halfway down its back in filmy lumps like soaked cotton batting. It had been injured, perhaps when a fisherman had hooked it and tossed it back, perhaps when a flood dashed it on rocks, and the fungus had spread from the injured site. I think of Loren Eisley's description of a scientist he met in the field, who was gleefully bearing a bloody jar squirming with yard after yard of some unthinkable parasite he had just found in the belly of a rabbit. Suddenly the lives of the parasites—some sort of hellish hagiography—come to mind. I remember the bloodworms and flukes, whose parasitic life cycles require the living bodies of as many as four hosts. How many of the grasshoppers that hurtled around me in the Lucas meadow bore inside their guts the immense coiled larvae of horsehair worms?

I received once as a gift a small, illustrated layman's guide to insect pests. These are insects that for one reason or another are in the way of human culture—or economics. By no means all are parasites. Nevertheless, the book reads like the devil's *summa theologica*. The various insects themselves include cottony-cushion scales, bean beetles, borers, weevils, bulb flies, thrips, cutworms, stink bugs, screwworms, sawflies, poultry lice, cheese skippers, cheese mites, cluster flies, puss caterpillars, itch mites, and long-tailed mealy bugs. Of cockroaches the book says, "When very abundant, they may also eat human hair, skin, and nails." (The key word, *skin*, is buried.) The full-color pictures show warbled beef and fly-blown gashes, blighted trees and blasted corn, engorged ticks and seething ham, pus-eyed hogs and the wormy nostrils of sheep.

In another book I learn that ten percent of all the world's species are parasitic insects. It is hard to believe. What if you were an inventor, and you made ten percent of your inventions in such a way that they could only work by harassing, disfiguring, or totally destroying the other ninety percent? These things are not well enough known.

There is, for instance, a species of louse for almost every species of everything else. In addition to sucking blood, lice may also eat hair, feathers, the dry scales of moths, and other lice. Birdbanders report that wild birds are universally infested with lice, to each its own. Songbirds often squat in the dust near ant hills and spray themselves with a shower of living ants; it is thought that the formic acid in the ants discourages the presence of lice. "Each species of auk has its own species of louse, found on all individuals examined." The European cuckoo is the sole host to three species of lice, and the glossy ibis to five, each specializing in eating a different part of the host's body. Lice live in the hollow quills of birds' feathers, in wart hog bristles, in Antarctic seals' flippers and pelican pouches.

Fleas are almost as widely distributed as lice, but much more catholic in their choice of hosts. Immature fleas, interestingly, feed almost entirely on the feces of their parents and other adults, while mature fleas live on sucked blood.

Parasitic two-winged insects, such as flies and mosquitos, abound. It is these that cause hippos to live in the mud and frenzied caribou to trample their young. Twenty thousand head of domestic livestock died in Europe from a host of black flies that swarmed from the banks of the Danube in 1923. Some parasitic flies live in the stomachs of horses, zebras, and elephants; others live in the nostrils and eyes of frogs. Some feed on earthworms, snails, and slugs; others attack and successfully pierce mosquitos already engorged on stolen blood. Still others live on such delicate fare as the brains of ants, the blood of nestling songbirds, or the fluid in the wings of lacewings and butterflies.

The lives of insects and their parasites are horribly entwined. The usual story is that the larva of the parasite eats the other insect alive in any of several stages and degrees of consciousness. It is above all parasitic *Hymenoptera*—which for the sake of simplicity I shall call wasps—that specialize in this behavior. Some species of wasps are so "practiced" as parasites that the female will etch a figure-eight design on the egg of another insect in which she has just laid her egg, and other wasps will avoid ovipositing on those marked, already parasitized eggs. There are over one hundred thousand species of parasitic wasps, so that, although many life histories are known, many others are still mysterious. British entomologist R. R. Askew says, "The field is wide open, the prospect inviting." The field may be wide open, but—although most of my favorite entomologists seem to revel in these creatures—the prospect is, to me at least, scarcely inviting.

Consider this story of Edwin Way Teale's. He brought a monarch butterfly caterpillar inside to photograph just as it was about to pupate. The pale green caterpillar had hung itself upside-down from a leaf, as monarch caterpillars have done from time immemorial, in the form of a letter J.

"All that night it remained as it was. The next morning, at eight o'clock, I noticed that the curve in the 'J' had become shallower. Then, suddenly, as though a cord within had been severed, the larva straightened out and hung limp. Its skin was baggy and lumpy. It began to heave as the lumps within pushed and moved. At 9:30 A.M., the first of the six white, fat-bodied grubs appeared through the skin of the caterpillar. Each was about three eighths of an inch in length." This was the work of a parasitic wasp.

There is a parasitic wasp that travels on any adult female praying mantis, feeding on her body wherever she goes. When the mantis lays her eggs, the wasp lays hers, inside the frothy mass of bubbles before it hardens, so that the early-hatching wasp larvae emerge inside the case to eat the developing mantis eggs. Others eat cockroach eggs, ticks, mites, and houseflies. Many seek out and lay eggs on the caterpillars of butterflies and moths; sometimes they store paralyzed, living caterpillars, on which eggs have been laid, in underground burrows where they stay "fresh" for as long as nine months. Askew, who is apparently very alert, says, "The mass of yellowish cocoons of the braconid *Apanteles glomeratus* beneath the shrivelled remains of a large white butterfly caterpillar are a familiar sight."

There are so many parasitic wasps that some parasitic wasps have parasitic wasps. One startled entomologist, examining the gall made by a vegetarian oak gall wasp, found parasitism of the fifth order. This means that he found the remains of an oak gall wasp which had a parasitic wasp which had another which had another which had another which had another, if I count it aright.

Other insect orders also include fascinating parasites. Among true bugs are bed-bugs, insects that parasitize dozens of species of bats, and those that parasitize bed-bugs. Parasitic beetles as larvae prey on other insects, and as adults on bees and kangaroos. There is a blind beetle that lives on beavers. The cone-nose bug, or kissing bug, bites the lips of sleeping people, sucking blood and injecting an excruciating toxin.

There is an insect order that consists entirely of parasitic insects called, singly and collectively, stylops, which is interesting because of the grotesquerie of its form and its effects. Stylops parasitize divers other insects such as leaf hoppers, ants, bees, and wasps. The female spends her entire life inside the body of her host, with only the tip of her bean-shaped body protruding. She is a formless lump, having no wings, legs, eyes, or antennae; her vestigial mouth and anus are tiny, degenerate, and nonfunctional. She absorbs food—her host—through the skin of her abdomen, which is "inflated, white, and soft."

The sex life of a stylops is equally degenerate. The female has a wide, primitive orifice called a "brood canal" near her vestigial mouthparts, out in the open air. The male inserts his sperm into the brood canal, whence it flows into her disorganized body and fertilizes the eggs that are floating freely there. The hatched larvae find their way to the brood canal and emerge into the "outside world."

The unfortunate insects on which the stylops feed, although they live normal life spans, frequently undergo inexplicable changes. Their colors brighten. The gonads of males and females are "destroyed," and they not only lose their secondary sexual characteristics, they actually acquire those of the opposite sex. This happens especially to bees, in which the differences between the sexes are pronounced. "A stylopsised insect," says Askew, "may sometimes be described as an intersex."

Finally, completing this whirlwind survey of parasitic insects, there are, I was surprised to learn, certain parasitic moths. One moth caterpillar occurs regularly in the *horns* of African ungulates. One adult, winged moth lives on the skin secretions between the hairs of the fur of the three-fingered sloth. Another adult moth sucks mammal blood in southeast Asia. Last of all, there are the many eye-moths, which feed as winged adults about the open eyes of domestic cattle, sucking blood, pus, and tears.

Let me repeat that these parasitic insects comprise ten percent of all known animal species. How can this be understood? Certainly we give our infants the wrong idea about their fellow creatures in the world. Teddy bears should come with tiny stuffed bear-lice; ten percent of all

baby bibs and rattles sold should be adorned with colorful
blowflies, maggots, and screw-worms. What kind of devil's
tithe do we pay? What percentage of the world's species
that are *not* insects are parasitic? Could it be, counting bacteria and viruses, that we live in a world in which half the
creatures are running from—or limping from—the other
half?

The creator is no puritan. A creature need not work for a
living; creatures may simply steal and suck and be blessed
for all that with a share—an enormous share—of the sunlight and air. There is something that profoundly fails to
be exuberant about these crawling, translucent lice and
white, fat-bodied grubs, but there is an almost manic
exuberance about a creator who turns them out, creature
after creature, and sets them buzzing and lurking and flying and swimming about. These parasites are our companions
at life, wending their dim, unfathomable ways into the
tender tissues of their living hosts, searching as we are
simply for food, for energy to grow and breed, to fly or
creep on the planet, adding more shapes to the texture of
intricacy and more life to the universal dance.

Parasitism: this itch, this gasp in the lung, this coiled
worm in the gut, hatching egg in the sinew, warble-hole in
the hide—is a sort of rent, paid by all creatures who live
in the real world with us now. It is not an extortionary
rent: Wouldn't you pay it, don't you, a little blood from the
throat and wrists for the taste of the air? Ask the turtle.
True, for some creatures it is a slow death; for others, like
the stylopsised bee, it is a strange, transfigured life. For
most of us Western humans directly it is a pinprick or
scabrous itch here and there from a world we learned early
could pinch, and no surprise. Or it is the black burgeoning
of disease, the dank baptismal lagoon into which we are

dipped by blind chance many times over against our wishes, until one way or another we die. Chomp. It is the thorn in the flesh of the world, another sign, if any be needed, that the world is actual and fringed, pierced here and there, and through and through, with the toothed conditions of time and the mysterious, coiled spring of death.

Outright predators, of course, I understand. I am among them. There is no denying that the feats of predators can be just as gruesome as those of the unlovely parasites: the swathing and sipping of trapped hummingbirds by barn spiders, the occasional killing and eating of monkeys by chimpanzees. If I were to eat as the delicate ladybug eats, I would go through in just nine days the entire population of Boys Town. Nevertheless, the most rapacious lurk and charge of any predator is not nearly so sinister as the silent hatching of barely visible, implanted eggs. With predators, at least you have a chance.

One night this summer I had gone looking for muskrats, and was waiting on the long pedestrian bridge over the widest part of the creek. No muskrat came, but a small event occurred in a spider's web strung from the lower rung of the bridge's handrail. As I watched, a tiny pale-green insect flew directly into the spider's web. It jerked violently, bringing the spider charging. But the fragile insect, which was no larger than a fifth of the spider's abdomen, extricated itself from the gluey strands in a flurry, dropped in a deadfall to the hard bridge surface a foot below, stood, shook itself, and flew away. I felt as I felt on the way back from lobar pneumonia, stuffed with penicillin and taking a few steps outside: *vive la chance.*

Recently I have been keeping an informal list of the ones that got away, of living creatures I have seen in various states of disarray. It started with spiders. I used to see a number of daddy-longlegs, or harvestmen, in the summer, and I got in the idle habit of counting their legs. It didn't take me long to notice that hardly ever did an adult of any size cross my path which was still hitting on all eight cylinders. Most had seven legs, some had six. Even in the house I noticed that the larger spiders tended to be missing a leg or two.

Then last September I was walking across a gravel path in full sunlight, when I nearly stepped on a grasshopper. I poked its leg with a twig to see it hop, but no hop came. So I crouched down low on my hands and knees, and sure enough, her swollen ovipositor was sunk into the gravel. She was pulsing faintly—with a movement not nearly so strained as the egg-laying mantis's was—and her right antenna was broken off near the base. She'd been around. I thought of her in the Lucas meadow, too, where so many grasshoppers leaped about me. One of those was very conspicuously lacking one of its big, springlike hind legs—a grasslunger. It seemed to move fairly well from here to there, but then of course I didn't know where it had been aiming.

Nature seems to catch you by the tail. I think of all the butterflies I have seen whose torn hind wings bore the jagged marks of birds' bills. There were four or five tiger swallowtails missing one of their tails, and a fritillary missing two thirds of a hind wing. The birds, too, who make up the bulk of my list, always seem to have been snatched at from behind, except for the killdeer I saw just yesterday, who was missing all of its toes; its slender shank ended in a smooth, gray knob. Once I saw a swallowtailed sparrow, who on second look proved to be a sparrow from whose tail the central wedge of feathers had been torn. I've seen a completely tailless sparrow, a tailless robin, and a tailless grackle. Then my private list ends with one bob-tailed and one tailless squirrel, and a muskrat kit whose tail bore a sizeable nick near the spine.

The testimony of experts bears out the same point: it's rough out there. Gerald Durrell, defending the caging of animals in well-kept zoos, says that the animals he collects from the wild are all either ridden with parasites, recovering from various wounds, or both. Howard Ensign Evans finds the butterflies in his neck of the woods as tattered as I do. A southwest Virginia naturalist noted in his journal for April, 1896, "Mourning-cloaks are plentiful but broken, having lived through the winter." Trappers have a hard time finding unblemished skins. Cetologists photograph the scarred hides of living whales, striated with gashes as long as my body, and hilly with vast colonies of crustaceans called whale lice.

Finally, Paul Siple, the Antarctic explorer and scientist, writes of the Antarctic crab-eater seal, which lives in the pack ice off the continent: "One seldom finds a sleek silvery adult crab-eater that does not bear ugly scars—or two-foot long parallel slashes—on each side of its body, received when it managed somehow to wriggle out of the jaws of a killer whale that had seized it."

I think of those crab-eater seals, and the jaws of the killer whales lined with teeth that are, according to Siple, "as large as bananas." How did they get away? How did not one or two, but most of them get away? Of course any predator that decimates its prey will go hungry, as will any parasite that kills its host species. Predator and prey offenses and defenses (and fecundity is a defense) usually operate in such a way that both populations are fairly balanced, stable in the middle as it were, and frayed and nibbled at the edges, like a bitten apple that still bears its seeds. Healthy caribou can outrun a pack of wolves; the wolves cull the diseased, old, and injured, who stray behind the herd. All this goes without saying. But it is truly startling to realize how on the very slender bridge of chance some of the most "efficient" predators operate. Wolves literally starve to death in valleys teeming with game. How many crab-eater seals can one killer whale *miss* in a lifetime?

Still, it is to the picture of the "sleek silvery" crab-eater seals that I return, seals drawn up by scientists from the Antarctic ice pack, seals bearing again and again the long gash marks of unthinkable teeth. Any way you look at it, from the point of view of the whale or the seal or the crab, from the point of view of the mosquito or copperhead or frog or dragonfly or minnow or rotifer, it is chomp or fast.

III

It is chomp or fast. Earlier this evening I brought in a handful of the gnawed mock-orange hedge and cherry tree leaves; they are uncurling now, limp and bluish, on the top of this desk. They didn't escape, but their time was almost up anyway. Already outside a corky ring of tissue is thickening around the base of each leaf stem, strangling each leaf one by one. The summer is old. A gritty, colorless dust cakes the melons and squashes, and worms fatten within on the bright, sweet flesh. The world is festering with suppurating sores. Where is the good, whole fruit? The world "Hath really neither joy, nor love, nor light,/Nor certitude, nor peace, nor help for pain." I've been there, seen it, done it, I suddenly think, and the world is old, a hungry old man, fatigued and broken past mending. Have I walked too much, aged beyond my years? I see the copperhead shining new on a rock altar over a fetid pool where a forest should grow. I see the knob-footed killdeer, the tattered butterflies and birds, the snapping turtle festooned with black leeches. There are the flies that make a wound, the flies that find a wound, and a hungry world that won't wait till I'm decently dead.

"In nature," wrote Huston Smith, "the emphasis is in what is rather than what ought to be." I learn this lesson in a new way every day. It must be, I think tonight, that in a certain sense only the newborn in this world are whole, that as adults we are expected to be, and necessarily, somewhat nibbled. It's par for the course. Physical wholeness is not something we have barring accident; it is itself accidental, an accident of infancy, like a baby's fontanel or the egg-tooth on a hatchling. Are the five-foot silver eels that migrate as adults across meadows by night actually scarred with the bill marks of herons, flayed by the sharp teeth of bass? I think of the beautiful sharks I saw from a shore, hefted and held aloft in a light-shot wave. Were those sharks sliced with scars, were there mites in their hides and worms in their hearts? Did the mockingbird that plunged from the rooftop, folding its wings, bear in its buoyant quills a host of sucking lice? Is our birthright and heritage to be, like Jacob's cattle on which the life of a nation was founded, "ring-streaked, speckled, and spotted" not with the spangling marks of a grace like beauty rained down from eternity, but with the blotched assaults and quarryings of time? "We are all of us clocks," says Eddington, "whose faces tell the passing years." The young man proudly names his scars for his lover; the old man alone before a mirror erases his scars with his eyes and sees himself whole.

Through the window over my desk comes a drone, drone, drone, the weary winding of cicadas' horns. If I were blasted by a meteorite, I think, I could call it blind chance and die cursing. But we live creatures are eating each other, who have done us no harm. We're all in this Mason jar together, snapping at anything that moves. If the pneumococcus bacteria had flourished more vitally, if it had colonized my other lung successfully, living and being fruitful after its created kind, then I would have died my death, and my last ludicrous work would have been an Easter egg, an Easter egg painted with beaver and deer, an Easter egg that was actually in fact, even as I painted it and the creatures burgeoned in my lung, fertilized. It is ridiculous. What happened to manna? Why doesn't everything eat manna, into what rare air did the manna dissolve that we harry the free live things, each other?

An Eskimo shaman said, "Life's greatest danger lies in the fact that men's food consists entirely of souls." Did he say it to the harmless man who gave him tuberculosis, or to the one who gave him tar paper and sugar for wolfskin and seal? I wonder how many bites I have taken, parasite and predator, from family and friends; I wonder how long I will be permitted the luxury of this relative solitude. Out here on the rocks the people don't mean to grapple, to crush and starve and betray, but with all the good will in the world, we do, there's no other way. We want it; we take it out of each other's hides; we chew the bitter skins the rest of our lives.

But the sight of the leeched turtle and the frayed flighted things means something else. I think of the green insect shaking the web from its wings, and of the whale-scarred crab-eater seals. They demand a certain respect. The only way I can reasonably talk about all this is to address you directly and frankly as a fellow survivor. Here we so incontrovertibly are. *Sub specie aeternitatis* this may all look different, from inside the blackened gut beyond the narrow craw, but now, although we hear the buzz in our ears and the crashing of jaws at our heels, we can look around as those who are nibbled but unbroken, from the shimmering vantage of the living. Here may not be the cleanest, newest place, but that clean timeless place that vaults on either side of this one is noplace at all. "Your fathers did eat manna in the wilderness, and are dead." There are no more chilling, invigorating words than these of Christ's, "Your fathers did eat manna in the wilderness, and are dead."

Alaskan Eskimos believe in many souls. An individual soul has a series of afterlives, returning again and again to earth, but only rarely as a human. "Since its appearances as a human being are rare, it is thought a great privilege to be here as we are, with human companions who also, in this reincarnation, are privileged and therefore greatly to be respected." To be here as we are. I love the little facts, the ten percents, the fact of the real and legged borers, the cuticle-covered, secretive grubs, the blister beetles, blood flukes and mites. But there are plenty of ways to pile the facts, and it is easy to overlook some things. "The fact is," said Van Gogh, "the fact is that we are painters in real life, and the important thing is to breathe as hard as ever we can breathe."

So I breathe. I breathe at the open window above my desk, and a moist fragrance assails me from the gnawed leaves of the growing mock orange. This air is as intricate as the light that filters through forested mountain ridges and into my kitchen window; this sweet air is the breath of leafy lungs more rotted than mine; it has sifted through the serrations of many teeth. I have to love these tatters. And I must confess that the thought of this old yard breathing alone in the dark turns my mind to something else.

I cannot in all honesty call the world old when I've seen it new. On the other hand, neither will honesty permit me suddenly to invoke certain experiences of newness and beauty as binding, sweeping away all knowledge. But I am thinking now of the tree with the lights in it, the cedar in the yard by the creek I saw transfigured.

That the world is old and frayed is no surprise; that the world could ever become new and whole beyond uncertainty was, and is, such a surprise that I find myself referring all subsequent kinds of knowledge to it. And it suddenly occurs to me to wonder: were the twigs of the cedar I saw really bloated with galls? They probably were; they almost surely were. I have seen those "cedar apples" swell from that cedar's green before and since: reddish-gray, rank, malignant. All right then. But knowledge does not vanquish mystery, or obscure its distant lights. I still now and will tomorrow steer by what happened that day, when some undeniably new spirit roared down the air, bowled me over, and turned on the lights. I stood on grass like air, air like lightning coursed in my blood, floated my bones, swam in my teeth. I've been there, seen it, been done by it. I know what happened to the cedar tree, I saw the cells in the cedar tree pulse charged like wings beating praise. Now, it would be too facile to pull everything out of the hat and say that mystery vanquishes knowledge. Although my vision of the world of the spirit would not be altered a jot if the cedar had been purulent with galls, those galls actually do matter to my understanding of this world. Can I say then that corruption is one of beauty's deep-blue speckles, that the frayed and nibbled fringe of the world is a tallith, a prayer shawl, the intricate garment of beauty? It is very tempting, but I honestly cannot. But I can, however, affirm that corruption is not beauty's very heart. And I can I think call the vision of the cedar and the knowledge of these wormy quarryings twin fiords cutting into the granite cliffs of mystery, and say that the new is always present simultaneously with the old, however hidden. The tree with the lights in it does not go out; that light still shines on an old world, now feebly, now bright.

I am a frayed and nibbled survivor in a fallen world, and I am getting along. I am aging and eaten and have done my share of eating too. I am not washed and beautiful, in control of a shining world in which everything fits, but instead am wandering awed about on a splintered wreck I've come to care for, whose gnawed trees breathe a delicate air, whose bloodied and scarred creatures are my dearest companions, and whose beauty beats and shines not *in* its imperfections but overwhelmingly in spite of them, under the wind-rent clouds, upstream and down. Simone Weil says simply, "Let us love the country of here below. It is real; it offers resistance to love."

I am a sacrifice bound with cords to the horns of the world's rock altar, waiting for worms. I take a deep breath, I open my eyes. Looking, I see there are worms in the horns of the altar like live maggots in amber, there are shells of worms in the rock and moths flapping at my eyes. A wind from noplace rises. A sense of the real exults me; the cords loose; I walk on my way.

CHAPTER 14

Northing

I

IN SEPTEMBER the birds were quiet. They were molting in the valley, the mockingbird in the spruce, the sparrow in the mock orange, the doves in the cedar by the creek. Everywhere I walked the ground was littered with shed feathers, long, colorful primaries and shaftless white down. I garnered this weightless crop in pockets all month long, and inserted the feathers one by one into the frame of a wall mirror. They're still there; I look in the mirror as though I'm wearing a ceremonial headdress, inside-out.

In October the great restlessness came, the *Zugunruhe*, the restlessness of birds before migration. After a long, unseasonable hot spell, one morning dawned suddenly cold. The birds were excited, stammering new songs all day long.

Titmice, which had hidden in the leafy shade of mountains all summer, perched on the gutter; chickadees staged a conventicle in the locusts, and a sparrow, acting very strange, hovered like a hummingbird inches above a roadside goldenrod.

I watched at the window; I watched at the creek. A new wind lifted the hair on my arms. The cold light was coming and going between oversized, careening clouds; patches of blue, like a ragged flock of protean birds, shifted and stretched, flapping and racing from one end of the sky to the other. Despite the wind, the air was moist; I smelled the rich vapor of loam around my face and wondered again why all that death—all those rotten leaves that one layer down are black sops roped in white webs of mold, all those millions of dead summer insects—didn't smell worse. When the wind quickened, a stranger, more subtle scent leaked from beyond the mountains, a disquieting fragrance of wet bark, salt marsh, and mud flat.

The creek's water was still warm from the hot spell. It bore floating tulip leaves as big as plates, and sinking tulip leaves, downstream, and out of sight. I watched the leaves fall on water, first on running water, and then on still. It was as different as visiting Cornwall, and visiting Corfu. But those winds and flickering lights and the mad cries of jays stirred me. I was wishing: colder, colder than this, colder than anything, and let the year hurry down!

The day before, in a dry calm, all the summer's ants took wing and swarmed, shining at the front door, at the back door, all up and down the road. I tried in vain to induce them to light on my upraised arm. Now at the slow part of the creek I suddenly saw migrating goldfinches in flocks hurling themselves from willow to willow over the reeds. They ascended in a sudden puff and settled, spreading slowly, like a blanket shaken over a bed, till some impulse tossed them up again, twenty and thirty together in sprays, and they tilted their wings, veered, folded, and spattered down.

I followed the goldfinches downstream until the bank beside me rose to a cliff and blocked the light on the willows and water. Above the cliff rose the Adams' woods, and in the cliff nested—according not only to local observation but also to the testimony of the county agricultural agent—hundreds of the area's copperheads. This October restlessness was worse than any April's or May's. In the spring the wish to wander is partly composed of an unnamable irritation, born of long inactivity; in the fall the impulse is more pure, more inexplicable, and more urgent. I could use some danger, I suddenly thought, so I abruptly abandoned the creek to its banks and climbed the cliff. I wanted some height, and I wanted to see the woods.

The woods were as restless as birds.

I stood under tulips and ashes, maples, sourwood, sassafras, locusts, catalpas, and oaks. I let my eyes spread and unfix, screening out all that was not vertical motion, and I saw only leaves in the air—or rather, since my mind was also unfixed, vertical trails of yellow color-patches falling from nowhere to nowhere. Mysterious streamers of color unrolled silently all about me, distant and near. Some color chips made the descent violently; they wrenched from side to side in a series of diminishing swings, as if willfully fighting the fall with all the tricks of keel and glide they could muster. Others spun straight down in tight, suicidal circles.

Tulips had cast their leaves on my path, flat and bright as doubloons. I passed under a sugar maple that stunned me by its elegant unself-consciousness: it was as if a man on fire were to continue calmly sipping tea.

In the deepest part of the woods was a stand of ferns. I had just been reading in Donald Culross Peattie that the so-called "seed" of ferns was formerly thought to bestow the gift of invisibility on its bearer, and that Genghis Khan wore such a seed in his ring, "and by it understood the speech of birds." If I were invisible, might I also be small, so that I could be borne by winds, spreading my body like a sail, like a vaulted leaf, to anyplace at all? Mushrooms erupted through the forest mold, the fly amanita in various stages of thrust and spread, some big brown mushrooms rounded and smooth as loaves, and some eerie purple ones I'd never noticed before, the color of Portuguese men-of-war, murex, a deep-sea, pressurized color, as if the earth heavy with trees and rocks had pressed and leached all other hues away.

A squirrel suddenly appeared, and, eying me over his shoulder, began eating a mushroom. Squirrels and box turtles are immune to the poison in mushrooms, so it is not safe to eat a mushroom on the grounds that squirrels eat it. This squirrel plucked the nibbled mushroom cap from its base and, holding it Ubangi-like in his mouth, raced up the trunk of an oak. Then I moved, and he went into his tail-furling threat. I can't imagine what predator this routine would frighten, or even slow. Or did he take me for another male squirrel? It was clear that, like a cat, he seemed always to present a large front. But he might have fooled me better by holding still and not letting me see what insubstantial stuff his tail was. He flattened his body against the tree trunk and stretched himself into the shape of a giant rectangle. By some trick his legs barely protruded at the corners, like a flying squirrel's. Then he made a wave run down his tail held low against the trunk, the same flicking wave, over and over, and he never took his eyes from mine. Next, frightened more—or emboldened?—he ran up to a limb, still mouthing his mushroom cap, and, crouching close to the trunk, presented a solid target, coiled. He bent his tail high and whipped it furiously, with repeated snaps, as if a piece of gluey tape were stuck to the tip.

When I left the squirrel to cache his mushroom in peace, I almost stepped on another squirrel, who was biting the base of his tail, his flank, and scratching his shoulder with a hind paw. A chipmunk was streaking around with the usual calamitous air. When he saw me he stood to investigate, tucking his front legs tightly against his breast, so that only his paws were visible, and he looked like a supplicant modestly holding his hat.

The woods were a rustle of affairs. Woolly bears, those orange-and-black-banded furry caterpillars of the Isabella moth, were on the move. They crossed my path in every direction; they would climb over my foot, my finger, urgently seeking shelter. If a skunk finds one, he rolls it over and over on the ground, very delicately, brushing off the long hairs before he eats it. There seemed to be a parade of walking sticks that day, too; I must have seen five or six of them, or the same one five or six times, which kept hitching a ride on my pants leg. One entomologist says that walking sticks, along with monarch butterflies, are able to feign death—although I don't know how you could determine if a walking stick was feigning death or twigginess. At any rate, the female walking stick is absolutely casual about her egg-laying, dribbling out her eggs "from wherever she happens to be, and they drop willy-nilly"—which I suppose might mean that my pants and I were suddenly in the walking-stick business.

I heard a clamor in the underbrush beside me, a rustle of an animal's approach. It sounded as though the animal was about the size of a bobcat, a small bear, or a large snake. The commotion stopped and started, coming ever nearer.

The agent of all this ruckus proved to be, of course, a towhee.

The more I see of these bright birds—with black backs, white tail bars, and rufous patches on either side of their white breasts—the more I like them. They are not even faintly shy. They are everywhere, in treetops and on the ground. Their song reminds me of a child's neighborhood rallying cry—ee-ock-ee—with a heart-felt warble at the end. But it is their call that is especially endearing. The towhee has the brass and grace to call, simply and clearly, "tweet." I know of no other bird that stoops to literal tweeting.

The towhee never saw me. It crossed the path and kicked its way back into the woods, cutting a wide swath in the leaf litter like a bulldozer, and splashing the air with clods.

The bark of trees was cool to my palm. I saw a hairy woodpecker beating his skull on a pine, and a katydid dying on a stone.

I could go. I could simply angle off the path, take one step after another, and be on my way. I could walk to Point Barrow, Mount McKinley, Hudson's Bay. My summer jacket is put away; my winter jacket is warm.

In autumn the winding passage of ravens from the north heralds the great fall migration of caribou. The shaggy-necked birds spread their wing tips to the skin of convection currents rising, and hie them south. The great deer meet herd on herd in arctic and subarctic valleys, milling and massing and gathering force like a waterfall, till they pour across the barren grounds wide as a tidal wave. Their coats are new and fine. Their thin spring coats—which had been scraped off in great hunks by the southern forests and were riddled with blackfly and gadfly stings, warble and botfly maggots—are gone, and a lustrous new pelage has appeared, a luxurious brown fur backed by a plush layer of hollow hairs that insulate and waterproof. Four inches of creamy fat cover even their backs. A loose cartilage in their fetlocks makes their huge strides click, mile upon mile over the tundra south to the shelter of trees, and you can hear them before they've come and after they've gone, rumbling like rivers, ticking like clocks.

The Eskimos' major caribou hunt is in the fall, when the deer are fat and their hides thick. If some whim or weather shifts the northern caribou into another valley, some hidden, unexpected valley, then even to this day some inland Eskimo tribes may altogether starve.

Up on the Arctic Ocean coasts, Eskimos dry the late summer's fish on drying racks, to use throughout the winter as feed for dogs. The newly forming sea ice is elastic and flexible. It undulates without cracking as the roiling sea swells and subsides, and it bends and sags under the Eskimos' weight as they walk, spreading leviathan ripples out toward the horizon, so that they seem to be walking and bouncing on the fragile sheath of the world's balloon. During these autumn days Eskimo adults and children alike play at cat's cradle, a game they have always known. The intricate string patterns looped from their fingers were thought to "tangle the sun" and so "delay its disappearance." Later when the sun sets for the winter, children will sled down any snowy slope, using as sleds frozen seal embryos pulled with thongs through the nose.

These northings drew me, present northings, past northings, the thought of northings. In the literature of arctic exploration, the talk is of northing. An explorer might scrawl in his tattered journal, "Latitude 82° 15′ N. We accomplished 20 miles of northing today, in spite of the shifting pack." Shall I go northing? My legs are long.

A skin-colored sandstone ledge beside me was stained

with pokeberry juice, like an altar bloodied. The edges of the scarlet were dissolved, faded to lymph like small blood from a wound. As I looked, a maple leaf suddenly screeched across the rock, arched crabwise on its points, and a yellow-spotted dog appeared from noplace, bearing in its jaws the leg of a deer. The hooves of the deer leg were pointed like a dancer's toes. I have felt dead deer legs before; some local butchers keep them as weapons. They are greaseless and dry; I can feel the little bones. The dog was coming towards me on the path. I spoke to him and stepped aside; he loped past, looking neither to the right nor the left.

In a final, higher part of the woods, some of the trees were black and gray, leafless, but wrapped in fresh green vines. The path was a fairway of new gold leaves strewn at the edges with bright vines and dotted with dark green seedlings pushing up through the leaf cover. One seedling spruce grew from a horse's hoofmark deep in dried mud.

There was a little hollow in the woods, broad, like a flat soupbowl, with grass on the ground. This was the forest pasture of the white mare Itch. Water had collected in a small pool five feet across, in which gold leaves floated, and the water reflected the half-forgotten, cloud-whipped sky. To the right was a stand of slender silver-barked tulip saplings with tall limbless trunks leaning together, leafless. In the general litter and scramble of these woods, the small grazed hollow looked very old, like the site of druidical rites, or like a theatrical set, with the pool at center stage, and the stand of silver saplings the audience in thrall. There at the pool lovers would meet in various guises, and there Bottom in his ass's head would bleat at the reflection of the moon.

I started home. And one more event occurred that day, one more confrontation with restless life bearing past me.

I approached a long, slanting mown field near the house. A flock of forty robins had commandeered the area, and I watched them from a fringe of trees. I see robins in flocks only in the fall. They were spaced evenly on the grass, ten yards apart. They looked like a marching band with each member in place, but facing in every direction. Distributed among them were the fledglings from summer's last brood, young robins still mottled on the breast, embarking on their first trip to unknown southern fields. At any given moment as I watched, half of the robins were on the move, sloping forward in a streamlined series of hops.

I stepped into the field, and they all halted. They stopped short, drew up, and looked at me, every one. I stopped too, suddenly as self-conscious as if I were before a firing squad. What are you going to do? I looked over the field, at all those cocked heads and black eyes. I'm staying here. You all go on. I'm staying here.

A kind of northing is what I wish to accomplish, a single-minded trek toward that place where any shutter left open to the zenith at night will record the wheeling of all the sky's stars as a pattern of perfect, concentric circles. I seek a reduction, a shedding, a sloughing off.

At the seashore you often see a shell, or fragment of a shell, that sharp sands and surf have thinned to a wisp. There is no way you can tell what kind of shell it had been, what creature it had housed; it could have been a whelk or a scallop, a cowrie, limpet, or conch. The animal is long since dissolved, and its blood spread and thinned in the general sea. All you hold in your hand is a cool shred of shell, an inch long, pared so thin it passes a faint pink light, and almost as flexible as a straight razor. It is an essence, a smooth condensation of the air, a curve. I long for the North where unimpeded winds would hone me to such a pure slip of bone. But I'll not go northing this year. I'll stalk that floating pole and frigid air by waiting here. I wait on bridges; I wait, struck, on forest paths and meadow's fringes, hilltops and banksides, day in and day out, and I receive a southing as a gift. The North washes down the mountains like a waterfall, like a tidal wave, and pours across the valley; it comes to me. It sweetens the persimmons and numbs the last of the crickets and hornets; it fans the flames of the forest maples, bows the meadow's seeded grasses, and pokes its chilling fingers under the leaf litter, thrusting the springtails and earthworms, the sowbugs and beetle grubs deeper into the earth. The sun heaves to the south by day, and at night wild Orion emerges looming like the Specter of the Brocken over Dead Man Mountain. Something is already here, and more is coming.

II

A few days later the monarchs hit. I saw one, and then another, and then others all day long, before I consciously understood that I was witnessing a migration, and it wasn't until another two weeks had passed that I realized the enormity of what I had seen.

Each of these butterflies, the fruit of two or three broods of this summer, had hatched successfully from one of those emerald cases that Teale's caterpillar had been about to form when the parasitic larvae snapped it limp, eating their way out of its side. They had hatched, many of them, just before a thunderstorm, when winds lifted the silver leaves of trees and birds sought the shelter of shrubbery, uttering cries. They were butterflies, going south to the Gulf states or farther, and some of them had come from Hudson's Bay.

Monarchs were everywhere. They skittered and bobbed,

rested in the air, lolled on the dust—but with none of their usual insouciance. They had but one unwearying thought: South. I watched from my study window: three, four . . . eighteen, nineteen, one every few seconds, and some in tandem. They came fanning straight towards my window from the northwest, and from the northeast, materializing from behind the tips of high hemlocks, where Polaris hangs by night. They appeared as Indian horsemen appear in movies: first dotted, then massed, silent, at the rim of a hill.

Each monarch butterfly had a brittle black body and deep orange wings limned and looped in black bands. A monarch at rest looks like a fleck of tiger, stilled and wide-eyed. A monarch in flight looks like an autumn leaf with a will, vitalized and cast upon the air from which it seems to suck some thin sugar of energy, some leaf-life or sap. As each one climbed up the air outside my window, I could see the more delicate, ventral surfaces of its wings, and I had a sense of bunched legs and straining thorax, but I could never focus well into the flapping and jerking before it vaulted up past the window and out of sight over my head.

I walked out and saw a monarch do a wonderful thing: it climbed a hill without twitching a muscle. I was standing at the bridge over Tinker Creek, at the southern foot of a very steep hill. The monarch beat its way beside me over the bridge at eye level, and then, flailing its wings exhaustedly, ascended straight up in the air. It rose vertically to the enormous height of a bankside sycamore's crown. Then, fixing its wings at a precise angle, it glided *up* the steep road, losing altitude extremely slowly, climbing by checking its fall, until it came to rest at a puddle in front of the house at the top of the hill.

I followed. It panted, skirmished briefly westward, and then, returning to the puddle, began its assault on the house.

It struggled almost straight up the air next to the two-story brick wall, and then scaled the roof. Wasting no effort, it followed the roof's own slope, from a distance of two inches. Puff, and it was out of sight. I wondered how many more hills and houses it would have to climb before it could rest. From the force of its will it would seem it could flutter through walls.

Monarchs are "tough and powerful, as butterflies go." They fly over Lake Superior without resting; in fact, observers there have discovered a curious thing. Instead of flying directly south, the monarchs crossing high over the water take an inexplicable turn towards the east. Then when they reach an invisible point, they all veer south again. Each successive swarm repeats this mysterious dogleg movement, year after year. Entomologists actually think that the butterflies might be "remembering" the position of a long-gone, looming glacier. In another book I read the geologists think that Lake Superior marks the site of the highest mountain that ever existed on this continent. I don't know. I'd like to see it. Or I'd like to be it, to feel when to turn. At night on land migrating monarchs slumber on certain trees, hung in festoons with wings folded together, thick on the trees and shaggy as bearskin.

Monarchs have always been assumed to taste terribly bitter, because of the acrid milkweed on which the caterpillars feed. You always run into monarchs and viceroys when you read about mimicry: viceroys look enough like monarchs that keen-eyed birds who have tasted monarchs once will avoid the viceroys as well. New studies indicate that milkweed-fed monarchs are not so much evil-tasting as literally nauseating, since milkweed contains "heart poisons similar to digitalis" that make the bird ill. Personally, I like an experiment performed by an entomologist with real spirit.

He had heard all his life, as I have, that monarchs taste unforgettably bitter, so he tried some. "To conduct what was in fact a field experiment the doctor first went South, and he ate a number of monarchs in the field. . . . The monarch butterfly, Dr. Urquhart learned, has no more flavor than dried toast." Dried toast? It was hard for me, throughout the monarch migration, in the middle of all that beauty and real splendor, to fight down the thought that what I was really seeing in the air was a vast and fluttering tea tray for shut-ins.

It is easy to coax a dying or exhausted butterfly onto your finger. I saw a monarch walking across a gas station lot; it was walking south. I placed my index finger in its path, and it clambered aboard and let me lift it to my face. Its wings were faded but unmarked by hazard; a veneer of velvet caught the light and hinted at the frailest depth of lapped scales. It was a male; his legs clutching my finger were short and atrophied; they clasped my finger with a spread fragility, a fineness as of some low note of emotion or pure strain of spirit, scarcely perceived. And I knew that those feet were actually tasting me, sipping with sensitive organs the vapor of my finger's skin: butterflies taste with their feet. All the time he held me, he opened and closed his glorious wings, senselessly, as if sighing.

The closing of his wings fanned an almost imperceptible redolence at my face, and I leaned closer. I could barely scent a sweetness, I could almost name it . . . fireflies, sparklers—honeysuckle. He smelled like honeysuckle; I couldn't believe it. I knew that many male butterflies exuded distinctive odors from special scent glands, but I thought that only laboratory instruments could detect those odors compounded of many, many butterflies. I had read a list of the improbable scents of butterflies: sandalwood, chocolate, heliotrope, sweet pea. Now this live creature here on my finger had an odor that even I could sense—this flap actually smelled, this chip that took its temperature from the air like any envelope or hammer, this programmed wisp of spread horn. And he smelled of honeysuckle. Why not caribou hoof or Labrador tea, tundra lichen or dwarf willow, the brine of Hudson's Bay or the vapor of rivers milky with fine-ground glacial silt? This honeysuckle was an odor already only half-remembered, a breath of the summer past, the Lucas cliffs and overgrown fence by Tinker Creek, a drugged sweetness that had almost cloyed on those moisture-laden nights, now refined to a wary trickle in the air, a distillation pure and rare, scarcely known and mostly lost, and heading south.

I walked him across the gas station lot and lowered him into a field. He took to the air, pulsing and gliding; he lighted on sassafras, and I lost him.

For weeks I found paired monarch wings, bodiless, on the grass or on the road. I collected one such wing and freed it of its scales; first I rubbed it between my fingers, and then I stroked it gently with the tip of an infant's silver spoon. What I had at the end of this delicate labor is lying here on this study desk: a kind of resilient scaffolding, like the webbing over a hot-air balloon, black veins stretching the merest something across the nothingness it plies. The integument itself is perfectly transparent; through it I can read the smallest print. It is as thin as the skin peeled from sunburn, and as tough as a parchment of flensed buffalo hide. The butterflies that were eaten here in the valley, leaving us their wings, were, however, few: most lived to follow the valley south.

The migration lasted in full force for five days. For those five days I was inundated, drained. The air was alive and unwinding. Time itself was a scroll unraveled, curved and still quivering on a table or altar stone. The monarchs

clattered in the air, burnished like throngs of pennies, here's
one, and here's one, and more, and more. They flapped and
floundered; they thrust, splitting the air like the keels of
canoes, quickened and fleet. It looked as though the leaves of
the autumn forest had taken flight, and were pouring down
the valley like a waterfall, like a tidal wave, all the leaves of
hardwoods from here to Hudson's Bay. It was as if the
season's color were draining away like lifeblood, as if the year
were molting and shedding. The year was rolling down, and a
vital curve had been reached, the tilt that gives way to headlong rush. And when the monarchs had passed and were
gone, the skies were vacant, the air poised. The dark night
into which the year was plunging was not a sleep but an
awakening, a new and necessary austerity, the sparer climate
for which I longed. The shed trees were brittle and still, the
creek light and cold, and my spirit holding its breath.

III

Before the aurora borealis appears, the sensitive needles
of compasses all over the world are restless for hours, agitat-
ing on their pins in airplanes and ships, trembling in desk
drawers, in attics, in boxes on shelves.

I had a curious dream last night that stirred me. I visited
the house of my childhood, and the basement there was
covered with a fine sifting of snow. I lifted a snow-covered
rug and found underneath it a bound sheaf of ink drawings
I had made when I was six. Next to the basement, but un-
attached to it, extended a prayer tunnel.

The prayer tunnel was a tunnel fully enclosed by solid
snow. It was cylindrical, and its diameter was the height of
a man. Only an Eskimo, and then only very rarely, could
survive in the prayer tunnel. There was, however, no exit

or entrance; but I nevertheless understood that if I—if almost anyone—volunteered to enter it, death would follow after a long and bitter struggle. Inside the tunnel it was killingly cold, and a hollow wind like broadswords never ceased to blow. But there was little breatheable air, and that soon gone. It was utterly without light, and from all eternity it snowed the same fine, unmelting, wind-hurled snow.

I have been reading the apophthegmata, the sayings of fourth- and fifth-century Egyptian desert hermits. Abba Moses said to a disciple, "Go and sit in your cell, and your cell will teach you everything."

A few weeks before the monarch migration I visited Carvin's Cove, a reservoir in a gap between Tinker and Brushy mountains, and there beside the forest path I saw, it occurs to me now, Abba Moses, in the form of an acorn. The acorn was screwing itself into the soil. From a raw split in its husk burst a long white root that plunged like an arrow into the earth. The acorn itself was loose, but the root was fixed: I thought if I could lift the acorn and stand, I would heave the world. Beside the root erupted a greening shoot, and from the shoot spread two furred, serrated leaves, tiny leaves of chestnut oak, the size of two intricate grains of rice. That acorn was pressured, blown, driven down with force and up with furl, making at once a power dive to grit and *grand jeté en l'air*.

Since then the killing frost has struck. If I got lost now on the mountains or in the valley, and acted foolishly, I would be dead of hypothermia and my brain wiped smooth as a plate long before the water in my flesh elongated to crystal slivers that would pierce and shatter the walls of my cells. The harvest is in, the granaries full. The broadleaf trees of the world's forests have cast their various fruits: "Oak, a nut; Sycamore, achenes; California Laurel, a drupe; Maple, a samara; Locust, a legume; Pomegranate, a berry;

Buckeye, a capsule; Apple, a pome." Now the twin leaves of the seedling chestnut oak on the Carvin's Cove path have dried, dropped, and blown; the acorn itself is shrunk and sere. But the sheath of the stem holds water and the white root still delicately sucks, porous and permeable, mute. The death of the self of which the great writers speak is no violent act. It is merely the joining of the great rock heart of the earth in its roll. It is merely the slow cessation of the will's sprints and the intellect's chatter: it is waiting like a hollow bell with stilled tongue. *Fuge, tace, quiesce.* The waiting itself is the thing.

Last year I saw three migrating Canada geese flying low over the frozen duck pond where I stood. I heard a heart-stopping blast of speed before I saw them; I felt the flayed air slap at my face. They thundered across the pond, and back, and back again: I swear I have never seen such speed, such single-mindedness, such flailing of wings. They froze the duck pond as they flew; they rang the air; they disappeared. I think of this now, and my brain vibrates to the blurred bastinado of feathered bone. "Our God shall come," it says in a psalm for Advent, "and shall not keep silence; there shall go before him a consuming fire, and a mighty tempest shall be stirred up round about him." It is the shock I remember. Not only does something come if you wait, but it pours over you like a waterfall, like a tidal wave. You wait in all naturalness without expectation or hope, emptied, translucent, and that which comes rocks and topples you; it will shear, loose, launch, winnow, grind.

I have glutted on richness and welcome hyssop. This distant silver November sky, these sere branches of trees, shed and bearing their pure and secret colors—this is the real world, not the world gilded and pearled. I stand under wiped skies directly, naked, without intercessors. Frost winds have lofted my body's bones with all their restless sprints to an airborne raven's glide. I am buoyed by a calm and effortless longing, an angled pitch of the will, like the set of the wings of the monarch which climbed a hill by falling still.

There is the wave breast of thanksgiving—a catching God's eye with the easy motions of praise—and a time for it. In ancient Israel's rites for a voluntary offering of thanksgiving, the priest comes before the altar in clean linen, empty-handed. Into his hands is placed the breast of the slain unblemished ram of consecration: and he waves it as a wave offering before the Lord. The wind's knife has done its work. Thanks be to God.

CHAPTER 15

The Waters of Separation

"FAIR WEATHER cometh out of the north: with God is
terrible majesty."

Today is the winter solstice. The planet tilts just so to
its star, lists and holds circling in a fixed tension between
veering and longing, and spins helpless, exalted, in and
out of that fleet blazing touch. Last night Orion vaulted
and spread all over the sky, pagan and lunatic, his shoulder
and knee on fire, his sword three suns at the ready—for
what?

267.

And today was fair, hot, even; I woke and my fingers were hot and dry to their own touch, like the skin of a stranger. I stood at the window, the bay window on which one summer a waxen-looking grasshopper had breathed puff puff, and thought, I won't see this year again, not again so innocent; and longing wrapped round my throat like a scarf. "For the Heavenly Father desires that we should see," said Ruysbroeck, "and that is why He is ever saying to our inmost spirit one deep unfathomable word and nothing else." But what is that word? Is this mystery or coyness? A cast-iron bell hung from the arch of my rib cage; when I stirred it rang, or it tolled, a long syllable pulsing ripples up my lungs and down the gritty sap inside my bones, and I couldn't make it out; I felt the voiced vowel like a sigh or a note but I couldn't catch the consonant that shaped it into sense. I wrenched myself from the window. I stepped outside.

Here by the mock-orange hedge was a bee, a honeybee, sprung from its hive by the heat. Instantly I had a wonderful idea. I had recently read that ancient Romans thought that bees were killed by echoes. It seemed a far-fetched and pleasing notion, that a spoken word or falling rock given back by cliffs—that airy nothing which nevertheless bore and spread the uncomprehended impact of something— should stun these sturdy creatures right out of the air. I could put it to the test. It was as good an excuse for a walk as any; it might still the bell, even, or temper it true.

I knew where I could find an echo; I'd have to take my chances on finding another December bee. I tied a sweater around my waist and headed for the quarry. The experiment didn't pan out, eaxactly, but the trip led on to other excursions and vigils up and down the landscape of this brief year's end day.

It was hot; I never needed the sweater. A great tall cloud moved elegantly across an invisible walkway in the upper air, sliding on its flat foot like an enormous proud snail. I smelled silt on the wind, turkey, laundry, leaves . . . my God what a world. There is no accounting for one second of it. On the quarry path through the woods I saw again the discarded aquarium; now, almost a year later, still only one side of the aquarium's glass was shattered. I could plant a terrarium here, I thought; I could transfer the two square feet of forest floor *under* the glass to *above* the glass, framing it, hiding a penny, and saying to passers-by look! look! here is two square feet of the world.

I waited for an hour at the quarry, roving, my eyes filtering the air for flecks, until at last I discovered a bee. It was wandering listlessly among dried weeds on the stony bank where I had sat months ago and watched a mosquito pierce and suck a copperhead on a rock; beyond the bank, fingers of ice touched the green quarry pond in the shade of the sheared bare cliffs beyond. The setup was perfect. Hello! I tried tentatively: Hello! faltered the cliffs under the forest; and did the root tips quiver in the rock? But that is no way to kill a creature, saying hello. Goodbye! I shouted; Goodbye! came back, and the bee drifted unconcerned among the weeds.

It could be, I reasoned, that ancient Roman naturalists knew this fact that has escaped us because it works only in Latin. My Latin is sketchy. *Habeas corpus!* I cried; *Deus absconditus! Veni!* And the rock cliff batted it back: *Veni!* and the bee droned on.

That was that. It was almost noon; the tall cloud was gone. To West Virginia, where it snubbed on a high ridge, snared by trees, and sifted in shards over the side? I watched the bee as long as I could, catching it with my eyes and losing it, until it rose suddenly in the air like a lost balloon and vanished into the forest. I stood alone. I still seemed to hear the unaccustomed sound of my own voice honed to a quaver by rock, thrown back down my throat and cast dying around me, lorn: could that have been heard at Hollins Pond, or behind me, across the creek, up the hill the starlings fly over? Was anybody there to hear? I felt again the bell resounding faint under my ribs. I'm coming, when I can. I quit the quarry, my spurt of exuberance drained, my spirit edgy and taut.

The quarry path parallels Tinker Creek far upstream from my house, and when the woods broke into clearing and pasture, I followed the creek banks down. When I drew near the tear-shaped island, which I had never before approached from this side of the creek, a fence barred my way, a feeble wire horse fence that wobbled across the creek and served me as a sagging bridge to the island. I stood, panting, breathing the frail scent of fresh water and feeling the sun heat my hair.

The December grass on the island was blanched and sere, pale against the dusty boles of sycamores, noisy underfoot. Behind me, the way I had come, rose the pasture belonging to Twilight, a horse of a perpetually different color whose name was originally Midnight, and who one spring startled the neighborhood by becoming brown. Far before me Tinker Mountain glinted and pitched in the sunlight. The Lucas orchard spanned the middle distance, its wan peach limbs swept and poised just so, row upon row, like a stageful of thin innocent dancers who will never be asked to perform; below the orchard rolled the steers' pasture yielding to flood plain fields and finally the sycamore log bridge to the island where in horror I had watched a green frog sucked to a skin and sunk. A fugitive, empty sky vaulted overhead, apparently receding from me the harder I searched its dome for a measure of distance.

Downstream at the island's tip where the giant water bug clasped and ate the living frog, I sat and sucked at my own dry knuckles. It was the way that frog's eyes crumpled. His mouth was a gash of terror; the shining skin of his breast and shoulder shivered once and sagged, reduced to an empty purse; but oh those two snuffed eyes! They crinkled, the comprehension poured out of them as if sense and life had been a mere incidental addition to the idea of eyes, a filling like any jam in a jar that is soon and easily emptied; they flattened, lightless, opaque, and sank. Did the giant water bug have the frog by the back parts, or by the hollow of the thigh? Would I eat a frog's leg if offered? Yes.

In addition to the wave breast of thanksgiving, in which the wave breast is waved before the Lord, there is another voluntary offering performed at the same time. In addition to the wave breast of thanksgiving, there is the heave shoulder. The wave breast is waved before the altar of the Lord; the heave shoulder is heaved. What I want to know is this: Does the priest heave it *at* the Lord? Does he *throw* the shoulder of the ram of consecration—a ram that, before the priest slayed and chunked it, had been perfect and whole, not "Blind, or broken, or maimed, or having a wen, or scurvy, or scabbed . . . bruised, or crushed, or broken, or cut"—does he hurl it across the tabernacle, between the bloodied horns of the altar, at God? Now look what you made me do. And then he eats it. This heave is a violent, desperate way of catching God's eye. It is not inappropriate. We are people; we are permitted to have dealings with the creator and we must speak up for the creation. God *look* at what you've done to this creature, look at the sorrow, the cruelty, the long damned waste! Can it possibly, ludicrously be for *this* that on this unconscious planet with my innocent kind I play softball all spring, to develop my throwing arm? How high, how far, could I heave a little shred of frog shoulder at the Lord? How high, how far, how long until I die?

I fingered the winterkilled grass, looping it round the tip of my finger like hair, ruffling its tips with my palms. Another year has twined away, unrolled and dropped across nowhere like a flung banner painted in gibberish. "The last act is bloody, however brave be all the rest of the play; at the end they throw a little earth upon your head, and it's all over forever." Somewhere, everywhere, there is a gap, like the shuddering chasm of Shadow Creek which gapes open at my feet, like a sudden split in the window or hull of a high-altitude jet, into which things slip, or are blown, out of sight, vanished in a rush, blasted, gone, and can no more be found. For the living there is rending loss at each opening of the eye, each *augenblick*, as a muskrat dives, a heron takes alarm, a leaf floats spinning away. There is death in the pot for the living's food, fly-blown meat, muddy salt, and plucked herbs bitter as squill. If you can get it. How many people have prayed for their daily bread and famished? They die their daily death as utterly as did the frog, *people*, played with, dabbled upon, when God knows they loved their life. In a winter famine, desperate Algonquian Indians "ate broth made of smoke, snow, and buckskin, and the rash of pellagra appeared like tattooed flowers on their emaciated bodies—the roses of starvation, in a French physician's description; and those who starved died covered with roses." Is this beauty, these gratuitous roses, or a mere display of force?

Or is beauty itself an intricately fashioned lure, the cruelest hoax of all? There is a certain fragment of an ancient and involved Eskimo tale I read in Farley Mowat that for years has risen, unbidden, in my mind. The fragment is a short scenario, observing all the classical unities, simple and cruel, and performed by the light of a soapstone seal-oil lamp.

A young man in a strange land falls in love with a young woman and takes her to wife in her mother's tent. By day the women chew skins and boil meat while the young man hunts. But the old crone is jealous; she wants the boy. Calling her daughter to her one day, she offers to braid her hair; the girl sits pleased, proud, and soon is strangled by her own hair. One thing Eskimos know is skinning. The mother takes her curved hand knife shaped like a dancing skirt, skins her daughter's beautiful face, and presses that empty flap smooth on her own skull. When the boy returns that night he lies with her, in the tent on top of the world. But he is wet from hunting; the skin mask shrinks and slides, uncovering the shriveled face of the old mother, and the boy flees in horror, forever.

Could it be that if I climbed the dome of heaven and scrabbled and clutched at the beautiful cloth till I loaded my fists with a wrinkle to pull, that the mask would rip away to reveal a toothless old ugly, eyes glazed with delight?

A wind rose, quickening; it seemed at the same instant to invade my nostrils and vibrate my gut. I stirred and lifted my head. No, I've gone through this a million times, beauty is not a hoax—how many days have I learned not to stare at the back of my hand when I could look out at the creek? Come on, I say to the creek, surprise me; and it does, with each new drop. Beauty is real. I would never deny it; the appalling thing is that I forget it. Waste and extravagance go together up and down the banks, all along the intricate

fringe of spirit's free incursions into time. On either side of
me the creek snared and kept the sky's distant lights, shaped
them into shifting substance and bore them speckled down.

This Tinker Creek! It was low today, and clear. On the
still side of the island the water held pellucid as a pane, a
gloss on runes of sandstone, shale, and snail-inscribed clay
silt; on the faster side it hosted a blinding profusion of
curved and pitched surfaces, flecks of shadow and tatters
of sky. These are the waters of beauty and mystery, issuing
from a gap in the granite world; they fill the lodes in my
cells with a light like petaled water, and they churn in my
lungs mighty and frigid, like a big ship's screw. And these
are also the waters of separation: they purify, acrid and laving, and they cut me off. I am spattered with a sop of ashes,
burnt bone knobs, and blood; I range wild-eyed, flying over
fields and plundering the woods, no longer quite fit for
company.

Bear with me one last time. In the old Hebrew ordinance
for the waters of separation, the priest must find a red heifer,
a red heifer unblemished, which has never known the yoke,
and lead her outside the people's camp, and sacrifice her,
burn her wholly, without looking away: "burn the heifer in
his sight; her skin, and her flesh, and her blood, with her
dung, shall he burn." Into the stinking flame the priest casts
the wood of a cedar tree for longevity, hyssop for purgation,
and a scarlet thread for a vein of living blood. It is from
these innocent ashes that the waters of separation are made,
anew each time, by steeping them in a vessel with fresh
running water. This special water purifies. A man—any
man—dips a sprig of hyssop into the vessel and sprinkles—
merely sprinkles!—the water upon the unclean, "upon him
that touched a bone, or one slain, or one dead." So. But I
never signed up for this role. The bone touched me.

I stood, alone, and the world swayed. I am a fugitive and

a vagabond, a sojourner seeking signs. Isak Dinesen in Kenya, her heart utterly broken by loss, stepped out of the house at sunrise, seeking a sign. She saw a rooster lunge and rip a chameleon's tongue from its root in the throat and gobble it down. And then Isak Dinesen had to pick up a stone and smash the chameleon. But I had seen that sign, more times than I had ever sought it; today I saw an inspiriting thing, a pretty thing, really, and small.

I was standing lost, sunk, my hands in my pockets, gazing toward Tinker Mountain and feeling the earth reel down. All at once I saw what looked like a Martian spaceship whirling towards me in the air. It flashed borrowed light like a propeller. Its forward motion greatly outran its fall. As I watched, transfixed, it rose, just before it would have touched a thistle, and hovered pirouetting in one spot, then twirled on and finally came to rest. I found it in the grass; it was a maple key, a single winged seed from a pair. Hullo. I threw it into the wind and it flew off again, bristling with animate purpose, not like a thing dropped or windblown, pushed by the witless winds of convection currents hauling round the world's rondure where they must, but like a creature muscled and vigorous, or a creature spread thin to that other wind, the wind of the spirit which bloweth where it listeth, lighting, and raising up, and easing down. O maple key, I thought, I must confess I thought, o welcome, cheers.

And the bell under my ribs rang a true note, a flourish as of blended horns, clarion, sweet, and making a long dim sense I will try at length to explain. Flung is too harsh a word for the rush of the world. Blown is more like it, but blown by a generous, unending breath. That breath never ceases to kindle, exuberant, abandoned; frayed splinters spatter in every direction and burgeon into flame. And now when I sway to a fitful wind, alone and listing, I will think, maple key. When I see a photograph of earth from space, the planet so startlingly painterly and hung, I will think, maple key. When I shake your hand or meet your eyes I will think, two maple keys. If I am a maple key falling, at least I can twirl.

Thomas Merton wrote, "There is always a temptation to diddle around in the contemplative life, making itsy-bitsy statues." There is always an enormous temptation in all of life to diddle around making itsy-bitsy friends and meals and journeys for itsy-bitsy years on end. It is so self-conscious, so apparently moral, simply to step aside from the gaps where the creeks and winds pour down, saying, I never merited this grace, quite rightly, and then to sulk along the rest of your days on the edge of rage. I won't have it. The world is wilder than that in all directions, more dangerous and bitter, more extravagant and bright. We are making hay when we should be making whoopee; we are raising tomatoes when we should be raising Cain, or Lazarus.

Ezekiel excoriates false prophets as those who have "not gone up into the gaps." The gaps are the thing. The gaps are the spirit's one home, the altitudes and latitudes so dazzlingly spare and clean that the spirit can discover itself for the first time like a once-blind man unbound. The gaps are the clifts in the rock where you cower to see the back parts of God; they are the fissures between mountains and cells the wind lances through, the icy narrowing fiords splitting the cliffs of mystery. Go up into the gaps. If you can find them; they shift and vanish too. Stalk the gaps. Squeak into a gap in the soil, turn, and unlock—more than a maple—a universe. This is how you spend this afternoon, and tomorrow morning, and tomorrow afternoon. *Spend* the afternoon. You can't take it with you.

I live in tranquility and trembling. Sometimes I dream. I am interested in Alice mainly when she eats the cooky that makes her smaller. I would pare myself or be pared that I too might pass through the merest crack, a gap I know is there in the sky. I am looking just now for the cooky. Sometimes I open, pried like a fruit. Or I am porous as old bone, or translucent, a tinted condensation of the air like a watercolor wash, and I gaze around me in bewilderment, fancying I cast no shadow. Sometimes I ride a bucking faith while one hand grips and the other flails the air, and like any daredevil I gouge with my heels for blood, for a wilder ride, for more.

There is not a guarantee in the world. Oh your *needs* are guaranteed, your needs are absolutely guaranteed by the most stringent of warranties, in the plainest, truest words: knock; seek; ask. But you must read the fine print. "Not as the world giveth, give I unto you." That's the catch. If you can catch it it will catch you up, aloft, up to any gap at all, and you'll come back, for you will come back, transformed in a way you may not have bargained for—dribbling and crazed. The waters of separation, however lightly sprinkled, leave indelible stains. Did you think, before you were caught, that you needed, say, life? Do you think you will keep your life, or anything else you love? But no. Your needs are all met. But not as the world giveth. You see the needs of your own spirit met whenever you have asked, and you have learned that the outrageous guarantee holds. You see the creatures die, and you know you will die. And one day it occurs to you that you must not need life. Obviously. And then you're gone. You have finally understood that you're dealing with a maniac.

I think that the dying pray at the last not "please," but "thank you," as a guest thanks his host at the door. Falling from airplanes the people are crying thank you, thank you, all down the air; and the cold carriages draw up for them on the rocks. Divinity is not playful. The universe was not made in jest but in solemn incomprehensible earnest. By a power that is unfathomably secret, and holy, and fleet. There is nothing to be done about it, but ignore it, or see. And then you walk fearlessly, eating what you must, growing wherever you can, like the monk on the road who knows precisely how vulnerable he is, who takes no comfort among death-forgetting men, and who carries his vision of vastness and might around in his tunic like a live coal which neither burns nor warms him, but with which he will not part.

I used to have a cat, an old fighting tom, who sprang through the open window by my bed and pummeled my chest, barely sheathing his claws. I've been bloodied and mauled, wrung, dazzled, drawn. I taste salt on my lips in the early morning; I surprise my eyes in the mirror and they are ashes, or fiery sprouts, and I gape appalled, or full of breath. The planet whirls alone and dreaming. Power broods, spins, and lurches down. The planet and the power meet with a shock. They fuse and tumble, lightning, ground fire; they part, mute, submitting, and touch again with hiss and cry. The tree with the lights in it buzzes into flame and the cast-rock mountains ring.

Emerson saw it. "I dreamed that I floated at will in the great Ether, and I saw this world floating also not far off, but diminished to the size of an apple. Then an angel took it in his hand and brought it to me and said, 'This must thou eat.' And I ate the world." All of it. All of it intricate, speckled, gnawed, fringed, and free. Israel's priests offered the wave breast and the heave shoulder together, freely, in